REMAKING EUROPE IN THE MARGINS

Remaking Europe in the Margins
Northern Europe after the Enlargements

Edited by

CHRISTOPHER S. BROWNING
University of Birmingham, UK

Routledge
Taylor & Francis Group

LONDON AND NEW YORK

First published 2005 by Ashgate Publishing

Reissued 2019 by Routledge
2 Park Square, Milton Park, Abingdon, Oxon, OX14 4RN
52 Vanderbilt Avenue, New York, NY 10017

Routledge is an imprint of the Taylor & Francis Group, an informa business

A Library of Congress record exists under LC control number:

ISBN 13: 978-0-8153-9145-6 (hbk)
ISBN 13: 978-1-138-62036-0 (pbk)
ISBN 13: 978-1-351-15032-3 (ebk)

Contents

PART IV: FUTURE MOTORS OF REGIONAL COOPERATION

PART V: CONCLUSION

List of Contributors

Clive Archer is Research Professor in the Department of Politics and Philosophy at Manchester Metropolitan University and is Director of the Manchester European Research Institute. His most recent book is *Norway outside the European Union* (2005).

Christopher S. Browning is ESRC Research Fellow at the Department of Political Science and International Studies at the University of Birmingham. His research interests include the role of margins in international relations, the construction of European political space and the issues of identity and foreign policy in Northern Europe. His most recent book is *Constructivism, Narrative and Foreign Policy. A Case Study of Finland* (2005).

Thomas Christiansen is Senior Lecturer and Project Leader at the European Institute for Public Administration, Maastricht (NL). He is a member of the Steering Committee of the ECPR Standing Group on the European Union, and co-editor of the *Europe in Change* Series at Manchester University Press. He has published widely on various aspects of institutional politics in the EU. His most recent book is *Rethinking European Foreign Policy* (2005), edited together with Ben Tonra.

Pertti Joenniemi is Senior Research Fellow at the Danish Institute for International Studies, Department of European Studies. He is co-editor of the NEBI Yearbook on North European and Baltic Sea Integration (Springer Verlag). His most recent book is *The Nordic Peace* (2003), edited together with Clive Archer.

Frank Möller is Research Fellow at Tampere Peace Research Institute, University of Tampere, Finland, and co-editor of *Cooperation and Conflict: Journal of the Nordic International Studies Association*. His most recent book is *Encountering the North: Cultural Geography, International Relations and Northern Landscapes* (2003), edited together with Samu Pehkonen.

Sergei Prozorov is Professor of International Relations at the University of Petrozavodsk, Russia. He received his Ph.D. from the University of Tampere, Finland. He is author of *Political Pedagogy of Technical Assistance: A Study in Historical Ontology of Russian Postcommunism* (2004). His research interests include poststructuralist political philosophy, Russian political thought, EU-Russian relations and theories of postcommunist transformation.

Alexander Sergounin is Professor and Chair of the Department of International Relations and Political Science, Nizhny Novgorod Linguistic University, Russia. His research interests include: international relations history and theory, Russia-EU relations and Russian foreign policy making. His most recent publications include *Russia and the European Union's Northern Dimension: Clash or Encounter of Civilisations?* (2003), which he co-authored with Pertti Joenniemi, and *Russian Foreign Policy Thinking: Problems of National and International Security* (2003).

Carl-Einar Stålvant is Senior Lecturer in political science at the Institute for Security and Strategy at the Swedish National Defence College. He has served in a number of university assignments and public administration positions. His research focuses on Baltic Sea affairs, European Integration, Swedish and Nordic foreign policy as well as military-civilian relations.

Stanislav Tkachenko is Associate Professor at the Department of European Studies, School of International Relations at Saint-Petersburg State University. Since 1997 he has served as the Vice-Dean of the Department of International Relations and since 2003 as Vice-Rector of Saint-Petersburg State University for International Relations. His research focuses on European monetary integration, the foreign policy of the Russian Federation, and international political economy.

Marius Vahl is a Research Fellow at the Centre for European Policy Studies (CEPS) in Brussels and a Ph.D. candidate at the Catholic University of Leuven. His thesis focuses on EU-Russia relations. At CEPS he works in the Wider Europe Programme on relations between the expanding European Union and its neighbours, in particular focusing on EU relations with the Eastern neighbours and with EFTA. He has published extensively on EU neighbourhood policy, including on EU relations with Russia, Ukraine, Moldova and EFTA, as well as on the Northern Dimension initiative, Europeanisation and conflict prevention, and regional cooperation in the Black Sea region.

Acknowledgements

This book has benefited from generous financial assistance from several sources. It was initially conceived as part of a project funded by the Danish Social Science Research Council (DSSRC), which was coordinated by Pertti Joenniemi and Christopher Browning at Copenhagen Peace Research Institute (COPRI) (before it was merged into the Danish Institute for International Studies), and Professor Edward Rhodes at Rutgers University. The project, entitled, 'Westphalia or New Hansa? The US, the EU and the Unfolding of Political Space and World Order: The Case of the European North', sought to explore the unfolding geopolitics of Europe and the North and to account for the role played by the major external powers in the region. As a part of this project, DSSRC funding enabled the organisation of two workshops, one at Rutgers University (January 2003), the other held in Copenhagen (September 2003), during which the idea behind this edited volume germinated. Invaluable support was also received from the School of Social Sciences at the University of Birmingham, to host a final workshop in June 2004 that brought together the contributors to the volume and that was aimed at finalising the manuscript. The authors would like to thank all the people who attended these events. Finally, the manuscript was completed whilst the Editor was a Research Fellow on the New Security Challenges Programme of the UK's Economic and Social Research Council (ESRC).

Chapter 1

Introduction:
Remaking Europe in the Margins

Christopher S. Browning

Introduction

From the perspective of Central and Western Europe the European North has traditionally been seen as of little importance in the broader outlines of European and world politics. Usually considered to be peripheral, marginal and even remote, Northern Europe has been seen as more of an object of international and European politics, than as a subject with its own constitutive voices and capacities to shape broader European developments. Understood this way, unless one has a particular interest in the region as such, there would appear to be little worth in devoting time to studying it.

This book, however, departs from a different premise. Being understood as marginal, peripheral or remote should not be equated with a lack of subjectivity or capacity to influence. On the contrary, this chapter (and book) will argue that a position in the margins often entails particular resources for action that enable the margins to play a significant role in shaping the nature of the whole. That is to say that developments in Northern Europe can at times impact on the nature of Europe more broadly. Or put another way, and as Ardener (1987) has pointed out in respect of the idea of remoteness, often it is only through their interaction with perceived remote places that are conceptualised as different from the norm that centres are able to gain a sense of their own essence and identity. Whilst such a view means accepting that the centre may objectify and try to use the margins for its own purposes, it also indicates a certain capacity of the margins to influence the centre.

Although the theoretical arguments for this perspective will be developed below, it is important to signal them here because they underpin the claim that the dual enlargements of the EU (to the Baltic States and Poland) and NATO (to the Baltic States) within Northern Europe in 2004, are likely to have significant effects both within the region, but also within Europe more generally.

The book starts from the view that the dual enlargement and the War on Terrorism are raising important questions for various actors in Europe, not least the EU and the various states of Europe. Without being too dramatic, it might be argued that a 'teachable' (Prizel, 1998, p.2) or 'formative' (Ringmar, 1996, pp.85-5) moment is unfolding as a result of which accepted understandings, policies and orientations developed during the post-Cold War period are not as applicable as before and are in need of revision. For example, after the post-Cold War celebration of postmodernity, de-bordering and the re-integration of a Europe 'whole and free', in the last few years modernity seems to have been making a comeback. This is clearest in the general re-securitisation of political discourse since 11 September 2001, and the growing tendency within Europe to see borders as lines of exclusion and defence, rather than of interaction and adventure.

Change can also be seen, however, to the extent to which the previously dominant 'East-West' framework of thinking about European geopolitics is being challenged by new ways of dividing Europe into variously defined 'New' and 'Old' camps. Most notable, here, has been Donald Rumsfeld's provocative categorisation of 'New Europe' as equating with a pro-American stance, with 'Old Europe' depicted as being somewhat anti-American and slow to adapt to the changing world. What is particularly notable about Rumsfeld's Old/New discourse from our perspective, however, is that it appears to enable a number of actors previously doomed to positions at the fringes of European politics to gain a more central place in the European constellation as a result of their steadfast support of the United States. In other words, the discourse entails a certain potential to reframe the nature of European geopolitics.

Similarly, the dual enlargement also raises significant questions in that with the expansion of the EU and NATO, for a number of countries in Europe it appears that the post-Cold War transition process has come to an end, or at the least has reached its closing stages. One important issue raised in this context, and especially in light of the reframing of international politics around the War on Terrorism, is whether discursive structures of 'returning to the West' will any longer be relevant as a way for the new member states to locate themselves in Europe and in relation to the key issues on the international agenda. Or put another way, one of the key questions raised by the dual enlargement and the War on Terrorism is whether thinking about European politics primarily through an East-West lens is any longer as pertinent as it used to be. If it is not, then this raises significant challenges for how many states in Europe are able to position themselves within the unfolding European geopolitical scene, whilst it also raises questions regarding how we should conceptualise Europe more generally.

Whether or not the period we are living through should be seen as being a teachable or formative moment is, of course, a matter for discussion, and it is probably something that will only become clear at some point in the future. However, what is evident is that over recent years, and not least following the dual enlargement and the War on Terrorism, rather fundamental questions connected to the issues noted above have come onto the agenda of European politics. In this context the concerns of this book are twofold.

Challenges for Northern Europe

In the first instance, the book is concerned with analysing what the dual enlargement and the War on Terrorism will mean for Northern Europe. The central question to be addressed in this context is what unfolding developments will mean for the future of regional cooperation and the development of a regional subjectivity.

For example, the perceived tendency back towards the concerns of modernism raises important challenges. Not least, this is because out of all the regions of Europe it is arguably in the North where the most progress has been made in pushing politics beyond statist security concerns to embrace ideas of debordering, multiplicity and regionality. In the post-Cold War period if any region has moved beyond the concerns of sovereignty to embrace ideas of neomedievalism, it is Northern Europe, where a multitude of overlapping spaces of governance and of transnational identities have been forged. As various prominent scholars have noted, Northern Europe has been something of a postmodern playground, where scholars well versed in critical understandings of international politics have played a hands-on role in how the region has developed (Neumann, 1994; Wæver, 1997). This raises questions of how Northern Europe will develop in the future. With the dual enlargement, the War on Terrorism and the return to the fore of questions of security, will the region continue to develop in the rather innovative ways in which it has to date? Or are regional cooperation and the construction of a regional subjectivity actually in danger of being undermined?

One of the central concerns, in this regard, relates to the attitudes of the different states of the region towards continuing to develop regional cooperation. For example, in the post-Cold War period the Baltic States have had much to gain by adopting a positive attitude to regional cooperation, not least because it has been seen as enhancing their prospects of EU and NATO membership. In a sense, regional cooperation in the North could be conceptualised as having been something of a training ground where they could prove they were responsible international citizens worthy of EU and NATO membership. This, however, raises the question of whether their enthusiasm for regional cooperation will wane now that membership has been gained, and now that they can approach the central forums of European politics through more direct avenues. Similar concerns also exist regarding the Nordic states, whilst it has also become common to question whether the states of Northern Europe will have sufficient common interests to make a focus on regional cooperation worth prioritising in the future.

Donald Rumsfeld's recent division of Europe into New and Old states has further compounded such concerns, a division that splits the countries of Northern Europe into separate camps and has led to a potential interesting realignment (amongst other possible realigments). Thus, in the post-Cold War period it was rather common to subdivide Northern Europe into the Nordic States, the Baltic States, Germany, Poland and Russia. However, the New/Old distinction leads to a rather different categorisation, with the Baltic States and Poland somewhat interestingly aligned alongside Russia as a part of New Europe, and with the Nordic countries also split as a result of Denmark's much more pro-American policy stance. In contrast, Finland, Germany, Norway and Sweden have rather firmly located themselves in Old Europe, or tried to distance themselves from the debate altogether.

Economically the region also appears increasingly divided between the progressivist social democratic models of Germany and the Nordic states, and the more neoliberal orientations of Poland, the Baltic States, and to some extent also Russia. Economic competition between the countries (and their different socio-economic models) has become marked, with various complaints being raised on all sides about unfair trading practices or advantages, points highlighted in some of the chapters.

Taking these points together, there is reason to question whether, with the process of transformation and transition apparently now over for the Baltic States and Poland, regional cooperation in the North will be undermined to some extent. Put another way, whilst the transition process has been actively supported by the Nordic states and Germany out of a combination of reasons of idealism and security concerns (with promoting regional cooperation being a central element of this), with the region now 'secure' and 'stable', will motivation for regional cooperation on the part of these states dissipate? Linked here is a rather interesting theoretical question about the relationship between security and cooperation, and the extent to which security concerns have been central in legitimising and providing focus for endeavours of region building and cross-border cooperation in the North (see Browning and Joenniemi, 2004). In other words, it seems to be precisely when the major security issues of the region look set to be solved that the future of regional cooperation (as a state-led enterprise) appears to be in question.

In turn, however, this leads to the question that if states are to some extent losing interest, is space in turn opening for other actors (such as towns, cities, civil society, etc.) to take the lead and become more prominent in setting the regional agenda? On these various issues related to the question of what impact the dual enlargement and the War on Terrorism will have on regional cooperation in the European North, the book includes analyses from various perspectives. Whilst some of the chapters take a cautious view of the prospects for regional cooperation in the future, others are more optimistic.

The North and European Geopolitics

However, whilst the dual enlargement and the War on Terrorism may be having an impact on Northern Europe, *the second theme of the book analyses how developments in Northern Europe may in turn impact upon the developing construction of Europe, Russia and the EU.* In this respect, the theoretical framework of the book stems from a view that whilst developments at the centre can clearly affect what happens in the margins of Europe, those margins also have some ability to 'bite back' and to reconstitute the whole (Parker, 2000, p.8). To put it another way, developments in Northern Europe are pro-active, not only reactive. It is important to lay out the theoretical groundwork for this claim, in order to highlight just how it is that even margins and peripheries can at times exert rather significant influence over broader processes, in our case of Europe-making.

As Shields (1991, p.276) points out, being on the 'margin' is usually associated with exclusion from the 'centre', and as such is also usually equated with a position of powerlessness and objectification. In discourses of modernity and in the major theories of international politics, being on the margins is equated with a lack of influence, and even a lack of subjectivity in international affairs. A position in the margins is usually seen as something from which one should try to escape, by trying to instead get closer to the core. A prime example of this way of thinking is precisely the recent case of the enlargement of the EU and NATO in 2004, where one of the key arguments for the applicants in favour of membership was that influence would be best attained through sitting at the tables where the decisions are made. Today, similar debates can now be heard in Finland and Sweden, where some pro-NATO politicians have warned that remaining outside the Alliance will condemn these countries to a position of marginality – this clearly being understood highly negatively. In the case of Finland, similar debates have been apparent also in respect of the EU, with some critics, like Erkki Liikanen, Finland's European Commissioner, of the government's seemingly less proactive and more critical European policies worried that the country is in danger of moving towards the 'outer orbit' of the EU and becoming simply a 'footnote country' (Liikanen cited in *Helsingin Sanomat International Edition*, 19 June 2003).

Whilst it has to be said that there may be good reasons for aspiring for a position at the centre, and whilst being at the centre may entail gaining a voice and influence in some contexts, the implication that a position in the margins entails a lack of these things is arguably misplaced. As argued by Parker (2000, p.8), there is a need to 'dissociate marginality from the idea of *inferiority* to, or *dependence* upon, a corresponding core'. Margins, Parker argues, can actually possess considerable influence and power in their own right. This power, he contends, stems from their uncertain status on the edge: located in the shadows of the boundaries between the inside and outside of any particular order, their belonging and incorporation within any given entity is always open to question. Parker makes the point by referring to elections, noting that whilst parties can usually take the loyalty of their core supporters for granted, they frequently have to make considerable efforts to secure the votes of the undecided, or the less loyal – those who feel that they may have other options available to them (Parker, 2000, pp.12-13).

However, similar arguments can also be made if we turn our attention to questions of territoriality and the growing literature on borders. As Ruggie (1993) points out, in modernist understandings territory tends to be conceptualised as clearly demarcated into neatly defined spaces, the borders between which are understood to be impermeable and clear cut. Such a view of territory is depicted on political maps of the world, where different countries are marked by different colours, and where there is no mixing or blurring of boundaries – despite realities on the ground. As Ruggie points out, in modernist understandings power is seen as projected from a centre evenly across the state's territory, and as such those on the margins are not seen to have distinct resources of their own, but are largely understood as subordinate to the designs and strategies of the centre. Borders, in this understanding, serve to simplify and standardise political space, and as such this understanding leaves little room for thinking about political space and borders in more differentiated terms (Walters, 2002, pp.565-6).

Over the past decade or so, such an understanding of territoriality and the characteristics thereby assumed of borders has been greatly criticised. Increasingly, and not least in view of processes of globalisation, state borders have been re-reconceptualised. Instead of focusing on borders as lines of division and walls of separation, different metaphors have often been invoked depicting borders as fuzzy zones, frontiers and intermediary spaces of interaction and exchange.[1] Understood in this way, margins near, at, on, or transcending the border need to be understood as 'substantive territories in their own right', that, whilst closely linked and defined by the centre(s) to which they are marginal, also exist as sites of action themselves (Parker, 2000, p.7). The fact that margins are connected to that which lies beyond the boundary provides them with a certain amount of constitutive power in regard to the centre. Put somewhat more theoretically, and extrapolating from Shields (1991, pp.276-8), it might be argued that the very connections that exist across borders in the margins, on the one hand, begin to point to how the very definition of the centre is dependent upon what happens at the margins, whilst on the other hand, also exposes the relativism underlying universalist modernist discourses on the role of territory and borders in the constitution of political space.

Put in more practical terms, this is to say that what happens in Northern Europe, the way in which borders between the states of the region, and not least between the EU states and Russia, operate and are conceptualised, will also have implications for the construction of European geopolitical space more generally. On the one hand, it should be noted that there has been some instrumentalist recognition on the part of major actors (EU, US, Russia) that developments in the Northern periphery may be worth transposing to other parts of Europe. Thus, at a policy level it is notable how the EU, US and Russia have each highlighted Northern Europe as a special case that needs to be utilised and learnt from in dealing with problems elsewhere in Europe and in the world more generally, and as such have at times talked of the region as a laboratory for experimenting with different forms of governance.

More fundamentally, however, postmodern developments in Northern Europe have also challenged the very figure and subjectivity of the EU and Russia, whether they have welcomed this or not. For example, there has been much discussion in Europe of whether the EU is moving in an increasingly statist

---

[1]   For an overview of some of these debates see, Newman (2000), Paasi (2003).

direction, or if it is instead developing more along the lines of multilevel networks and interlocking dimensions. Whilst the modernist statist discourse has strengthened in recent years, elements of dimensionalism also remain significant. Importantly, Northern Europe has not just been a recipient of these different debates, but has also arguably played a notable role regarding just how Europe (and Russia) unfolds. This is to say that the wide array of projects of regional cooperation that have developed in Northern Europe since the end of the Cold War have fundamentally re-conceptualised the nature of borders in the region (including EU borders), and as such significantly problematise any Westphalian aspirations that may exist at the EU centre. The impact of this is arguably rather fundamental since to the extent that the North has been an agent of postmodernism, it has also helped to open the debate concerning in what sense the EU can and should be aspiring to be an international actor. Similarly, these developments also problematise the extent to which the EU can be seen to possess a definitive territorial edge, beyond which its responsibilities for governance diminish. Moreover, what stands for the EU also stands for Russia as well.

On the one hand, therefore, the book aims to show how Northern Europe has been seen by the EU and Russia (and also the US to some extent) as something of a repository of informative and innovative experiences and as a testing ground for unconventional policy departures. On the other hand, however, the book also poses challenges to dominant understandings by indicating that power and influence can also be located at the margins. Whilst understanding this may also offer the EU (and Russia) alternative ways of conducting policy, the argument extends beyond this in that it is contended that developments in Northern Europe may not just impact on the policies of the European centres, but to some extent also impact on the very nature and subjectivity of those centres, which in turn impacts on the nature of the broader European constellation.

Structure of the Book

In order to achieve the various aims laid out above, the book is divided into four parts. The first part deals with *Regional Perspectives* and aims to provide a background to current debates and issues facing Northern Europe in the current climate. In chapter 2, Archer problematises some of the principal dynamics that have underlain regional cooperation in the post-Cold War period. More particularly, he argues that whilst Liberal Institutionalist ideas have been a driving force of regional cooperation, in view of the dual enlargement and the War on Terrorism, it now appears that the 'Liberal' and 'Institutionalist' elements of Liberal Institutionalism are no longer operating in sync, especially in regard to Russia. Ultimately, this raises questions for the future possible trajectories of Northern Europe. In chapter 3, Möller takes a closer look at attempts to create a Northern subjectivity in order to overcome some of the divides of the Cold War period. Möller argues this has been problematic (and ultimately unsuccessful) because the goal of creating a Northern subjectivity has been built around the perceived need for a homogenous regional story and memory. This, he indicates, has not only been ineffective, but has also entailed plays of power on the part of Western partners, which in turn has limited the development of Northern subjectivity and regional cooperation. Looking at different discourses of the region's artistic community, he instead points to a way out of the dilemma that involves re-conceptualising Northern subjectivity in a more heterogeneous and open manner.

The second part of the book focuses on the *North and the Construction of Europe*. The aim of this section is to broaden the frame and to analyse how developments in Northern Europe can have an impact on European developments more generally. At the same time, however, the chapters also demonstrate how this is a two way process in that developments and actions by actors beyond the region can also serve to limit and shape the Northern agenda. In chapter 4, Vahl looks at how EU experiences of the European Economic Area (EEA) agreement with Norway, and the Northern Dimension (ND) initiative for promoting regional cooperation (not least with Russia), have to some extent been seen as models by the EU in developing its new European Neighbourhood Policy. Key questions addressed relate to the extent to which Northern solutions should be seen as being unique or are more broadly applicable. In chapter 5, Christiansen focuses on recent EU debates largely related to the Constitutional Convention. In this regard, he points towards two longer-term processes of 'constitutionalisation' and 'territorialisation' that have become evident in recent debates and that indicate an emergent statist-type of discourse for the EU's development. Ultimately, these processes raise questions about the future nature of the EU, which in turn raises questions for regional cooperation in the North, and not least across the EU border with Russia. In chapter 6, through an analysis of different discourses related to the EU's ND, Browning draws out three different models (Westphalian, Imperial, Neomedieval) of future European governance. The chapter seeks to show how developments in Northern Europe may impact on which model(s) are more likely to provide a guide to the future shape of European governance, and the way in which the EU relates to its borders and those on the margins of, and outside, the EU.

The third part of the book looks at *Russian Perspectives* on developments in Northern Europe, the aim being to see how Russia has reacted to developments in the North, whilst at the same time looking at how those developments are in turn shaping the nature of Russian subjectivity. In chapter 7, Sergounin provides an overview of Russian perspectives on regional cooperation initiatives in Northern Europe and points to a number of obstacles and opportunities that exist on both sides in order to enhance the process. He argues that the North and the idea of Northernness holds significant attraction for Russia, not least by providing it with a new avenue into European debates and European political space, whilst at the same time developments in the North have also pushed Russia to rethink its previously rather negative stance towards matters of regionalisation and decentralisation. In chapter 8, Prozorov adopts a revisionist and challenging perspective arguing that it is not so much Russia as the EU that poses some of the main problems for further developing regional cooperation in Northern Europe. More specifically, however, he highlights how regionalisation processes in the EU and post-communist Russia follow substantively divergent logics, and that as such often the EU and Russia fail sufficiently to understand each other's concerns.

The fourth part of the book focuses on the *Future Motors of Regional Cooperation*. The aim of this section is to look to the future and to point towards where some of the new dynamics driving regional and European integration may lie. In chapter 9, Joenniemi provides a theoretically developed account of the role of cities in promoting regional cooperation in the North, but also beyond. He highlights how cities have the potential to escape the statist preoccupation with security and sovereignty and may further contribute to a move towards a much more post-Westphalian system of governance in Europe. As regards the North, it seems that with the dual enlargement space may have opened up for other actors, aside from the state, to take a more proactive approach to regional cooperation. In chapter 10, Tkachenko takes a more particular look at the role that cities can play in fostering regional cooperation. This is achieved through a case study of the paradiplomacy of St. Petersburg. Whereas it is often argued that processes of globalisation and decentralisation have the tendency to undermine the position of the state, Tkachenko argues that in the case of St. Petersburg the city's paradiplomatic activities can be seen to contribute to the modern Russian project, and as such are actively being promoted by Moscow. In chapter 11, Stålvant adopts a broader perspective on regional cooperation in Northern Europe since the end of the Cold War. The chapter argues that regional cooperation in the 1990s was driven by idealistic concerns of post-Cold War 'regionalisation', which were promoted in a rather spontaneous bottom-up way by civil society actors, and more security-led concerns of 'stabilisation', which were promoted top-down by the states of the region. Following the War on Terrorism and the dual enlargement, however, Stålvant argues that a new phase of 'normalisation' is apparent as a result of which the idealised and security concerns that informed regional cooperation in the past, will be replaced by more pragmatic and economic rationales. Stålvant argues that this experience raises important questions for the future of regional cooperation in the North, but also perhaps provides salutary lessons for the EU as it tries to develop its relations with its new post-enlargement neighbours.

Finally, in the concluding chapter Browning and Joenniemi draw together a number of themes and arguments made throughout the book related to the future prospects for regional cooperation in the North, but also related to what the Northern experience says about the construction of European space more generally. The chapter argues that both the EU and Russia appear trapped in separate 'internal/external security paradoxes' that perhaps limit how far they can go in the North, but which at the same time mean they are unable to escape a number of important dilemmas raised by Northern conditions.

References

Ardener, Edwin (1987), 'Remote Areas: Some Theoretical Considerations', in Anthony Jackson (ed.), *Anthropology at Home*, London, Tavistock Publications, pp. 38-54.

Browning, Christopher S. and Joenniemi, Pertti (2004b), 'Regionality Beyond Security? The Baltic Sea Region after Enlargement', *Cooperation and Conflict*, Vol. 39(3), pp. 233-53.

Helsingin Sanomat International Edition, 'Commissioner Liikanen warns Finland not to be a mere footnote in EU', 19 June 2003. Available at http://www.helsinki-hs.net.

Neumann, Iver B. (1994), 'A Region-building Approach to Northern Europe', *Review of International Studies*, Vol. 20 (1), pp. 53-74.

Newman, David (2000), 'Boundaries, Territoriality and Postmodernity: Towards Shared or Separate Spaces', in Martin Pratt and Janet Allison Brown (eds.), *Borderlands Under Stress*, London, Kluwer Law International, pp. 17-34.

Paasi, Anssi (2003), 'Boundaries in a Globalizing World', in Kay Anderson, Mona Domosh, Steve Pile and Nigel Thrift (eds.), *Handbook of Cultural Geography*, London, Sage, pp. 462-72.

Parker, Noel (2000), 'Integrated Europe and its "Margins": Action and Reaction', in Noel Parker and Bill Armstrong (eds.), *Margins in European Integration*, Houndmills, Macmillan Press, pp. 3-27.

Prizel, Ilya (1998), *National Identity and Foreign Policy: Nationalism and Leadership in Poland, Russia, and Ukraine*, Cambridge, Cambridge University Press.

Ringmar, Erik (1996) *Identity, Interest and Action: A Cultural Explanation of Sweden's Intervention in the Thirty Years War*, Cambridge, Cambridge University Press.

Ruggie, John Gerard (1993), 'Territoriality and Beyond: Problematizing Modernity in International Relations', *International Organization*, Vol. 47(1), pp. 139-74.

Shields, Rob (1991), *Places on the Margin: Alternative Geographies of Modernity*, London, Routledge.

Wæver, Ole (1997), 'The Baltic Sea: A Region after Post-Modernity', in Pertti Joenniemi (ed.), *Neo-Nationalism or Regionality: The Restructuring of Political Space Around the Baltic Rim*, Stockholm, NordREFO, pp. 293-342.

Walters, William (2002), 'Mapping Schengenland: Denaturalizing the Border', *Environment and Planning D: Society and Space*, Vol. 20(5), pp. 561-80.

PART I

REGIONAL PERSPECTIVES

Chapter 2

Regional Security, the War on Terrorism and the Dual Enlargements

Clive Archer[1]

Introduction

The broad assumption of this chapter is that, over the years, security thinking in the Nordic – and later Baltic – region, while being dominated by Realist assumptions for much of the Cold War period, was penetrated by other views, especially Liberal Institutionalist ones, arising from the domestic politics of some of the Nordic states. In the post-Cold War period these ideas have been given a freer range, though it now appears that they have been challenged by the effects of the War on Terrorism and the dual enlargement of the EU and NATO on the region.

The claim will be examined that the alternative view is basically a Liberal Institutionalist one, whilst noting that this has entailed a dual set of potentially contradictory elements. These aspects will be illustrated by analysing them in respect of the aftermath of 9/11 and the dual enlargement. This study is not undertaken in the belief that a Realist and a Liberal Institutionalist approach are the main, let alone the only, ways of understanding international politics. To the contrary, even the liberal tradition in the study of international relations involves many aspects (Jackson and Sørensen, 1999, pp.108-26), whilst the Constructivist approach, evident elsewhere in this book, also has a presence.

The motivation lies elsewhere. Early in the 1990s the works of John Mearsheimer (1991) provided a bleak picture of a Future Europe where a Realist (some would say Neo-realist, but there was little new about it) story unfolded. Events in the Balkans may have provided a partial vindication of the view that states' incapacity to stay out of the clutches of anarchy brings mistrust and a reliance on self-help.[2] However, a view of the Baltic Sea region from 1989 until the dual enlargement of 2004 shows a region with the potential for conflict – there

---

[1] The author is grateful to Chris Browning and Erik Männik for their comments on earlier drafts.

[2] Mearsheimer's two main consequences of international anarchy were: 'little room for trust among states... [and] each state must guarantee its own survival since no other actor will provide its security' (1991, p.148).

were new states being born, discontented minorities, poorly controlled militias, border disputes and wide socio-economic disparities in a small area – but one where there has been substantial political and economic change with remarkably little conflict. The contention is that this was partly because governments in the region took on a Liberal Institutionalist foreign policy (though they did not ignore the realities of power) and that this was also backed by the rapid growth of interdependence in the region. However, differences in the development of the factors that support the Liberal Institutionalist agenda, and the impact of outside events on the region, could mean a slightly different outcome in the next fifteen years.

The Theoretical Background

What can be expected from a Liberal Institutionalist approach to the study of security issues and their policy consequences? Jackson and Sørensen (1999, pp.108-26) list four sorts of liberal approaches to the study of international relations: Sociological Liberalism (pluralism with a stress on transnational relations), Interdependence Liberalism (where functional and neo-functional theories of integration dominate), Institutional Liberalism (where international institutions, especially international organisations and regimes, have modified the assumptions of crude anarchy in international relations) and Republican Liberalism (in which the ideas of the democratic peace prevail). The main independent variable in the first three is based in the form of the relationship between states and societies, which in one way or another makes them more inter-dependent and less likely to resort to conflict. In contrast, the independent variable in the latter (and, to an extent, Sociological Liberalism) is the form of government of the states involved in any relationship (democracy producing a greater propensity to peace with another democracy; pluralism encouraging transnational links). The first strand allows for the importance of non-governmental actors in the system, whereas the last three forms are predominantly state-centric, though Interdependence Liberalism allows considerable space for non-governmental actors. The view in this chapter is that Sociological and Republican Liberalism, with their reference to domestic factors, can be usefully linked in the case study, as can Interdependence and Institutional Liberalism, both of which stress the institutional links between states.[3] However, there can be a tension between the strands of Liberal Institutionalism as suggested by each part of the name.

---

[3]   Russett and Oneal (2001, pp.24-9) consider that three elements make up the international agenda of liberal theories. These elements are: the promotion of democracy, bolstering national economies through complex interdependence and constructing a web of international institutions. Here the second and third elements are conflated.

Starting with the *institutionalist* element, this entails a strong belief in cooperation, especially through international institutions, not least international organisations. Keohane and Martin (1995, p.42) conclude that 'institutions can provide information, reduce transaction costs, make commitments more credible, establish focal points for coordination and, in general, facilitate the operation of reciprocity'. They can also socialise decision-makers into the habit of cooperation and the expectation of trust (Archer, 2001a, pp.99-102). While these institutions could be non-governmental, there is recognition that the dominant actors in international relations are still sovereign states and that for institutions to work they should, at least, be backed by governments. The important element in this part of the approach is that the outcome, in terms of relationships between states, is positively affected by the form, extent and basis of that relationship.

In the case of the North European area, there has been a test of the notion that the knitting together of states in a web of institutions, with a wide range of links, and a freeing up of interactions between states and societies, especially in economic terms, would bring a more trust-based and enduring relationship between the states involved. In Jackson and Sørensen's terms, this would be the dual effect of Interdependence Liberalism and Institutional Liberalism at work. By weakening both their borders and the factors that prevented cross-border cooperation, the states help provide the environment for increased trade and transnational links. Increased interdependence and a wide range of common institutions could have a substantial impact on relations between societies by breaking away from what Mitrany (1966, p.125) called 'the traditional link between authority and a definite territory'. This functionalist approach 'treats the promotion of welfare as an indirect approach to the prevention of warfare', to use Claude's somewhat dramatic expression (1968, pp.34-5). At least, there is an expectation of a positive benefit to the general relations between states and societies of increased social and economic intercourse.

The second element, reflecting more the *liberal* aspect, contains two points, both of which relate to the political nature of the states involved rather than the form of their relationship. The first reflects the consequences of the states involved being democratic. It is the notion that democratic states at least do not go to war with each other and can also form a zone of peace and/or a security community (Doyle, 1995; Russett, 1993; Deutsch *et al.*, 1957; Adler and Barnett, 1998). The other point concerns the society of the states involved; they are sufficiently liberal and pluralistic in terms of human rights and fundamental freedoms to allow a wide range of non-state political, social and economic activity which can also stretch across frontiers. This accepts the notion that the state is not the only actor in international relations, it allows for the importance of non-state actors (Keohane and Nye, 1971), and reflects the Sociological Liberalist side of Liberal Institutionalism. In the end this is reflected in a greater attachment to what Held (1993) calls the democratisation of the society of states, involving not just the greater involvement of representative institutions, but also enhanced stress on human rights and fundamental freedoms within states.

The existence of the basis for a democratic peace in a region can be fairly easily assessed. The indicator is one of democracy, though its nature is not always so clear, especially concerning states that are in the process of transition from obvious non-democracy. In the relationship between any two states, there must also be a mutual appreciation of each other's status. One way of keeping a check on others is through the various international institutions that concern themselves with democracy, human rights and fundamental freedoms, such as the Council of Europe, the Organization for Security and Cooperation in Europe (OSCE), the European Union and, at the non-governmental level, Amnesty International and Freedom House. An assessment of zones of peace and security communities needs a more extensive evaluation of factors such as trade, transactions, and, most importantly, mutual perceptions.[4] Any estimation of the evolution of security communities will thus consist, not just of a record of 'objective' factors, but also of some notion of how groups understand each other, a concern of most Constructivist writers (see, for example, Williams, 2001). An important element in building security communities and zones of peace is that of feeling that those in neighbouring states are sufficiently similar so that trust can be easily established. If countries had a similar political, economic and social profile, as did the Nordic states during the latter part of the twentieth century, then the controls and barriers between them can be drawn down considerably. Should states and societies have similar economic and political profiles and aims, but different social structures, then some economic barriers can be taken down. If there are social differences, or the society is at a stage of considerable change, trust may be more difficult to maintain.

The above two elements are often conflated into one understanding of Liberal Institutionalism, and indeed there are overlaps between the two. However, in this analysis the tensions are shown between the two aspects in the Liberal Institutionalist elements of the security policies of the Nordic, and latterly and to a limited extent, the Baltic States, and also in the various historical phases covered.

---

[4]   Adler and Barnett (1998, p. 29) list three 'tiers' in a framework for understanding the emergence of security communities. The first consists of 'precipitating factors that encourage states to orient themselves in each other's direction and coordinate their policies'. For Northern Europe this might be seen as the events of 1989-91 that changed the internal political nature, and external orientation, of the former communist countries around the Baltic Sea. However, the response of the three Baltic States and the Nordic countries was very different, let alone that of Russia. The second tier consists of the '"structural" elements of power and ideas and the process elements of transactions, international organizations, and social learning'; while the third tier is the development of trust and collective identity formation.

The Cold War Background

During this period the whole area was enmeshed in a Cold War understanding of security that was heavily state-oriented and Realist in its nature. The three Baltic republics were parts of the Soviet Union and, until the late 1980s, were not actors on the international scene. However, the Nordic states developed a 'minor key' in their security policies that resembled certain elements of a Liberal Institutionalist approach to international relations. There was an acceptance of the policy consequences of the Realist 'reality' that dominated the Cold War, as well as some differences between the three Scandinavian states and Finland. The strategic attention of the Scandinavian states was directed primarily to the United States and its presence in Europe and their defence policies (even that of Sweden) were predicated on that presence, while the over-riding security concern for Finland was the attitude of the Soviet Union.

Broadly speaking decision-makers in the Nordic states had little choice during the Cold War years but to accept the policy-consequences of being part of the East-West divide. There was an attempt in 1948 to create a 'Nordic Defence Union' by the three Scandinavian states (Denmark, Norway and Sweden) but, as the Cold War divisions deepened in Europe, this failed and Denmark and Norway, with Iceland, joined NATO, and only Sweden remained outside any alliance (though secretly cooperating with NATO; see SOU, 1994). Meanwhile, Finland had signed the Treaty of Friendship, Cooperation and Mutual Assistance with the Soviet Union which, though not an alliance, created some restrictions on the development of Finnish security policy.

While Cold War rhetoric dominated the security discourse of all the Nordic states during this time – their politicians had to react to crises, plans for re-armament, nuclear weapons, and proposals for reinforcements and integration into alliances – they also managed to keep alive another discourse that talked more about restraint on military activities, a distancing from nuclear weapons, a wider view of security than just a stress on defence, and protecting society and not just the state. Holst (1985, p.274) wrote about 'an element of escapism in the attitudes that are particularly prevalent in the smaller nations', but also these small, front-line states adopted a 'partial propitiation by which an ally [Norway and Denmark] seeks to reduce the common adversary's incentives to attack' (Joffe, 1985, p.230). Many of these elements could be seen in Swedish security policy, but there were also aspects in the so-called 'base and ban' policies of Denmark and Norway,[5] and in what became regarded as 'the Nordic balance' (Brundtland 1966, pp.30-63). This latter expression was used to encompass the pattern of the Nordic security

---

[5]   The 'base' policy was the refusal by Denmark and Norway to have foreign bases on their metropolitan territory. The 'ban' element refers to the restrictions that Denmark, Iceland and Norway placed on having nuclear weapons on their territory and on holding certain allied military exercises in the vicinity of the frontiers with Warsaw Treaty Organization states (Boel, 1988, pp.38-88; Riste, 2001, pp.212-17).

policies (three members of NATO but with some policy restraints, Sweden's armed non-alliance, and Finland's non-alliance and its close relationship with the Soviet Union) and what seemed to be the effort of all Nordic policy-makers not to adopt any policy that would have a negative impact on the security policies of their Nordic neighbours.[6]

This approach was underpinned by what Nils Andrén (1967, p.17) called 'cobweb integration' of the states and societies 'with a fine-meshed net of small interdependencies that is being spun over the Nordic countries' and which continued apace from the establishment of the Nordic Council in 1952. The ideas behind this 'minor key' of security policy were sometimes exported – they can, for example, be found in small state cooperation within NATO (Joffe, 1985), in meetings of the Socialist International and in the Palme Report (Independent Commission on Disarmament and Security Matters, 1982). There was also an interchange of ideas with the West German Social Democrats, not least in such international forums as the Palme and Brundtland Commissions. The genesis of these ideas can be found in the peace movements, the churches and in the labour movements of the Scandinavian states, with the values that were practised in domestic politics being seen fit and ready for externalisation, especially by the 1980s (Archer, 2003, pp.14-16).

In security terms, Liberal Institutionalism placed some emphasis on absolute rather than comparative capabilities and on the role of international institutions 'in changing conceptions of self-interest' (Keohane, 1993, p.271). Furthermore, a move to a 'non-zero sum game' approach, where a potential opponent's loss is not always a benefit, is considered, as is cooperation, often through institutions, as an alternative to self-help in pursuing security. However, during the Cold War, little consideration was given by the Nordic states to changing the political system of the Warsaw Pact states – the existence of a Communist bloc was taken as a given. The hope was that institutions could be built to bridge the two blocs in Europe. Indeed, the existence of these blocs provided small states such as the Nordics with the stable context for their activities. Indeed, the Norwegian defence (and later foreign) minister and academic, Johan Jørgen Holst, saw the Atlantic Alliance as a mechanism that allowed Norway and Denmark to pursue aspects of this 'minor key' security policy: 'Participation in a multinational alliance enables the small state to pursue their idealistic visions of equity and world order rather than succumb to ignoble "realism" or escapism of adherence to the principles of *sauve qui peut*' (1985, p.283). This view explains why Finland, whose resources were spent on maintaining its precarious relations with the Soviet Union, was perhaps the Nordic state least able to have an active 'minor key'. Sweden's surer geo-strategic position, its greater resources and perhaps its covert dealings with NATO,

---

[6]   Sometimes the Nordic states seemed to be at odds, as when Finland pursued plans for a Nordic Nuclear Weapons Free Zone, by which 'Norway and Denmark would be decoupled from NATO's nuclear strategy' (Lodgaard and Berg, 1982, p.78).

gave it the opportunity to develop an alternative security policy, an element welcomed by the dominant Social Democrats.

Post-Cold War

In the early 1990s all the Nordic states reconsidered their security situation in government and/or parliamentary reports that had a number of factors in common. First, they recognised that the end of the Cold War had changed the security situation, not only in Europe, but also for their own countries (Ministry for Foreign Affairs, 1995; Ministry of Defence (Denmark), 1992; Ministry of Defence (Sweden), 1995; NOU, 1992). The fear of a bipolar conflict, possibly nuclear, in Europe had disappeared and was replaced by an emphasis on new threats and uncertainties. These were listed as, *inter alia*, ethnic conflict, mass migration, threats to the environment, international crime, and the spread of disease, and all for which the traditional defence establishment and the armaments of the Cold War were not especially useful. Nevertheless, there were some Cold War 'leftovers' that remained of concern, such as the residual armed forces of the Russian Federation (which may, or may not, be under Moscow's control), degrading weaponry from the Cold War, and the proliferation of weapons, including those of mass destruction, not just to states, but also to non-governmental groups including terrorists. So the two threat scenarios overlapped. In a way, Northern Europe was becoming more secure – there was no longer the threat of being the battleground between NATO and the Warsaw Pact – but was also becoming, like the rest of Europe, more risky. An old nuclear submarine or power station could implode; refugees could 'flood' in from a collapsing Russia, mafia groups could extend their activities to the North, and terrorists might want to attack installations. The referent of security was no longer as state-based as during the Cold War, but was more focused on society or groups within the nation. Despite these general worries, a particular concern of the Nordic states during the first half of the 1990s was a possible security vacuum in the Baltic States, that is in the periphery of Norden. It is no coincidence that Finland started to provide military assistance to Estonia in 1992 – long before NATO was ready to even consider anything similar. The Swedish Moderate government of Carl Bildt assumed a similar stance to Finland. By helping the Baltic States, the Nordics achieved a threefold goal: they supported state-building in the Baltic States to prevent internal collapse of the new countries; they prevented the Baltic States from falling back into Russia/CIS (thus keeping a *cordon sanitaire* between themselves and the bulk of Russia); and they helped to restrain potential Russian neo-imperialist impulses.

However, all five Nordic states took some time to re-adjust in security terms to the end of the Cold War, despite what could have been interpreted as a triumph (or at least an opportunity) for their brand of security. It seemed that a more comprehensive and cooperative approach to security was being accepted across Europe and in such institutions as the UN, NATO, the CSCE/OSCE and the WEU.

Indeed, these institutions were becoming the instruments for a Liberal Institutionalist approach to security and after a while the Nordic states were pressing for regional institutions (Barents Euro-Arctic Council and the Council of the Baltic Sea States).

The slowness of change is explicable by a number of factors. The main one seems to be the relative proximity of Russia. Finland, with its long border with Russia, has been slowest in changing its defence posture (while its general security and foreign policy have altered rapidly); Norway, with a short border with north-west Russia, is trying to reform its defence posture, but the prospect of a troublesome Russia keeps making a re-appearance in the defence debate (Neumann, 2001). In contrast, Sweden is 'cushioned' by Finland against the immediate effects of adverse events in Russia, while Denmark considers itself to be far away. Furthermore, the political process in the countries and the consensus mode of policy-making, which is often deliberative and requires reports by commissions, is cumbersome. This is a factor all have in common. Also, some of the governments (especially those of Sweden and Norway) may have been cautious about concepts of security that included entities other than the nation-states as referents.

Nevertheless, the emergence of the Baltic States provided an incentive and a test case for the Liberal Institutionalist approach: it encouraged a generous non-zero-sum approach, the use of institutions, and a transfer of knowledge and experience.

The Baltic States themselves started with a fairly 'zero-sum game' approach to security, seeing Russia and minority groups within their states as possible threats to their delicate independence. Over the decade, the discourse used by officials changed considerably and started to reflect the sort of security issues discussed in Nordic, EU and NATO documents (Männik 2004, pp.27-28). What is harder to detect is the extent to which this new discourse reflects the deep-seated thoughts of even the Baltic decision-makers (let alone their voters). Have the Baltic States' governments learnt new lessons or have they just learnt to say what is expected? A closer examination shows that the change in rhetoric was related to the prospects of receiving, in 1997, invitations to join the EU and/or NATO, and later, to the post-'9/11' war on terrorism. This would suggest a change in the calculations made by decision-makers as to what other countries wanted to hear from them. Subsequently, the 'new threats' that became the main centre of security discourse after 1997, were then crystallised into the war on terrorism after 9/11 in 2001. Nevertheless the Russian Federation remained as a dominant threat to much of the population and many politicians (at least in Estonia) up to 2003, though less and less was it seen as a direct military threat (Männik 2005, Ch.4).

The position of the three new Baltic States evinced a response from the Nordic states in the concept of the 'near neighbourhood', meaning the Baltic Sea region and the Baltic States in particular. During the 1990s this concept was developed individually and collectively by the Nordic states (Baltic Sea States Summit, 1996; Hansen, 1995; Försvarsdepartementet, 1996). It was partly a reflection of the new set of circumstances in which they found themselves – as they looked out across the Baltic Sea they saw potential friends rather than adversaries. It also mirrored a policy outcome of the new European world of risks and dangers. If nothing was done, the Baltic region could become another Balkans with governments suppressing minorities, groups breaking away and attacking each other, and crime and disease rampant. Apart from any immediate effect on the Nordic region, there would also be a 'knock-on' effect should Russia become involved. For the Nordic states, there was a logic to dealing with disease, criminality and refugees in Tallinn rather than Tampere, or Vilnius rather than Västerås; there was also sense in giving the Russian authorities less opportunity to interfere in the Baltic States. The methods used were familiar to the Nordic states: the functionalist approach encouraging interdependence between all the Baltic States and an encouragement of pluralism in especially the Baltic States and Poland that would cement links between societies and help underpin democracy. The implicit Mitranian reading of the situation was that individuals and groups would offer less of a threat to states in which they held a material interest. There was perhaps the hope that not only would functional links bring a close relationship between the Baltic States and the Nordic countries such that there would be no security issues between them, but that this process might be extended to Russia (Hjertonsson, 1997, p.61). However, that presumed a willing partner and perhaps a certain amount of risk-taking by the Baltic States which they were not prepared to assume, at least before having the cover of NATO and EU membership.

The Nordic approach to the Baltic Sea area was based on the four elements of the liberal approach to international relations noted above. There was an enhancement of pluralism and society-to-society links (Sociological Liberalism) and an encouragement of democratic forces in Russia, as well as underpinning democracy in the Baltic States (Republican Liberalism). Most of all, the Nordic states embedded functional links with and between the Baltic States, especially through trade and foreign direct investment (FDI) (Interdependence Liberalism), whilst they also built regional international institutions enveloping the Baltic Sea states and other groups within the Northern region more generally (Institutional Liberalism). Denmark joined Germany to sponsor the Council of the Baltic Sea States (CBSS), Norway was midwife to the Barents Euro-Arctic Council (BEAC), Finland launched the Northern Dimension initiative (NDI) within the European Union, and the Nordic states engaged the Baltic States in Nordic cooperation and encouraged the formation of the Baltic Council. Institutionalism and encouraging investment (for example through the Nordic Investment Bank) were dominant in the policies of the Nordic states towards the other Baltic Sea countries. The encouragement of FDI, together with straightforward aid, presumed that ameliorating the sharp socio-economic distinctions between the north and south-east coasts of the Baltic Sea would have a positive effect on relations between all the states involved, as well as benefiting Nordic business interests. The creation of the CBSS, BEAC and the NDI presumed that institutions mattered quite considerably. The sort of programmes involved in the Nordic 'neighbourhood' policies assumed that institution-building, both within the states and between them, would make a difference to the external policies of these states. There was also an element of passing on to the Baltic States the (presumed successful) experience of the Nordic states in security matters, though it became clear along the way that, in defence terms at least, this was not always appropriate. Nevertheless, the Nordic states were the first states to initiate military assistance to the Baltic States.

During the 1990s the Nordic countries' approach to their 'near neighbourhood' was thus a full-blown Liberal Institutionalist one, though with a special emphasis on the Institutionalist side that included a stress on the institutions, not just of international organisations, but also of trade and investment. Nevertheless, there was also a concern to spread liberal values and this was addressed in a manifestation of Sociological and Republican Liberalism, though both of these were conducted with some caution, especially by Sweden and Norway, as it meant moving away from a statist view of international relations, allowing other actors a greater say. This is not to say that the Nordic states were unaware of the conditions of power in the region. Indeed, Denmark in particular was a staunch advocate of the three Baltic States being taken into NATO, whereas Norway was concerned about the effect of such membership on Russia – an example of its 'Russia first' policy (Archer, 1998, pp.25-8). All the Nordic states were aware that Russia and its relations with the three Baltic States was key to peace in the region, and it is noticeable that the CBSS, BEAC and the NDI all included Russia in one form or another.

The War on Terrorism

After the events in the United States of 11 September 2001, international politics became more focused on what became known as the war on terrorism, the conflict in Afghanistan and the one in Iraq. The US Bush administration took a robust stance in all these cases and by Iraq, its leadership was more of the 'with us or against us' type. Even in the relatively quiet corner of Northern Europe, these events have had their effect. The countries there could have sat out all these conflicts, perhaps sending humanitarian aid where needed. This has not been the case. Indeed, Poland has been leading the Central-South Multi-National Division in Iraq, whilst the three Baltic States also have made contributions to the 'coalitions of the willing' in both Afghanistan and Iraq. Likewise, Norwegian armed forces have been seen in Afghanistan and Iraq, Denmark has sustained casualties in both areas, and even Finland and Sweden have a presence in ISAF in Afghanistan, as well as their sizeable presence in KFOR in Serbia-Montenegro.

This reaction could be seen in Realist terms with the Baltic States, in particular, 'bandwagoning' in favour of the dominant world and NATO power, the United States. The Danes and Norwegians could be seen as doing likewise, but with some ability to distance themselves, as a result of normative/value considerations, from aspects of the Iraq enterprise in particular. Lacking any formal defence ties to the

US, Sweden and Finland were able to avoid any commitment to a conflict that seemed to offer no direct threat. At least the conflict in Afghanistan could be seen as a struggle against forces that exported most of the world's heroin and Islamic fundamentalism, both of which could have adverse effects on Europe.

There is a problem for the Nordic and Baltic States. The adoption of a Liberal Institutionalist security agenda has allowed them to tackle security issues arising in the Baltic region during the 1990s, whether these were related to Russia or to broader societal threats and insecurities. It even has application when these countries have engaged themselves in the Balkans. For example, tying the former-Yugoslav republics together and to the wider Europe via institutions and spreading democracy within their borders, it has been hoped, could do for that area what the process has done for the Baltic region. This may be wishful thinking on their behalf, but it is appropriate for small states in Northern Europe that have nothing to give but their values and some peacekeeping forces (Archer, 1994, pp.374-81).

However, it is not so easy to respond to the main threat – coming from fundamentalist Islamic groups – identified in the war on terrorism. Their centre is hard to identify and is certainly outside Europe, whilst their demands are equally difficult to discern and are not open to immediate amelioration by an application of a liberal agenda. This forces the Northern European states back to the more traditional responses of tightening up defences, which include police activities as well as military ones, or participating in conflicts such as those in Afghanistan and/or Iraq. In these cases, Denmark's, Norway's, and Sweden's move away from a sole concentration on 'defence of the homeland' towards more mobile forces has allowed these countries to participate in operations abroad quite different from traditional peacekeeping operations, even if all the governments had reservations about participating in the Iraq operation before a suitable UN resolution, or participating at all, in the case of Sweden. Poland and the Baltic States had fewer scruples and, perhaps spurred on by the prospect of NATO membership, contributed to the forces in Iraq with few reservations.

Nevertheless, there are elements of the war on terrorism addressed by the Liberal Institutionalist approach. The comprehensive security agenda has been confirmed, as has a wider set of referent objects of security (the individual, family, religious groups, the nation, and the state). This would suggest a wide range of instruments (from 'soft' to 'hard') to be used in this conflict, a concept well-rooted in Nordic thinking (Archer, 2001b). Furthermore, the concept of the 'indivisibility of security', central to much liberal thinking about security, would suggest that conflicts left to fester in Sudan, Palestine or Kashmir, repressive regimes in Afghanistan (or, indeed, Saudi Arabia) cannot be isolated in their effects. Sooner or later, even the quiet corners of Europe in Spain or Sweden can be affected. It is, therefore, not unexpected that the Nordic states at least, have been taking another approach to this 'war'. All of them have engaged themselves in attempting to encourage political settlements of the conflicts that are seen as the tinder of terrorism, especially the Palestine-Israel conflict. The success of this engagement, even when assisted by the US in the case of the 'Oslo process', has been a hostage to the attitude of the parties involved, and it has not involved directly those forces that have been behind many of the terrorist outrages. Furthermore, when some people from Palestine or Chechnya have been engaged in a dialogue by Nordic states, even unofficially by non-governmental groups, the response of the Israeli and Russian governments has been to chastise the Nordic (and, in the Chechen case, Baltic) governments for dealing with terrorists.

When looking at Northern Europe, there has thus been a differentiated response to the 'war on terrorism'. After an initial dispute about Iraq, Russia has signed up to the US agenda, with President Putin vowing to fight terrorism wherever it may be. Especially after the Beslan school siege, this could involve Russia taking preventative action abroad, something that the Baltic States would view with some concern. Denmark and Norway, joined by the three Baltic States, have engaged themselves in Iraq and Afghanistan at a modest level within NATO. Finland, Germany and Sweden have limited their involvement to the NATO-led operation in Afghanistan. All the EU states around the Baltic, plus Norway, have contributed to the European Union's own operations against terrorism through Europol and similar cooperation (Europol, 2004).

The very immediacy of terrorism has overshadowed the efforts of the Nordic states to provide long-term solutions by dealing with the roots of terror in conflicts in the world outside Europe and North America. There is also the point that some aspects of the grievances espoused by those dubbed as terrorists are not open to treatment by the liberal agenda. To the extent that actions taken against the West are inspired by its very materialism and lifestyle, it is hard for a group of some of the most materially successful countries to deal with such a threat, short of renouncing their worldly goods. Nevertheless, the Nordic states are well aware that many of the groups behind international terrorism find fertile ground in the miserable economic, environmental and political conditions suffered by a large section of the world's population, and work through international organisations and non-governmental agencies (as well as using their own national and collective Nordic efforts) to try to alleviate this poverty. However, there is the feeling that, especially without the full-hearted support of the governments of the 'Golden Billion' citizens in the world – those that have a better life – little can be achieved. In this case the liberal agenda is limited by a lack of understanding and sympathy from the people and governments in countries that have a more effective capability to change the world than the small Nordic states.

Dual Enlargement

The dual enlargement of the EU and NATO to include the three Baltic States, as well as Poland, has seen some shifts in their approaches towards security. These states can now pursue their security agenda through NATO and, to some extent, the EU, and may seem to need the Nordic states less. The question arises as to whether these countries have pursued a more Liberal Institutionalist agenda on the way to membership simply as a guise, or whether they have actually believed what they were saying. This may prove an almost impossible question to answer (though see Männik 2005, Ch.4).

On the eve of joining NATO and the EU, the Baltic States and Poland, in response to US prompting, signed up to the US-led agenda on Iraq and the war on terrorism (Larrabee, 2003). This can be seen in fairly Realist terms – following the dominant power, especially with the expectation that such support could work two ways – or there may be a Liberal Institutionalist explanation. In this case, it can be seen as part of the socialising process of the institutions, particularly NATO. Poland, a recent NATO member, and the Baltic States, soon to be members, understood from the US and the UK that this was what was needed from 'good' alliance members (as opposed to France and, in this case, but not in the case of Afghanistan, Germany). Furthermore, the Baltic States' talk in the run-up to NATO membership of being security providers (and not just consumers) obliged them to act more globally, thus requiring them to think outside the Baltic box. In the latter case, the 'Institutionalist' element in Liberal Institutionalism might have had its effect on security policy, though it has been given a hefty push by US persuasion.

The dual enlargement of NATO and the EU will add a couple of new twists to the security picture in the region. Poland and the Baltic States have now achieved a major security aim, that of joining NATO and the EU. Any policy posture that was felt necessary to advance membership can be eased. NATO membership, together with EU membership, provides these four states with a certain amount of collective security, a point that seems to have helped them moderate their portrayal of Russia. Under present circumstances, the question of who might provide 'Article 5' security cover for the region does not seem to be asked, though the Alliance's configuration of forces would presumably allow it to deploy anywhere in Europe.

Membership of NATO and the EU by the Baltic States (and Poland) may seem likely to lessen their reliance on and involvement with the Nordic countries in the defence and security field. They may expect to be involved with a wider spectrum of alliance members. Nevertheless, the message from Brussels (the ESDP as well as NATO) may be similar to that to Denmark and Norway, which is to 'think regionally' and to link up with the North Sea states, the United Kingdom, Germany and the Netherlands. In the area of weapons procurement, this would also include Sweden. The Baltic States now have to rely on NATO for their national defence as their own resources are too limited to do anything but the basics for their part in collective defence systems.

For wider security considerations, the EU may play a more important role and one that fits in to the Liberal Institutionalist outlook. It will be through the EU that the new members will have the opportunity to establish better economic links with Russia, but a number of these institutions, such as the Northern Dimension Initiative (NDI), need agendas of value to all members. Interreg and the NDI will encourage closer societal links with north-west Russia, though they can also be subject to governmental indifference. This can scarcely be expected to bring about a security community for the whole region, including Kaliningrad and St. Petersburg, but it may form the basis for a more modest zone of peace. The danger is that the dual enlargement has entrenched both aspects of the Liberal Institutionalist agenda in the non-Russian part of Northern Europe, to the detriment of spreading it to the entire region.

Conclusions

Compared with most other parts of Europe, Northern Europe is relatively 'secure', both in more traditional defence of the realm terms, and in terms of the new security agenda. The governments there have identified new insecurities (drugs, crime, environmental hazards, and disease) and items on their lists would no doubt be echoed by most of their populations. More traditional threats to the homeland have either fallen off the agenda or are now covered by NATO, and to some extent EU, membership.

Has it been the case that the area is becoming/has become one of 'asecurity'? After all, Wæver (1998, p.71) reminds us that 'security and insecurity are not exhaustive options, and more attention needs to be given to a-security'. Pertti Joenniemi (2003, pp.204-5) claims that Norden 'constitutes a community of asecurity by default, and achieved that end-station already a long time ago'. This is compared with the EU that aspires for desecuritization by design in order to arrive at a state of asecurity as a result. The notion is that security is just off the agenda (and has been for some while) between the Nordic countries. The explanation is that the Nordic region created a complementary 'we' to national identity that was based on contacts in civil society: this allowed members of the region to drop security when they engaged with each other, and instead to deal with other (non-security) issues.

This may neglect the extent to which, especially during the Cold War, the Nordic governments considered each other's security both in positive terms (in order not to harm the security of other Nordic states by their own actions) or negatively (how the actions of other Nordic states might harm them). It may also be a sanguine view of the extent to which security between the states did go off the agenda in the Cold War period. Nevertheless, if we use the notion as a starting point, can we expect the Baltic region and the area of Northern Europe as a whole to become one of asecurity? The answer to this would depend on the extent and strength of societal links and their ability to knock security off the political agenda by prioritising other elements. Again, between governments, security issues (even narrowly defined) have been of interest in Nordic-Baltic relations, but this may now be less the case as the Baltic States find other NATO members with which to interact. Both the institutionalist and the liberal aspects of Liberal Institutionalism have been important here. Russia is included in many of the institutions in the region such as the BEAC, CBSS, NDI and Partnership for Peace. A more engaged official response to the work of these institutions by the Russian authorities would help these institutions' goals, though the involvement of Russian companies, civic groups and local authorities has already had a positive effect on their activities (Nordic Council, 2004). The building of functioning democracies in the Baltic States and Poland and the society-to-society transnational links have helped establish a level of trust between the countries and this has been confirmed and routinised by membership of institutions such as the CBSS, Partnership for Peace, the EU and NATO. However, doubts over the nature of democracy in Russia and difficulties in establishing societal links have hobbled the liberal aspect of the Liberal Institutionalist agenda, thereby showing its sometimes fragile nature and limitations. It has shown that often success in the institutional aspect of cooperation can be circumscribed by the weakness of democratic and societal institutions in one or more member state.

Furthermore, for either an area of security or a security community or even a region of asecurity to remain such still requires an iteration of conducive policies by the political elite and for a significant section of the population to keep rewarding them for their efforts. One aspect of this region is that it is becoming more cosmopolitan and one possible result, especially if minorities are not integrated into existing societies, is that external conflicts, hatreds and attitudes may test both the relative social peace of the area and its ability substantially to exclude security issues from its internal agenda.

To sum up, the Nordic states developed a minor theme bearing the imprint of Liberal Institutionalism in their Cold War security policies and this was given broader importance during the decade after the end of the Cold War. During that time the dual elements of liberalism and institutionalism worked together, especially in the inclusion of the Baltic States into a zone of cooperative security. The Baltic States themselves, and Poland, may have had a more traditional view of security, but came publicly to accept a security agenda more in line with that of the Nordic states and the EU. This was aided by the actions of Russia in withdrawing its troops from their territory and by their membership of NATO and the EU. However, the war on terrorism has produced a situation to which it is more difficult to apply the liberal security agenda, though the institutional element still has immediate relevance. The dual enlargement favours a Liberal Institutionalist approach between the members of the EEA and of NATO but this could exclude Sweden and Finland in some cases and seems to leave Russia on the side. Nevertheless, Russia can be and has been included in institution-building in the region, but its inclusion in a liberal grouping will depend on internal developments in Russia itself. However, the continued existence of common institutions that affect the wider security agenda can help maintain a common interest between all the North European states, though for trust to become embedded there will need to be further political development within Russia.

References

Adler, Emanuel and Barnett, Michael (eds.) (1998), *Security Communities*, Cambridge, Cambridge University Press.

Andrén, Nils (1967), 'Nordic integration', *Cooperation and Conflict*, (3-4), pp. 1-25.

Archer, Clive (1994), 'Conflict Prevention in Europe. The case of the Nordic States and Macedonia', *Cooperation and Conflict*, Vol. 29(4), pp. 367-86.

Archer, Clive (1998), *Norden and the Security of the Baltic States*, Oslo, Den norske atlanterhavskomite, Det sikkerhetspolitiske bibliotek nr. 4/1998.

Archer, Clive (2001a), *International Organizations*, London and New York, Routledge, 3rd edition.

Archer, Clive (2001b), 'The Northern Dimension as a soft-Soft Option for the Baltic States' Security', in Hanna Ojanen (ed.), *The Northern Dimension: Fuel for the EU?*, Helsinki and Berlin, Ulkopoliittinen instituutti and Institut für Europäische Politik, pp. 188-208.

Archer, Clive (2003), 'Introduction', in Clive Archer and Pertti Joenniemi (eds.), *The Nordic Peace*, Aldershot, Ashgate, pp. 1-23.

Baltic Sea States Summit (1996), *Presidents' Declaration, Visby, 3-4 May 1996*, mimeo.

Boel, Erik (1988), *Socialdemokratiets atomvåbenpolitik 1945-88*, Copenhagen, Akademisk Forlag.

Brundtland, Arne Olav (1966), 'The Nordic Balance', *Cooperation and Conflict*, (2), pp. 30-63.

Claude, Inis (1968), 'International Organization: the Process and the Institutions', in David Sills (ed.), *International Encyclopaedia of the Social Sciences*, New York, Macmillan and Free Press, Vol. 8, pp. 33-40.

Deutsch, Karl *et al.*, (1957), *Political Community and the North Atlantic Area*, Princeton, NJ, Princeton University Press.

Doyle, Michael (1995), 'On the Democratic Peace', *International Security*, Vol. 19(4), pp. 164-84.

Engelbrekt, Kjell (2002), *Security Policy Reorientation in Peripheral Europe*, Aldershot, Ashgate.

Europol (2004), 'Europol at a glance'. Available at http://www.europol.eu.int.

Försvarsdepartementet (1995), *Sverige I Europa och världen*, Stockholm, Försvarsdepartementet.

Hansen, Birthe (1995), 'Dansk Baltikumpolitik 1989-1995', in Svend Aage Christensen and Ole Wæver (eds.), *Dansk Udenrigspolitisk Årbog 1995*, Copenhagen, Dansk Udenrigspolitisk Institut, pp. 35-65.

Held, David (1993), 'Democracy from City-states to a Cosmopolitan Order?', in D. Held (ed.), *Prospects for Democracy: North, South, East, West*, Cambridge, Polity Press, pp. 13-52.

Hjertonsson, Ulf (1997), 'Sweden and Security in the Baltic Sea Region', in Bo Huldt and Ulrika Johannessen (eds.), *1st Annual conference on Baltic Sea Security and Cooperation*, Conference Papers, Stockholm, Utanrikspolitisk Institutet, pp. 59-62.

Holst, Johan Jørgen (1985), 'Lilliputs and Gulliver: Small States in a Great Power Alliance', in G. Flynn (ed.), *NATO's Northern Allies: The National Security Policies of Belgium, Denmark, the Netherlands, and Norway*, London, Croom Helm, pp. 258-86.

Independent Commission on Disarmament and Security Matters (1982), *Common Security: A Programme for Disarmament*, London, Pan.

Jackson, Robert and Sørensen, Georg (1999), *Introduction to International Relations*, Oxford, Oxford University Press.

Joenniemi, Pertti (2003), 'Norden Beyond Security Community', in Clive Archer and Pertti Joenniemi (eds.), *The Nordic Peace*, Aldershot, Ashgate, pp. 198-212.

Joffe, Josef (1985), 'The "Scandilux" Connection: Belgium, Denmark, the Netherlands and Norway in Comparative Perspective', in G. Flynn (ed.), *NATO's Northern Allies: The National Security Policies of Belgium, Denmark, the Netherlands, and Norway*, London, Croom Helm, pp. 224-57.

Keohane, Robert (1993), 'Institutionalist Theory and Realist Challenge After the Cold War', in David Baldwin (ed.), *Neorealism and Neoliberalism: The Contemporary Debate*, New York, Columbia University Press, pp. 269-300.

Keohane, Robert and Martin, L. (1995), 'The Promise of Institutionalist Theory', *International Security*, Vol. 20(1), pp. 39-51.

Keohane, Robert and Nye, Joseph (eds.) (1971), *Transnational Relations and World Politics*, Cambridge, Mass., Harvard University Press.

Larrabee, F. S. (2003) 'The Baltic States and NATO Membership', *Testimony Presented to the United States Senate Committee on Foreign Relations on April 3*, Santa Monica, RAND Corporation.

Lodgaard, Sverre, with Paul Berg (1982), 'Nordic Initiatives for a nuclear-free zone in Europe', in *SIPRI Yearbook 1982*, London, Taylor and Francis, pp. 78-80.

Männik, Erik (2004), 'Small States: Invited to NATO – Able to Contribute?', *Defense & Security Analysis*, Vol. 20(1), pp. 21-37.

Männik, Erik (2005), *Estonia's Integration into NATO: the opportunities and willingness of the small state*, PhD thesis submitted to the Manchester Metropolitan University.

Mearsheimer, John (1991), 'Back to the Future: Instability in Europe After the Cold War', in Sean Lynne-Jones (ed.), *The Cold War and After: Prospects for Peace*, Cambridge, Mass., MIT Press, pp. 141-92.

Ministry for Foreign Affairs (1995), *Security in a Changing World. Guidelines for Finland's Security Policy*, Helsinki, Ministry for Foreign Affairs.

Ministry of Defence (Denmark) (1992), *Rapport om Forsvarets fremtidige struktur og størrrelse*, Copenhagen, Ministry of Defence.

Ministry of Defence (Sweden) (1995), *Sweden in Europe and the World*, Stockholm, Ministry of Defence.

Mitrany, David (1961), *A Working Peace System*, Chicago, Quadrangle Books.

Neumann, Iver (2001), *Norge – en kritikk Begrepsmakt I Europa-debatten*, Oslo: Pax-forlag.

Nordic Council (2004), 'Russian Environmental Debate' *The Northern Dimension in an Enlarged EU – Nordic Council Theme Meeting 14-15 April 2004*. Available at http:www.norden.org/tema2004/uk/kg3.pdf.

NOU (Norges Offentlige Utredninger) (1992), *Forsvarskommisjonen av 1990*, Oslo, NOU 1992:12.

Riste, Olav (2001), *Norway's Foreign Relations – A History*, Oslo, Universitetsforlaget.

Russett, Bruce (1993), *Grasping the Democratic Peace: Principles for a Post-Cold War World*, Princeton, Princeton University Press.

Russett, Bruce and Oneal, John (2001), *Triangulating Peace. Democracy Interdependence and International Organizations*, New York and London, W.W. Norton & Company.

SOU (Statens Offentliga Utredningar) (1994), *Om kriget kommer...Förberedelser för mottagande av militärt bistand 1949-1969 (Betänkande av Neutralitetspolitikkommissionen, 1994:11)*, Stockholm, Statsrådsberedningen.

Wæver, Ole (1998), 'Insecurity, security and asecurity in the West-European non-war community', in E. Adler and M. Barnett (eds.), *Security Communities*, Cambridge, Cambridge University Press, pp. 69-118.

Williams, Michael C. (2001), 'The Discipline of the Democratic Peace: Kant, Liberalism and the Social Construction of Security Communities', *European Journal of International Relations*, Vol. 7(4), pp. 525-53.

Chapter 3

Rafting Nilas:
Subjectivity, Memory and the Discursive
Patterns of the North

Frank Möller

Nilas, a thin elastic crust of ice, easily bending on waves and swell and under pressure, thrusting in a pattern of interlocking 'fingers'. Has a matt surface and is up to 10 cm in thickness.

Rafting, pressure process whereby one piece of ice overrides another.

Finger rafting, a type of rafting whereby interlocking thrusts are formed, each floe thrusting 'fingers' alternately over and under each other.

– standard definitions published by the World Meteorological Organisation, here quoted from Scientific Committee on Antarctic Research, *Global Change and the Antarctic*, at http://www.antcrc.utas.edu.au/aspect/seaiceglossary.html.

Introduction

This chapter asks whether or not Northern subjectivity can be thought of without the existence of a collective memory. In other words, does the North have to be a community of memory in order to exert its own subjectivity and to impact on the European centre? Subjectivity means here the capability of groups of people to act together as a subject in international affairs, rather than being an object of someone else's politics. Collective subjectivity requires a feeling of togetherness linked to common interests and/or identities because otherwise people would not work together consistently and dependably. Derived from social memory studies it is argued here that this process cannot be thought of without the existence of a collective memory, which bridges temporal and spatial gaps in order to create the illusion of continuous identities. It is further argued that an all-encompassing collective memory is missing in the North. Different sets of memories of, for example, the Second World War and the Cold War compete with one another. The absence of a collective memory seems to limit the capability for collective action because it renders difficult the emergence of a we-feeling, in terms of which common interests could be defined and collective action could be pursued. This deficiency has been recognised by many policy-makers who, especially in the early 1990s, invoked a common historical heritage by referring to, among other things, the Hansa League. This may have been a useful starting point for region building, but from a long-term perspective it has failed. This is because the historical identity markers emphasised in the early stages of the region building process (Hansa League, Pomor trade and so on) have been too weak, being too remote from and too irrelevant to people's everyday lives to provide sufficient amalgam to bind the Northern people together.

However, rather than drawing the pessimistic conclusion that due to a lack of a collective memory the region building process in Europe's North is ultimately doomed to failure, it is suggested here that we should treat as an asset what at first sight seems to be a liability. That is to say deconstructing the ostensibly unifying stories and acknowledging the existence of diverse and ambivalent collective memories may result in a Northern subjectivity that is based on an appreciation of, rather than a reduction in, difference. Discourse over memories may be more important to collective Northern subjectivity than the construction of a necessarily artificial common memory. It is precisely here where the North can also impact on the European centre by cultivating a culture that, as Andreas Huyssen (1995, p.28) has put it in a different context, 'no longer feels the need to homogenise and is learning how to live pragmatically with real difference'. This learning process is relevant to the European integration process which is too often characterised by the desire for unitary positions. It is also relevant to security policy: the most pressing dangers of late modernity are said to require 'a form of security based on the appreciation and articulation rather than the normalisation or extirpation of difference' (Der Derian, 1995, p.27). To achieve this end this chapter argues that policy-makers can very effectively be supported by the arts, while the artistic community has also something to learn from politics.

The North Remembered

Regardless of deliberate attempts by several policy-makers to use historical metaphors to trigger region building, it can be argued that the region building process in Northern Europe has made the least progress regarding what may be called a mnemonic region, i.e. one that acknowledges that different groups of people have different sets of memories that are equally valuable. Memories of the North mirror different experiences with, conceptions of and emotional-geographical self-locations within, the North. These different Norths do not always relate to each other easily. The aim of region building, therefore, cannot be the construction of common memories. Rather than playing off a specific set of memories of the North against its competitors, the discursive strength of the North is to be found in its refusal of, and resistance to, simplistic approaches. Its potential for subjectivity lies in the simultaneous existence of memories of different Norths that are equally valuable. These different Norths are partially overlapping and partially separated from or ignorant of one another and may even be mutually exclusive. This results in a condition of tension that cannot be easily relaxed. It invites constant negotiation of the relationship between different conceptions and memories of the North. The North cannot be reduced to one reading without violating the subjectivity of those adhering to alternative interpretations.

Thus, different ideas of the North have a role to play in the Northern jigsaw puzzle – except that 'puzzle' (indicating distinct pieces, clearly separated from, but fitting neatly with one another) is not really the right word. As suggested by the Arctic metaphor used in the title of this chapter, the (memories of the) North can more aptly be seen as elastic and changeable. Its components can be thought of as partially overlapping and interlocking, bending when under pressure rather than immediately fracturing; shaped and influenced by the surrounding environment, yet maintaining distinctive features of their own (that can be integrated in their environment only at the price of their evaporation).

However one conceives of and remembers the North – e.g., the Arctic North, the Nordic North, 5 (Nordic states) + 3 (Baltic States), north-eastern Europe or even wider conceptions, or the sum of all these conceptions – the North is not a unified actor. One should therefore avoid naturalising 'the North' and bear in mind that it is characterised by its peripheral location in, and multidimensional relationship with, Europe (which is the main topic of this book). However, it is also characterised by complex internal centre/periphery dynamics that influence both Northern subjectivity and various region building processes. For example, appeals to the Hansa League legacy have often been depicted as a useful identity provider for the Nordic-Baltic region, but their relevance to the Arctic North seems to be only limited. References to Pomor trade, on the other hand, can be seen as the Arctic equivalent of an historical identity provider, but which in turn is not very relevant to the Baltic region. Both are perfect examples of the construction of collective memories in the light of present requirements, but they are also indicative of the lack of a more recent, inclusive identity provider for Northern Europe. They are also reminders that conflict, rather than cooperation, dominated international relations in the region throughout the 20th century, during which time Northern Europe seemed to display little of its own subjectivity – with the possible exception of the mutually reinforcing concepts of the Swedish welfare state and neutrality that were periodically admired from the outside. The attractiveness of the principle of 'equality at home and justice abroad' (Ruth, 1984, p.71) also shows that subjectivity does not always require centrality; indeed, a 'small-state position' at the periphery of the international system may be converted 'from a handicap into an asset' (Ruth, 1984, p.92). 'Periphery' certainly is a social construction reflecting discursive and material power relations. Like 'marginality', it is constructed, perceived and remembered as positive or negative only as a result of the meaning socially assigned to it, with positive and negative meanings occasionally coexisting (Palosaari and Möller, 2004).

For example, in the Mediterranean view, as expressed in classic Greek and Roman writings, the North 'represented both threat and salvation' (Lopez, 1999, p.314). Both representations are important ingredients of the Western imagination. This ambivalence can be traced back to the ancient Greek tales, including those about the regions beyond the travellers' own voyages. These writings frequently were projections of the travellers' own imagination, sometimes combined with hearsay; they reflected fears and hopes rather than empirical evidence: empty areas in terms of experience, generously furnished by the authors' conjectures. Although representations can be found of the Northern peoples as Cynocephali, fierce, barbaric and malevolent, the projections were not exclusively negative: that which was unknown to the writers/travellers was not necessarily depicted as a threat. Herodotus, writing in 440 B.C., explicitly excluded the Hyperboreans (i.e., those beyond the North winds) from those nations who 'were continually encroaching upon their neighbours'. Depictions of Hyperborea as a land with twenty-four hours a day of sunshine contrasted with representations of the Northern lands focusing on the permanent fall of 'feathers', i.e., snow – 'less, of course, in the summer than in the wintertime' – that 'prevent persons from penetrating into the remoter parts of the continent' and that were declared 'uninhabitable by reason of the severity of the winter'. Snow-covered mountains separated negatively-valued Northern regions from positively-valued areas still farther North, beyond the North wind. The Northern Ocean was often seen as a 'place of whirlpools (*Chaos* and *Maelstrom*) and rip tides' (Lopez, 1999, p.315), the Hyperborean Sea as unnavigable, the Northern winds as awesome and destructive. Pytheas de Massalia (380-310 B.C.), however, reportedly spoke of what he called Thule, a place six days sailing North of Britain, as a honey-producing agricultural country with fruit-eating and milk-drinking inhabitants that made a drink of grain and honey and threshed their grain in barns. The account of his journey is now lost and many different interpretations compete with one another as to which place Pytheas did actually visit.

This is not to suggest that the representations of Northern lands and peoples as peacefully living in plenty were more accurate than those depicting the North as a source of danger. The idealised representations of the North are no less products of the ideas prevalent in the centres than are the negative descriptions, and both construct the indigenous peoples 'within perspectives other than their own' (Shapiro, 2004, p.xii). What is important in the present context is that representations of the North as old as those suggested by the Greek and Roman writers, today serve as a repository for multifarious conceptions and memories of the North which can be utilised for present purposes. This is so due to the characteristics of collective memory that, before returning to the North, shall briefly be sketched.

Subjectivity and Collective Memory

Subjectivity requires collective memories be translated into a collective identity. The relation between identity and memory has been firmly established in the literature on social memory. While reviewing the literature on collective memory Olick and Robbins (1998, p.133) state that 'Memory is a central, if not the central, medium through which identities are constituted'. David Lowenthal (1985, p.197) adds that 'to know what we were confirms that we are'. Pierre Nora (2002) links the 'current upsurge in memory' to changes in the understanding of identity, where identity is changing from an individual property to a collective project. In international politics, the relationship between subjectivity and collective memory is important because collective memories connect the members of a community to the community's past members. By doing so, they provide the community with a sense of continuity, help establish this community in the first place and render possible acting in terms of a collective 'we'. Indeed, a 'memory of Self as a separate locus of thought and activity' (Wendt, 1999, p.225) characterises the identity of intentional actors. The connection between subjectivity and collective memory is important also because collective memories 'can help explain patterns in aggregate behaviour':

> As long as individuals see themselves as having an allegiance and commitment to the group, collective memories will be available as a resource for mobilizing collective action even if they are not believed, in a phenomenological sense, by individuals (Wendt, 1999, p.163).

Collective memory does not mean that each person has the same recollections of the same events, but rather that memory is acquired in discourse with others, discourse that may also include conflicts over meaning. Memory and subjectivity are treated here as projects pertaining to collectivities rather than individuals. Throughout the chapter, the rather vague term 'groups of people' is used in order not to essentialise them: the composition of groups changes over time and with it the collective memories of their members. Since each person is a member of many groups at the same time, they carry with them different memories of the same event that can be motivated in a given social context. Furthermore, collective memory:

> simplifies; sees events from a single, committed perspective; is impatient with ambiguities of any kind; reduces events to mythic archetypes. [...] Typically a collective memory, at least a significant collective memory, is understood to express some eternal or essential truth about the group – usually tragic. A memory, once established, comes to define that eternal truth, and, along with it, an eternal identity, for the members of the group (Novick, 2001, p.4).

While history is concerned with the past, memory is shaped by present requirements. While history acknowledges the historicity of events, memory often does not (ibid.). Memory has been collectivised only recently, owing to what Nora calls the acceleration and the democratisation of history. The latter resulted from international, domestic and ideological decolonisation, in the course of which 'traditional, long-term memories' were liberated from oppression or confiscation by totalitarian regimes (Nora, 2002). Apart from its temporal dimension, memory 'is equally a recollection of spaces past' (Johnson, 2003, p.6); it is 'a form of awareness' (Lowenthal, 1985, p.194) but, like identity, it is also an 'a-where-ness' (Osborne, 2001), maintained through geographical discourse and linked to notions of place. Like the times past, the spaces past are impervious to simplified interpretations.

Given the above assessment that the 20th century in Europe's North was characterised by conflict rather than cooperation, it does not require much theoretical sophistication to expect that a person that experienced the Second World War in, for example, neutral Sweden will remember the war differently to a person that experienced the same war in, say, occupied Estonia – and it may even be pondered if both persons actually remember the 'same' war. In early 1991, for example, the 'situation of the Second World War' was still said to persist in the Baltic countries (Meri, 1991, p.109). In particular, memories of such violent encounters as wars, occupations and deportations, experienced in parts of Northern Europe in abundance, are likely to 'deeply influence the perceptual predispositions of most citizens' (Jervis, 1976, p.266) even a long time after the events actually took place. Likewise, the indigenous peoples of the Arctic are not likely to have shared recollections with the political decision-makers in the capitals of the militarisation and nuclearisation of their land during the Cold War, and the earlier erection of national boundaries that cut their land into pieces. Thus, nation-building and nation-destroying will be remembered differently. Russian-speakers who moved to what they considered a Soviet republic can be expected to remember the Soviet times in Estonia, Latvia and Lithuania differently to the members of the titular nations. As has been argued in regard to Soviet Latvia, for example, 'Latvian memories conflicted with official versions of history'. Therefore, 'memory acquire[d] a central importance for the preservation of authenticity and truth as well as a peculiar poignancy' (Skultans, 1998, p.28). Today, with reversed premises, Russian-speakers' memories can be expected to deviate from the official version of history. Again, memory may acquire importance as a reservoir of authenticity, except that 'authenticity' does not seem to be the right word given the characteristics of collective memory, namely, that it is unreliable, fragmentary and constantly reshaped in the light of present requirements.

'There's not much history in these parts'

– a Moscow *dzhentelman* angler, responding to the idea to visit the Kola peninsula in search of the area's history (Took, 2004, p.340).

In a recent paper discussing the remnants of the past in the Baltic Sea region, Christian Wellmann (2004, p.282) states that 'sentiments against neighbours', a 'highly confrontational and often biased debate among the public' and the 'tabooing of issues' are still to be found: 'consensus building is hindered by traumata, myths, and hesitations to constructively deal with the past'. Even among intellectuals, domestic and cross-border dialogue on issues related to history and memory 'seems to be extremely difficult to initiate'. Thus, what can currently be witnessed is not so much a lack of history, but rather history – and its reworking in memory and myth – in abundance. If we understand a collective memory as a precondition for collective subjectivity and social action, then the temporal and spatial fragmentation of memories in Europe's North seems to be an obstacle to region building, mentally and otherwise. However, consensus building and the homogenisation of memories are inappropriate remedies.

In particular, memories of violent encounters inhibit the willingness to remember 'stories not only of suffering received but [also] of suffering inflicted', which is seen by Robert Bellah and associates (1984, p.153) as a precondition for a genuine community of memory. When addressed by politics, questions pertaining to history and memory have occasionally resulted in confrontation and conflict, rather than in cooperation and communication. A case in point is the *éclat* that followed a speech by the then Latvian Minister of Foreign Affairs, Sandra Kalniete, at the Leipzig Book Fair in 2004. Her claims that Nazism and Communism 'were equally criminal' and that there 'must never be a gradation between those philosophies just because one of them participated in the victory over the other' (Kalniete, 2004) could have been a starting point for an open-minded debate on the different experiences and memories which still separate different groups of people in the Baltic Sea region from one another. Yet, it was not, and instead resulted in cognitive closures and emotional fissures – not least due to the inclinations of segments of the West's political and societal elite to render their own mnemonic culture obligatory to others and to act as an 'erinnerungspolitischer Lehrmeister', a mnemo-political teacher (Güntner, 2004). For example, in April 2002 a US State Department official linked NATO membership of the Baltic States with, among other things, 'hard work [...] on complex domestic issues like dealing with the history of the Holocaust' (Conley, 2002), without mentioning in this context the equally complex issue of dealing with the history – and the memory – of the Soviet occupation.

The overall reluctance in the West to put much emphasis on the wrongs inflicted upon many people during the Soviet rule (Maier, 2001/2002) co-exists with the duty, emphasised by Kalniete, to 'reverse [the] mistake' of 'forever exculpat[ing] the sins of the Soviet system' because of the Soviet battle against

Fascism (Kalniete, 2004). What Nora calls '*ideological* decolonisation' in Eastern Europe, which enables formerly suppressed peoples to rediscover their memories, challenges Western Europe's intention to act as the model for the whole of Europe. This is not only in terms of political, economic and social organisation, but also with respect to the politics of memory by which Western Europe prescribes to the new EU member-states which aspects of their national past they have to emphasise in order to qualify for full membership of 'Europe' – even after their formal acceptance to the EU (Donskis, 2004, p.20). However, the more pressure the West exerts on the Baltics as to memory formation, the more likely is the official cultivation of particularistic memories (Welzer et al., 2002, p.191). Even if the cognitive dimension of memory in the new EU member-states is designed according to Western prescriptions, the emotional dimension of memory may still adhere to different readings of the past. It is important to note here that just because memories are different does not mean that they are wrong or even illegitimate. The appreciation of difference, emphasised elsewhere with respect to security (Möller, 2003), is equally important when it comes to representations of the past. What is required, then, is something else than the homogenisation of memories and the one-sided adaptation to the narrative prevalent in the West. Thus, even an agreement to disagree, modest as it may seem, would seem to be a step forward and a welcome replacement of attempts to naturalise one specific reading of the past by the acknowledgement that different groups of people may legitimately have different memories of the same historical event.

A constructive dialogue on the past is made difficult by two other things, one related to identity construction, the other to nation-state construction. First, the emphasis on crimes committed by the Soviet Union against the Baltic peoples, legitimate as it may be, fits neatly with the cultivation of the Russian Federation, the successor to the Soviet Union, as a negative reference point against which the independent Baltic States were constructed during the 1990s. In the Baltic States a significant ingredient of cultural identity is said to be the experience of '*living on the border* of Western civilization': 'living under the Soviets meant a "clash of civilizations" inside the mind of every single individual, the loss of personal integrity, and even the loss of the right to an authentic life-world' (Lauristin, 1997, pp.29, 37). Regaining an authentic life-world and gaining a post-Soviet identity required what Eviatar Zerubavel (2003, p.40), in a different context, has called the '*mental* integration of otherwise disconnected points in time into a seemingly single historical whole'. Social memory makes this integration possible. It connects past with present events but, as always, it does so in the light of present requirements reflecting, among other things, identity construction. Indeed, the cultivation of a particular past and its inscription in collective memory is 'a key area of cultural reproduction, of moral regulation and of identity maintenance' (Schöpflin, 1999, p.7).

Second, memory becomes politics when nationalised and naturalised so as to create the impression of a coherent state-nation nexus and to essentialise the concept of the nation-state. Like the printed media (Anderson, 1991) and visual culture (Shapiro, 2004), appeals to the past contribute to the essentialisation of the 'concept of the nation-state as a "natural" political entity' (Turnbull, 1996, p.411) and to the homogenisation of the national imaginary (Shapiro, 2004, p.105). For example, forms of commemoration such as war memorials symbolise self-other relations and perpetuate them by engraving them on the collective memory. Likewise, region building may be inhibited by the 'multiple sources of learning' to which young people are exposed, and which may result in the prioritisation of the national over the regional. From this it follows that 'nations may prevail a long time in the young people's mind maps', by becoming inscribed in their memories (Jukarainen, 2003, p.231). It is difficult to build regions if the primary thing one is made to remember is nations. Indeed, the dominance of national memory over other memories 'maintains the primacy of national over other kinds of identity for primary allegiance' (Olick and Robbins, 1998, p.127). This is a challenge to region building to which policy-makers have responded by using a variety of historical metaphors indicating, both the social constructedness of, and the existence of alternatives to, nation-states. However, their possibility to call into question the very social institution that gives them legitimacy seems to be limited and in need of support (more on which below).

The construction of a regional collective memory will compete for a long time with the construction of memory on the national level, with the former ideally acknowledging difference and the latter frequently suppressing it. The politics of memory is a component part of the permanent reproduction of states through discursive practice. Nation-building may be a more obvious object of states that regained their independence only recently, but established nation-states also rely on the same repertoire of discursive practices, among which 'historical discourse' (Lagerspetz, 1999, p.24) figures prominently, except that this particular discourse often assumes the form of stipulation (Sontag, 2002, p.86) or duty (Nora, 2002). It therefore seems to be optimistic to assume that policy-makers single-handedly would to able to initiate dialogues that ultimately could result in a regional community of memory. In the early 1990s many policy-makers were telling stories in order to discursively construct the region by referring to a common historical heritage. Although this narrative strategy may be seen as a genuine attempt at region building rather than nation building, it was problematic for two reasons. First, most of these stories were unifying and homogenising. This may have been an important trigger for the region building process, but it has not proven durable. Second, most policy-makers were initially interested in either the Barents Sea or the Baltic Sea region, not the North. The stories told to help integrate the Baltic region did not have much to say about the non-Baltic parts of the North, and vice versa. This has been corrected, to some extent, in the second half of the 1990s by introducing all-encompassing approaches to the North, for example, the European Union's Northern Dimension and the United States' Northern Europe Initiative, the latter of which explicitly intended to offer a framework for managing, rather than eliminating, differences (Asmus, 1999). These are promising but still fragile signs. It still seems to be necessary to assist those policy-makers who are genuinely interested in the North in a way that would help people regard the negotiation of different views on the past as an asset to region building, rather than as a liability to nation building.

Likewise, the academic community has been very active in region building (e.g., Kukk et al., 1992). As to the Arctic North, however, there has been criticism of those ingredients of the region building endeavours that treated the Northern lands as laboratories for theory testing, thus reducing the Northern peoples to objects of scientific curiosity (Lehtinen, 2003, p.51). The North as a social laboratory is perhaps not the rule. The Northern Europe Initiative, for example, has considered local interests while at the same time furthering US interests (Möller, 2002). But it is a necessary reminder that some people might benefit from, and therefore support region building, more than others. It is also a reminder that the region building processes in the Baltic Sea region and in the Barents Sea region are not necessarily mutually supportive. All the same, the academic community has been, and still is, an important actor in region building. As will be shown in the remainder of the chapter, the artistic community is another important actor. It is often neglected in academic treatments, but is emphasised here not least because of its capability of breaking with institutionalised forms of knowledge production. However, although the arts have succeeded in addressing memory in a way superior to policy-makers, they have to some extent failed to break with the habit of separating a Nordic-Baltic from an Arctic North. By so doing they have helped both maintain the image of compartmentalised Norths that are clearly separated from, ignorant of and unaffected by one another, and undermined the potential for overall Northern subjectivity.

Memory Games

> [The arts'] archives remain open to a process in which memory can never be constructed as definitive history (Shapiro, 2004, p.204).

Rather than reflecting the past, memory constructs and permanently reconstructs it. In this sense, memory can be said to function like language. To paraphrase George and Campbell (1990, p.273), to remember is to 'do': to engage in remembering is 'to give meaning to the activities which make up social reality', not only past reality but also present reality. Memory constructs rather than reflects the past and it functions through language and images such that to remember 'is, more and more, not to recall a story but to be able to call up a picture' (Sontag, 2002, p.89). We are living in a world dominated by images and a culture dominated by pictures and we receive most of the information we gather through our eyes. What and how we remember is partly dependent on the images we already carry with us. These images shape the perception of an event and its memorialisation.

By performing pluralistic and discursive, instead of monolithic and stipulating memory games, visual culture and the arts have often been capable of addressing questions pertaining to history and memory more adequately than has politics. Several exhibitions in the north have thematised the past and its representations in a variegated and occasionally ironic manner, acknowledging difference and change rather than establishing the one 'correct' interpretation. By so doing, they have effectively disrupted and subverted the strategies normally applied by nation-states to construct, on the basis of a linear historical narrative, homogeneous national cultures which then make the nation-state appear to be the natural form of political and social organisation. This is not to idealise the arts as a forum for staging political dissent and denationalising political narratives. Historically, the arts have frequently contributed to essentialising nation-states and the narratives on the basis of which they are constructed (Shapiro, 2004). As the following discussion shows, however, in Northern Europe the arts have presented mnemonic narratives below and beyond the nation-states that effectively counter the homogenising tendencies in the states' cultural policies.

The first exhibition to be discussed here brought together photographers from all the Baltic Sea littoral states.[1] Organised in 1996 and entitled *The Return of the Past – The End of Utopias?*, the exhibition and the participating artists mainly focused on private pasts: everyday life, family, childhood, home and place. Photographers such as Antanas Sutkus focused on ordinary people in their ordinariness rather than on people as model citizens or model workers, and thus created counter imagery to that of the photographs officially promoted by the authorities during Soviet times. Sutkus's archives of photographs of ordinary Lithuanian lives serve as a repository for those interested in the unofficial histories and memories of Soviet Lithuania. Other photographers used family albums as well as anonymous and historical photographs. They interrogated the (impression of) authenticity frequently emanating from amateur photography as opposed to the perfect glossy aesthetics of professional journals and propaganda photography. Reproducing the trivial aesthetics and banality of family albums, the photographers Ljudmila Fedorenko and Veronika Lapreye broke with the habit, prevalent in official Soviet photography, of producing solemn portraits and grand gestures. Ironically accepting the insignificance of family albums to anyone other than those depicted contrasted with the overall significance formerly assigned to photography as a part of the state's cultural governance and as a signifier for the glorious future. Through 'photo-archaeology', memory was reconstructed by deconstructing the photographic image (Straka, 1996, p.37). Fragments of and tears in portraits represented the nervous damage and feeling of helplessness, experienced by many people during Soviet times, resulting from 'the arbitrariness of a system which claim[ed] to be logical' (Skultans, 1998, p.104). They also represented fissures in personal biographies and uncertainties as to one's future, given the unpredictability of the social and economic transformation at that time. Wojciech Prazmowski

---

[1]   1st Ars Baltica Triennial of Photographic Art, *The Return of the Past – The End of Utopias?* Schleswig-Holsteinisches Landesmuseum Schloß Gottorf, Schleswig, 14 April-2 June 1996, and Haus am Waldsee, Berlin, 24 August-29 September 1996.

assembled pictures from family albums and old postcards to form multilayered installations depicting private and public lives and mirroring the condition of tension, characteristic of memory, between 'forever there' and 'forever lost'.

Bengt Olof Johansson and Winzer Klüglein altered historical photographs, respectively through technical interventions and by relying on the photographs' natural ageing process. They insisted on the changeability of the medium and the meaning assigned to historical images and responded to a photograph's characteristic difficulty in showing the passage of time. By storing the pictures on disks and CD-ROMs and instructing the viewer/buyer in manipulating the pictures, Johansson interfered with the conventional artist/viewer and producer/consumer cleavage. He offered the viewers the possibility to process historical images according to their own memories, experiences and taste and refused to present a final product and prescribe this product's meaning to the viewer. He thus respected that each person carries with them a unique emotional and cognitive baggage, irreducible to shared cultural patterns and partly impervious to cultural meaning prescribed by others. The links to the workings of social memory are apparent: memory is basically a private property, transformed into a collective project only by means of discourse. In the work of the photographer Kapa (Martti Kapanen) this discourse takes place within the photographs, representing 'the stratified nature of time in the picture' (Valjakka, 1996, p.99). Kapa, for example, makes contemporary photographs appear old and timeworn by scratching their surfaces. He transplants them, by means of manipulation during the negative and development phases, from the present to a time before the invention of the camera, and he looks at the present through the lens of the past by taking photographs of installations displaying details of gravestones.

The second exhibition to be discussed here, *Faster than History: Contemporary Perspectives on the Future of Art in the Baltic Countries, Finland and Russia*, followed an even more pluralistic, ironic and multilayered approach to the past.[2] Taking place in 2004, the exhibition had a narrower geographical, but a wider thematic focus and scope of genres. While the exhibition discussed above still followed, to some extent, national narratives, the artists participating in *Faster than History* challenged the national point of view more profoundly. For example, the members of the Latvian group of artists, F5, claimed that 'nationality is losing its importance' and their work 'is bound to neither time nor place' (cited in Isohanni, 2004b, p.7). The Lithuanian artists Egle Rakauskaite, Arunas Gudaitis and Laura Stasiulyte argued that, although their art reflects their nationality and mother tongue, they 'work on a local level' (cited in Isohanni, 2004a, p.6). Mikhail Jeleznikov's characterisation of his film about the 'Good People', 'Tales on the Marshes – Between a Bright Future and a Rosy Past', is a telling example of the pluralistic, non-dogmatic approach to the past characteristic of many artists participating in this exhibition:

---

2   Museum of Contemporary Art Kiasma, Helsinki, 31 January-2 May 2004.

While making this film I wanted to get a simplistic view of recent Russian history, without trying to reason, to justify or explain it. To see it with the innocent eyes of an alien, or a child. It turns out that this innocent film evokes quite different reactions in people; some take it as a joke, others say it's very true, and some are deeply insulted. My objective was none of these. Anyway, I'm glad if it makes somebody smile; history should sometimes be funny (Jeleznikov, 2004, p.124).

Minna Rainio and Mark Roberts' film, 'Borderlands', is a calm meditation about the Finnish-Russian border and its meaning to the people on both sides of it. It is not an ironic film, but a quiet and sober reflection on the ordinariness of borders. This ordinariness is perceived differently on both sides of the border and the film, divided between three screens, mirrors these differences by showing images from Finland on the left, images from Russia on the right and images from the border itself on the central screen, thus inviting different and equally valuable narratives. This particular border epitomises both the increasing immateriality of borders – there is no fence or iron curtain but just an eight-metre wide space and some border posts – and the power they still exert on the people on both sides, people that remain mostly invisible in the film just as they had been invisible to one another while the border was still tightly closed. Thus, rather than cross-border dialogue there are monologues on each side of the border, showing the preservation of one's own impressions, experiences and memories rather than their negotiation with others. By repeatedly taking photographs of the same place, Mart Viljus made street scenes in Tallinn communicate with themselves and by so doing reminded the beholder, not only of the changes in the physical environment, but also of one's own position in a continuously changing society. Just as the Baltic States during the 1990s, Finland in the 1930s was going through rapid modernisation, an expression of which was the city of Vyborg, lost to the Soviet Union in 1944. Liisa Roberts' 'What's the Time in Vyborg?' aims at cross-generation and cross-border dialogue about a city that inevitably raises different and contradictory memories; or, as the 8th grade Gymnasium student, Yana Klichuk, puts it: 'Vyborg itself is an intermediate state of being. It is precisely a state of being. One suspended between Finns, Russians, and Swedes. Everything is so intermixed, foggy, and disturbingly dim' (cited in Parshikov, 2004, p.252). It is a state of mind that invites memory games. It is, however, more important to participate in these games than to win.

Sheets of Nilas, Rafting Together

In conclusion, what this chapter has argued is that the arts have been able to address issues pertaining to history and memory in better ways than have been evident in political debates. As has further been argued, an increase in pluralistic memory games is required in order for Northern subjectivity to grow. This means, first of all, an increase in the awareness of the deficiencies in the region building process with respect to the emergence of a mnemonic region, i.e., one that does not unite its inhabitants on the basis of common memories, but rather one that acknowledges that different groups of people have different sets of memories that are equally valuable. As has been suggested above, the political community can benefit from the artistic community in the sense that the latter has effectively undermined the premise of the need for unitary stories and the prioritisation of the national over the regional and local. Politics thus can benefit from the memory games played in the arts. As has also been suggested, politics based on the appreciation of difference may even impact on and change the desire for unitary positions, which still characterises the European Union's attitude towards the past.

However, even though the exhibitions discussed above have partly broken with the logic of the nation-state, they have failed to address Northern Europe as a whole. This is evident in that the Arctic dimension of the North was mainly absent and has instead been addressed in separate exhibitions offering completely different views on memories of/in landscapes.[3] In turn, however, these exhibitions were largely ignorant of the Nordic-Baltic dimension. This exclusionary practice is not very useful. Here, the arts may learn from politics in the sense that politics has, to some extent, rejected the compartmentalisation of the North in favour of all-encompassing approaches. This would match the idea of the North addressed above in meteorological terms as sheets of nilas. While the arts have emphasised the elasticity and changeability of (the memories of) the North, the artificial separation of the Arctic North from the Nordic-Baltic North should be replaced with universal conceptions of the North: various sheets and fingers of nilas slowly rafting together in order for the North to both increase its own subjectivity and play a more prominent role in the construction of Europe.

References

Anderson, Benedict (1991), *Imagined Communities*. Extended and Revised Edition, New York, Verso.

Asmus, Ronald D. (1999), 'Address at the 4th Annual Stockholm Conference on Baltic Sea Region Security and Cooperation', 4 November 1999. Available at http://www.usemb.se/bsconf/1999/text/11asmus.html.

---

[3] *Strangers in the Arctic: 'Ultima Thule' and Modernity*, Rundetårn and Centralhallen Krystalgade, Copenhagen, 8 March-28 April 1996, and Pori Art Museum and Museum of Contemporary Art, Helsinki, 9 June-1 September 1996; *Yhteinen Maa / Gemensamt Land / A Land Shared: Contemporary and Applied Art of the Northern Peoples*, The Gallen-Kallela Museum, Espoo, 1 February-18 May 2003, Sámi Museum SIIDA, Inari, 18 June 2003-2 February 2004, and Wäinö Aaltonen Museum of Art, Turku, 19 March-30 May 2004.

Bellah, Robert N., Madsen, Richard., Sullivan, William M., Swidler, Ann and Tipton, Steven M. (1984), *Habits of the Heart: Individualism and Commitment in American Life*, Berkeley, Los Angeles and London, University of California Press.

Conley, Heather (2002), 'The United States and Northern Europe – A Continuing Commitment', Remarks to Stockholm Security Conference, 24 April 2002. Available at http://www.state.gov/p/eur/rls/rm/2002/9753pf.htm.

Der Derian, James (1995), 'The Values of Security: Hobbes, Marx, Nietzsche, and Baudrillard', in Ronnie D. Lipschutz (ed.), *On Security*, New York, Columbia University Press, pp. 24-45.

Donskis, Leonidas (2004), 'Faster than History yet Slower than a Lifetime', in Jari-Pekka Vanhala (ed.), *Faster than History: Contemporary Perspectives on the Future of Art in the Baltic Countries, Finland and Russia*, Helsinki, Museum of Contemporary Art Kiasma, pp. 17-22.

George, Jim and Campbell, David (1990), 'Patterns of Dissent and the Celebration of Difference: Critical Social Theory and International Relations', *International Studies Quarterly*, Vol. 34(3), pp. 269-93.

Güntner, Joachim (2004), 'Unkenntnis und ungleiches Gedenken. Gulag und Holocaust – Nachbetrachtungen zum Eklat von Leipzig', *Neue Zürcher Zeitung*, 3 April 2004. Available at http://www.nzz.ch/2004/04/03/fe/page-article9IISG.htm.

Herodotus (440 B.C.), *The History of Herodotus*, Book IV, Melpomene, translated by George Rawlinson. Available at http://classics.mit.edu/Herodotus/history.html.

Huyssen, Andreas (1995), *Twilight Memories: Marking Time in a Culture of Amnesia*, New York and London, Routledge.

Isohanni, Maria (2004a), 'Realistic Generation', *Kiasma*, No. 22, p. 6.

Isohanni, Maria (2004b), 'Serious Art From Latvia?' *Kiasma*, No. 22, p. 7.

Jelezkinov, Mikhail (2004), 'Tales of the Marshes – Between a Bright Future and a Rosy Past', in Jari-Pekka Vanhala (ed.), *Faster than History: Contemporary Perspectives on the Future of Art in the Baltic Countries, Finland and Russia*, Helsinki, Museum of Contemporary Art Kiasma, pp. 121-6.

Jervis, Robert (1976), *Perception and Misperception in International Politics*, Princeton, Princeton University Press.

Johnson, Nuala C. (2003), *Ireland, the Great War and the Geography of Remembrance*, Cambridge, Cambridge University Press.

Jukarainen, Pirjo (2003), 'Definitely Not Yet the End of Nations: Northern Borderlands Youth in Defence of National Identities', *Young*, Vol. 11(3), pp. 217-34.

Kalniete, Sandra (2004), 'Old Europe, New Europe', Speech given at the Leipzig Book Fair, 24 March 2004. Available at http://www.mdr.de/DL/1290734.pdf.

Kukk, Mare., Jervell, Sverre and Joenniemi, Pertti (eds.) (1992), *The Baltic Sea Region – A Region in the Making*, Oslo, Europa-programmet.

Lagerspetz, Mikko (1999), 'The Cross of Virgin Mary's Land: A Study in the Construction of Estonia's "Return to Europe"', *Idäntutkimus*, Vol. 6(3-4), pp. 17-28.

Lauristin, Marju (1997), 'Contexts of Transition', in Marju Lauristin and Peter Vihalemm with Karl Erik Rosengren and Lennart Weibull (eds.), *Return to the Western World:*

Cultural and Political Perspectives on the Estonian Post-Communist Transition, Tartu, Tartu University Press, pp. 25-40.

Lehtinen, Ari Aukusti (2003), 'Mnemonic North: Multilayered Geographies of the Barents Region', in Frank Möller and Samu Pehkonen (eds.), *Encountering the North: Cultural Geography, International Relations and Northern Landscapes*, Aldershot, Ashgate, pp. 31-56.

Lopez, Barry (1999), *Arctic Dreams: Imagination and Desire in a Northern Landscape*, London, The Harvill Press.

Lowenthal, David (1985), *The Past Is a Foreign Country*, Cambridge, Cambridge University Press.

Maier, Charles S. (2001/2002), 'Heißes und kaltes Gedächtnis. Zur politischen Halbwertzeit des faschistischen und kommunistischen Gedächtnisses', *Transit. Europäische Revue*, No. 22, pp. 153-65.

Meri, Lennart (1991), 'Estonia's Role in the New Europe', *International Affairs*, Vol. 67(1), pp. 107-10.

Möller, Frank (2002), 'Reconciling International Politics with Local Interests: The United States in Northern Europe', in Teresa Pohjola and Johanna Rainio (eds.), *The New North of Europe: Policy Memos*, Helsinki/Bonn, The Finnish Institute of International Affairs/Institut für Europäische Politik, pp. 77-81.

Möller, Frank (2003), 'Capitalizing on Difference: A Security Community or/as a Western Project', *Security Dialogue*, Vol. 34(3), pp. 315-28.

Nora, Pierre (2002), 'The Reasons for the Current Upsurge in Memory', *Tr@nsit-Virtuelles Forum*, No. 22. Available at http://www.univie.ac.at/iwm/t-22txt3.htm.

Novick, Peter (2001), *The Holocaust and Collective Memory: The American Experience*, London, Bloomsbury.

Olick, Jeffrey K. and Robbins, Joyce (1998), 'Social Memory Studies: From "Collective Memory" to the Historical Sociology of Mnemonic Practices', *Annual Review of Sociology*, Vol. 24, pp. 105-40.

Osborne, Brian S. (2001), 'Landscapes, Memory, Monuments, and Commemoration: Putting Identity in Its Place', *Canadian Ethnic Studies*, Vol. 33(3), pp. 39-78.

Palosaari, Teemu and Möller, Frank (2004), 'Security and Marginality: Arctic Europe after the Double Enlargement', *Cooperation and Conflict*, Vol. 39(3), pp. 255-81.

Parshikov, Aleksey (2004), 'Riddled with Crossroads', in Jari-Pekka Vanhala (ed.), *Faster than History: Contemporary Perspectives on the Future of Art in the Baltic Countries, Finland and Russia*, Helsinki, Museum of Contemporary Art Kiasma, pp. 248-55.

Ruth, Arne (1984), 'The Second New Nation: The Mythology of Modern Sweden', *Daedalus*, Vol. 113(2), pp. 53-96.

Schöpflin, George (1999), 'Uses of the Past in Inter-Ethnic Relations', *Idäntutkimus*, Vol. 6(3-4), pp. 7-16.

Shapiro, Michael J. (2004), *Methods and Nations: Cultural Governance and the Indigenous Subject*, New York and London, Routledge.

Skultans, Vieda (1998), *The Testimony of Lives: Narrative and Memory in Post-Soviet Latvia*, London and New York, Routledge.

Sontag, Susan (2002), *Regarding the Pain of Others*, New York, Farrar, Straus and Giroux.

Straka, Barbara (1996), 'Pandora's Box: The Handling of Things Past in Contemporary Photo Art', in Enno Kaufhold (ed.), *1st Ars Baltica Triennial of Photographic Art: The Return of the Past - The End of Utopias?* Cologne, Ars Baltica, pp. 32-49.

Took, Roger (2004), *Running with Reindeer: Encounters in Russian Lapland*, London, John Murray.

Turnbull, Phyllis (1996), 'Remembering Pearl Harbor: The Semiotics of the *Arizona* Memorial', in Michael J. Shapiro and Hayward R. Alker (eds.), *Challenging Boundaries: Global Flows, Territorial Identities*, Minneapolis and London, University of Minnesota Press, pp. 407-33.

Valjakka, Timo (1996), 'Travels in Time', in Enno Kaufhold (ed.), *1st Ars Baltica Triennial of Photographic Art: The Return of the Past – The End of Utopias?* Cologne, Ars Baltica, pp. 98-102.

Wellmann, Christian (2004), 'Overcoming the Remnants of the Past in the Baltic Sea Region: Considerations Derived from the Kaliningrad Case', in Konstantin K. Khudoley (ed.), *New Security Challenges as Challenges to Peace Research*, St Petersburg, St Petersburg State University Press, pp. 281-99.

Welzer, Harald., Moller, Sabine and Tschuggnall, Karoline (2002), *'Opa war kein Nazi'. Nationalsozialismus und Holocaust im Familiengedächtnis*, Frankfurt, Fischer.

Wendt, Alexander (1999), *Social Theory of International Politics*, Cambridge, Cambridge University Press.

Zerubavel, Eviatar (2003), *Time Maps: Collective Memory and the Social Shape of the Past*, Chicago and London, The University of Chicago Press.

PART II

THE NORTH AND THE CONSTRUCTION OF EUROPE

Chapter 4

Lessons from the North
for the EU's 'Near Abroad'

Marius Vahl

Introduction

The idea that EU policies towards Northern Europe could serve as a potential
model for the EU's relations with its other neighbours has emerged in recent times,
both in the Convention on the Future of the EU in 2002-2003, and in some of the
proposals for the EU's new 'European Neighbourhood Policy' (ENP). In this paper
I will focus on two particular EU policies towards non-EU members in Northern
Europe: the Northern Dimension (ND) initiative and the European Economic Area
(EEA). These two policies will be analysed in light of two broader themes: first,
how the EU organises its policy towards its neighbours more generally and,
second, the enlargement process and how the EU has attempted to developed
alternatives to EU membership.

The Northern Dimension represents a regional approach to the EU's
neighbours, and can be contrasted to a bilateral approach whereby the EU relates to
its neighbours on a country by country basis. A number of arguments can be raised
for and against a regional versus a bilateral approach. These will be analysed in
light of the experiences of the Northern Dimension, as well as EU policies towards
other regions in its immediate neighbourhood.

The Agreement on the European Economic Area between the EU and the three
EFTA states Iceland, Liechtenstein and Norway is the most comprehensive
agreement between the EU and any third country short of full EU membership. The
EEA has recently been discussed as a possible long-term goal in the EU's relations
with other neighbouring countries. The prospects of this, and how this is linked to
past and possible future EU enlargements, will be analysed by comparing the
proposals for a European Neighbourhood Policy with the EU's Southern and
Eastern neighbours with the realities of the EEA.

The Northern Dimension Model(s)

In order to analyse the Northern Dimension initiative as a potential model for EU policy towards other neighbouring regions and states it is necessary first to have a clear idea of what the Northern Dimension is. Diverging views on the ultimate scope and purpose of the initiative have been voiced since its gestation in the late 1990s. In view of these conceptual differences it is more correct to speak, not of one Northern Dimension model, but of several partially overlapping models.

In the speech that put the Northern Dimension on the EU's agenda in 1997, Finland's Prime Minister, Paavo Lipponen, claimed that the 'ultimate goal of an EU policy [for the Northern Dimension] is peace and stability, with prosperity and security shared by all nations [in the region]' (Lipponen, 1997). Such ambitious objectives were supported in a number of academic studies that called for a radical re-organisation of the EU's relations with neighbouring countries. A 'Europe of regions' in a structure of 'Olympic circles' would complement or even transform the current dominant approach of hub-and-spoke diplomacy in a structure of 'concentric circles', with the EU at the core, accession candidates occupying the 'inner circles' and non-candidates relegated to the outer circles (Emerson, 1999; Joenniemi, 1999). Such a regional approach, it was argued, could counteract the trend towards the creation of new dividing lines in Europe, and create stronger incentives for the countries in the 'outer circles' to converge on European norms and values.

While stating the need for a 'comprehensive strategy, an institutional framework and adequate financing arrangements', Lipponen (1997) pointed out that cooperation in Northern Europe was 'already organised well enough to make major new institutional arrangements unnecessary' and that therefore no new financing was required. Some observers noted early on in the process of establishing the Northern Dimension that a certain 'scaling down' of the initiative had occurred (Joenniemi, 1999), and was evident in the official documents from the EU on the Northern Dimension, one of which stated that 'the Commission considers that neither new permanent structures nor new budget lines should be considered' (European Commission, 1999). According to the first Action Plan for the Northern Dimension (2000-2003), adopted by the Feira European Council in June 2000, the 'aim [of the Northern Dimension] is to provide added value through reinforced co-ordination and complementarity in the EU and Member States' programmes and enhanced collaboration between the countries in Northern Europe'.

There were thus two clearly distinct Northern Dimension models proposed in the early phases of the initiative. Meanwhile, it appears that the ambitions concerning the Northern Dimension initiative have been lowered and that the discrepancy between these (perhaps) overly ambitious aims and the resources the EU has been willing to put into the initiative has been reduced.

The Northern Dimension in Practice

The Northern Dimension initiative could be assessed in terms of how it has dealt with the main contentious issues in the region. It is notable that many of these have been beyond the competencies of the EU as such, and that to the extent that they have been confronted, this has occurred without the direct involvement of the EU. Issues on this list include hard security matters, such as the withdrawal of Russian forces from the Baltic States, NATO enlargement (first to Poland and then to the Baltic States), and the possible extension of the CFE treaty in the region. On other issues, where the EU could have become involved, for example concerning the situation of the Russian-speaking minorities in Estonia and Latvia, these have been deferred to other international institutions, in this case to the OSCE and its commissioner for minorities. This was in part due to the allocation of the Northern Dimension portfolio to the external relations department in the European Commission, which further limited the possibility of a more comprehensive regional multilateral approach by excluding questions relating to enlargement and the enlargement candidates. While the Northern Dimension contributed to putting the special challenges of Kaliningrad on the agenda, it did not provide sufficient impetus to finding an early solution to the problem. This led to the 'crisis' of 2002, until then arguably the most serious crisis in the history of EU-Russia relations. While the regional approach has made inroads in Northern Europe, it is hard not to agree that the European Union is indeed a 'reluctant regionaliser' (Haukkala, 2001).

In spite of this, the Northern Dimension arguably provided 'added-value' beyond the 'minimalist model' and the limited aims of many, if not most, EU member states (Selliaas, 2002; Bonvincini et al., 2000). In political terms, the Northern Dimension has been appreciated by the EU's partners for its inclusive approach, with extensive consultations on priorities creating a sense of 'joint ownership' (European Commission, 2004). In operational terms, the main result of the Northern Dimension initiative is the Northern Dimension Environmental Partnership and its activities in Kaliningrad and St. Petersburg, financed in part by the Commission and the European Investment Bank. The creation of an additional programme can be criticised as going against the aim of improving coherence between the various initiatives in the region. There has also been criticism that the EU has not made use of existing institutions such as the Council of Baltic Sea States and the Barents-Euro Arctic Council (Catellani, 2001). Despite the insistence that no new financing would be made available, considerable funds (€110 million) were promised to the Northern Dimension Environmental Partnership in July 2002. Furthermore, the commitment to annual high-level conferences and the Second Action Plan for the period 2003-2006 entails that the Northern Dimension has become a going concern.

The relative success of the Northern Dimension initiative may be attributed to the fortuitous sequencing of EU presidencies, rather than reflecting a principled change in the EU's approach towards its 'near abroad.' The three Nordic EU member states – Finland, Sweden and Denmark – held the EU Presidency in autumn 1999, spring 2001 and autumn 2002, respectively. Their active support for the initiative ensured that the Northern Dimension became a fixture on the EU agenda. Indeed, it has been claimed that the principal lesson of the Northern Dimension initiative is the way Finland managed to 'customise' the Union and use its EU membership and its Presidency to promote stronger EU policies in areas of national interest (Ojanen, 1999). The Northern Dimension has been seen as an example of how an EU member state could use its membership and the presidency to promote its national interest, by turning a policy question of national importance into an EU project. This 'lesson' was an important reason for the Polish proposals for an 'Eastern Dimension' during 2002 (Cimoszewicz, 2002).

The 2004 EU enlargement transformed the rationale on which the Northern Dimension is based, as most of the questions of coherence and co-ordination of policies and programmes will be greatly reduced. Whereas the task until 2004 was to co-ordinate economic assistance programmes targeting member states, candidates and non-candidates, this is now limited to co-ordination between EU internal assistance and aid to Russia. This is unlikely to change much, as the key issues confronted so far in the Northern Dimension have been essentially bilateral EU-Russian affairs. From 2004 onwards, the Northern Dimension became essentially a regional element of EU-Russia bilateral cooperation.

This does not, however, spell the end of the utility of the regional approach in Northern Europe. Some of the key outstanding issues on the Northern Dimension initiative's agenda, such as energy and environmental security, involve third parties, notably Norway, but also Iceland, the US and Canada. This is reflected in the growing use of the term the 'Arctic Window' in official texts on the Northern Dimension. These indicate that the regional approach of the Northern Dimension could remain relevant also after 2004, although this utility seems in part to depend on widening the scope of, and participation in, the Northern Dimension initiative.

The Organisation of EU Policy Towards Its Neighbours

The regional approach exemplified by the Northern Dimension is, of course, not the only way in which the EU can organise its relations with its neighbours. In principle, the EU is faced with two principal ways in which to approach cooperation between itself and neighbouring countries, and indeed to third countries more generally: *bilateralism* or *multilateralism*.

According to a *bilateral approach*, EU policies, strategies, programmes, initiatives and economic assistance are targeted towards individual countries, and contractual arrangements between the EU and neighbouring countries are bilateral. In a *multilateral approach*, by contrast, political dialogue would take place between the EU and a group of neighbouring countries. There would be multilateral policy initiatives on, for instance, multi-national cross-border economic assistance programmes, and multilateral agreements between the EU and two or more neighbouring countries. Theoretically, there are an infinite number of ways in which the EU could organise its third country relations multilaterally, ranging from global to trilateral initiatives and from comprehensive arrangements to sector-by-sector cooperation. Here, focus will be on the *regional approach*, of which the Northern Dimension would be an example, in which cooperation primarily takes place between the EU and a smaller group of neighbouring countries, which together with parts of the EU constitute well-defined geographic and historical regions.

EU Neighbourhood Policies

So which of these two approaches – *bilateralism* or the *regional approach* – has the EU availed itself of in its policy towards its neighbours? At the most general level, the EU has divided its neighbours into about half a dozen groups, and has had different types of contractual agreements and economic assistance programmes with each of them.

The erstwhile EU candidates in Central and Eastern Europe constituted one group, with bilateral Europe Agreements and assistance through the PHARE, SAPARD and ISPA programmes. For the countries of the Western Balkans the EU has established a Stability and Association Process, with bilateral Stability and Association Agreements (SAAs) and assistance through the CARDS programme. Turkey and Andorra are part of the EU customs union through bilateral agreements. The countries of the Commonwealth of Independent States constitute another group, with bilateral Partnership and Cooperation Agreements and assistance through the TACIS programme. The countries of the Southern Mediterranean are in the process of concluding the so-called Euro-Mediterranean Association Agreement with the EU. The states of the European Free Trade Association (EFTA) are either part of the European Economic Area or have bilateral sectoral agreements with the EU.

The distinctions between the various agreements and programmes are marked, reflecting in particular the priority accorded to the enlargement process. There are large differences in terms of the economic assistance provided. In the EU's financial perspective for 2000-2006, the enlargement candidates received almost 1200 euro/capita, the Western Balkans approximately 200 euro/capita, while the CIS countries received on average 13 euro/capita in assistance from the EU budget (Council of the EU, 1999a). Although assistance is allocated on a 'group-by-group' basis, almost all support and most projects created are bilateral.

Integration between the EU and its neighbours is to a considerable extent a post-Cold War phenomenon. These arrangements are increasingly embedded in bilateral *association agreements* between the EU and the country concerned, with the number of third countries with which the EU has association agreements increasing from three, at the end of the 1980s, to more than twenty in 2004. Previous trade and cooperation agreements have successively been replaced with second generation association agreements, all of them providing for more comprehensive and deeper integration with the EU.[1] With further integration in the second and third pillars, the EU's neighbours are increasingly associating with the EU also in other domains, such as justice and home affairs and foreign, security and defence policy, either through their more comprehensive second generation agreements, or through new bilateral association arrangements.

Since around the time of the accession of two more Nordic states – Finland and Sweden – to the EU in 1995, the preference for bilateralism has been tempered by more active regional policies by the EU towards the Baltic region. This started with the preparation by the Commission of the Baltic Sea Region Initiative, presented to the CBSS summit in spring 1996 (Joenniemi, 1999), and was later followed by the Northern Dimension initiative. However, apart from this, regional approaches have been virtually absent in the EU's relations with its Eastern neighbours (European Commission, 2004), and the EU has, for instance, been unwilling to engage further with regional cooperation in the Black Sea region.

Regionalism, as seen in the Baltic region, arguably plays a more limited role in the EU's relations with the Balkans. Although regionalism was one of the main novelties of the Stability and Association process, this consists of regional cooperation among the countries of the region, rather than multilateral cooperation between the countries of the region and the EU itself (Whyte, 2001). Furthermore, a considerable part of EU policy towards South East Europe is channelled through institutions other than the EU, from organisations such as the UN, NATO, the OSCE and the international financial institutions, to initiatives such as the Stability Pact for South Eastern Europe launched in the wake of the 1999 Kosovo war, all of which include countries outside the EU. The regional approach was pioneered in the Mediterranean region with the launch of the so-called 'Barcelona Process' in 1995, later renamed the Euro-Mediterranean Partnership. This 'Southern Dimension' was explicitly used as a model for the Northern Dimension (Lipponen, 1997). The Euro-Mediterranean Partnership is a framework for bilateral and multilateral relations between the EU and its 12 Mediterranean partners initiated by the 1995 Barcelona Conference. The aims are broad and include creating a common area of peace and stability and the establishment of a Euro-Mediterranean free trade area. As in EU policy towards the Balkans, a key element of the Barcelona process is the upgrading of bilateral contractual relations between the EU and its Mediterranean partners.

---

[1]   The difference between Association Agreements and Trade and Cooperation agreements is mainly one of internal EU procedures, and not the scope of commitments made. Association agreements are based on Article 310 of the Treaty of Nice and require unanimity in the Council. Trade and cooperation agreements are based on Article 133 and require only a qualified majority in the Council. In spite of the connotations of closer relations in the term 'association', there is not necessarily a difference in substance between agreements concluded in accordance with Article 310 and those concluded on the basis of Article 133.

Bilateralism versus Multilateralism

What are then the major pros and cons of the various approaches available to the EU for its neighbourhood policy? A bilateral approach enables the Union and its partners to tailor cooperation according to the different needs and requirements of individual countries. Considering the widely diverging levels of economic, political and social development among the EU's neighbours, the emphasis on the principle of differentiation is easily justifiable. From the perspective of *Realpolitik*, a bilateral approach accentuates the power asymmetries between the EU and its smaller and/or weaker neighbours and thus makes it easier for the EU to shape the relationship and to determine common and cooperative policies. This asymmetric bilateralism, with the EU the policy-maker and the neighbours policy-takers stands, however, in sharp contrast to the EU's professed preference for multilateralism. In practice, it amounts to little more than EU unilateralism, with proclamations of equality acting merely as political window-dressing.

Beyond such ideological concerns, the proliferation of bilateral sectoral agreements, processes and initiatives is in practice becoming increasingly difficult for the EU institutions to manage. The growing complexity creates a significant burden of cooperation and co-ordination of policies and programmes, difficulties which are compounded by the multi-tiered nature of governance in Europe, as national policies, regional organisations and international financial institutions multiply the number of programmes to be co-ordinated. A bilateral approach could make it more difficult to develop and implement coherent EU policies, given the considerable interdependencies between not only the EU and its neighbours, but also among the neighbours themselves. That such differentiated bilateralism could lead to trade distortions as well as trade creation is well known: overlapping, non-congruent free trade agreements open up possibilities to free-ride for producers in third countries, requiring detailed rules of origin, to take one example (Brenton and Machin, 2002). Even if unintended, differential treatment may cause resentment among those neighbours who are accorded less favourable terms with the EU. The development of new bilateral arrangements with an increasing number of partner countries creates problems of precedence, with pressures for 'concessions' given by the EU to one country to be extended also to other countries. Instead of developing into a 'ring of friends', as called for by Commission President Prodi, (Prodi, 2002), there seems to be a growing sense of frustration with the EU among many of its neighbours. An inclusive regional approach could counter such developments.

Although the number of associates was reduced as a result of the 2004 enlargement, this does not spell the end for a continued demand for upgraded contractual relations. First, there is the continuing process of negotiating second generation agreements with the countries of the Euro-Mediterranean Partnership and the Stability and Association Process. Many of the countries with which the EU already has such second generation agreements are calling for either a revision of these or for new associations. The EU and Russia are discussing how to develop four 'Common Spaces' (on economics, external security, internal security, and research and education) which is quite likely to lead to new bilateral agreement(s), perhaps replacing the PCA. The EU-Russia relationship has already been upgraded institutionally, through the creation of the Permanent Partnership Council, which met for the first time in spring 2004. Ukraine is also calling for an association agreement as a stepping-stone towards membership, a long-term objective not yet endorsed by the EU, whilst Moldova has requested to be included in the Stability and Association Process with its prospects for full membership in the EU.

Finally, and in more general terms, many of the challenges the EU faces in its relations with neighbouring countries go beyond the concerns of individual partner countries. This is because they are either by nature, transnational, for instance energy and environmental issues, or because the neighbours face similar challenges, with the transition process in Central and Eastern Europe as the most obvious example, or because of shared aims in relations with the EU, with the goal of creating free trade as an example. Indeed, 'over the coming decade and beyond, the Union's capacity to provide security, stability and sustainable development to its citizens will no longer be distinguishable from its interest in close co-operation with the neighbours' (European Commission 2003).

The European Economic Area as a Model for the European Neighbourhood Policy

The potential of the EEA as a model for EU relations with its neighbours was discussed in the Convention on the Future of Europe in 2002- 2003, in connection with a provision for special arrangements with neighbouring countries. In its draft proposal for the EU Constitution of 18 October 2002, the European People's Party (EPP) suggested that the 'EU should offer institutionalised cooperation to States which can not become members for the time being. The EPP proposes the creation of a "European Partnership", open both to Eastern Europe and to Mediterranean countries – similar to the European Economic Area – but including a political component' (EPP, 2002). Questioned about relations between the EU and Russia, Spanish Socialist MEP Carlos Westendorp suggested 'a sort of EEA-EU arrangement with a political content' (Bolkenstein, 2004).

The EEA was also mentioned in the first Commission Communication of March 2003 on the 'Wider Europe.' This new policy was launched in 2002, focusing initially on the 'new neighbours' Belarus, Moldova and Ukraine. Renamed the 'European Neighbourhood Policy' (ENP), the initiative was subsequently expanded in stages to include also the EU's Southern Mediterranean partners, Russia, and the South Caucasus. According to the Commission, the long-term aim is 'an arrangement whereby the Union's relations with the neighbouring countries ultimately resemble the close political and economic links currently enjoyed with the EEA'.

The European Economic Area and the European Neighbourhood Policy

The EEA Agreement between the three EFTA states Norway, Iceland and Liechtenstein and the EU is an association agreement like many of the other agreements between the EU and its neighbours discussed above. However, the EEA differs from these other agreements in a number of ways which are of relevance if the EEA is to be used as a model for EU relations with its neighbours (Emerson et al., 2002). First, it could be noted that the EEA Agreement, in contrast to other association agreements, is a multilateral agreement. However, the three EFTA states are required to speak with one voice, and from the EU's point of view, these agreements thus consist of two parties, similar to other association agreements. From the associate's perspective the difference is, however, profound, as it makes agreement on any issue dependent on acceptance by the other two EFTA states.

Bilateral Action Plans covering a 3-5 year period are the principal instruments of the ENP, and the official documents emphasise the need for 'differentiation' between the ENP countries. The first seven Action Plans[2] were developed during 2004, in close consultation with the countries concerned. Endorsed by both sides, the Action Plans set out common objectives and a timetable for their achievement, and are to be reviewed annually through the existing institutional cooperation framework with the partner countries. The Commission has also suggested the possibility of entering into new European Neighbourhood Agreements as part of the ENP. The scope of these is to be examined after existing contractual agreements have been fully implemented. It is emphasised that these 'should not override the existing framework for EU relations' with the partner countries, and 'would supplement existing contractual relations where the EU and the neighbouring country have moved beyond the existing framework, taking on new entitlements and obligations' (European Commission, 2003).

The question of economic assistance has been high on the agenda for both the EEA and the ENP, although the former is unlikely to be seen as a model for the latter, as the flow of assistance is from the EFTA states to the EU in the EEA. It is envisaged that funding to the ENP countries would be increased 'significantly' through a new Neighbourhood Instrument (European Commission, 2004). This new instrument, partially inspired by the experience in Northern Europe and the Northern Dimension, will apply both inside and outside the external border of the Union, in order to avoid creating dividing lines in Europe.

More than a decade after it was signed the EEA agreement remains 'the most ambitious and the most complete agreement ever signed by the Community with a group of third countries' (Phinnemore, 1999). Through the EEA agreement, Norway, Iceland and Liechtenstein are essentially part of the EU's Single Market, with the partial exception of the common policies on trade, agriculture and fisheries. The EEA differs from most other EU agreements by being a 'dynamic'

---

[2] With Israel, Jordan, Morocco, Tunisia, the Palestinian Authority, Moldova and Ukraine.

agreement, with detailed provisions for the regular inclusion of new EU *acquis* into the agreement. Most other EU agreements with third countries are 'static', with substantial changes requiring re-negotiation of the entire agreement, or alternatively, a new agreement. One of the complaints of the EEA is exactly the dynamism inherent in the agreement. Critics claim that it has become more comprehensive and encompassing than originally envisaged, with new rules incorporated that fall outside the intended scope of the agreement (Nei til EU, 2001).

In the early ENP proposals it was suggested that the partner countries would be given 'a stake in the EU's internal market', with 'further integration and liberalisation to promote the free movement of persons, goods, services and capital', in return for approximation with EU law and economic reform more generally. While the ENP Strategy Paper calls for 'privileged relations' and 'enhanced preferential trade relations', it is clear that the extent of economic integration through the ENP has been scaled down and will fall far short of the EEA. Indeed, there are no direct references to the 'four freedoms' in the 2004 Strategy Paper, as there were in the 2003 Wider Europe Communication (Moshes and Haukkala, 2004). Considering that the ENP has a medium-term perspective, this seems realistic. As seen during the accession process of the new members in Central and Eastern Europe, adopting and implementing the Single Market rules and regulations is the most difficult part of the process. Few, if any of the states included in the ENP have the administrative and institutional capacity required to participate in the EEA.

The EEA has the most complex institutions of any EU association agreement. In addition to the regular institutions of EU associations, with a ministerial council, a committee of senior officials, and a joint parliamentary committee, an EFTA Surveillance Authority (ESA) and an EFTA Court have been established to monitor compliance by the EFTA states and to settle disputes that may arise. These thus play a somewhat similar role to that of the European Commission and the European Court of Justice *vis-à-vis* the Single Market and the EU member states. Although the EEA contains the right of reservation to specific directives and regulations, no EFTA state has ever used this right, often erroneously referred to as a 'veto-right', presumably because the political price was regarded as too high. The institutions of the EEA are frequently described as a 'bureaucratic monster', and there has also been concern about the role played by the ESA, which has been regarded as being too pro-active in ensuring compliance with the EEA, further contributing to the gradual expansion of the scope of the agreement. In contrast, monitoring of the ENP is to be undertaken within existing frameworks, complemented with periodic progress reports drawn up by the Commission. This has much more in common with the monitoring of EU accession candidates than with the EEA.

The EEA Agreement does not open for participation of EFTA representatives in the decision-making process in the EU Council of Ministers, although EFTA ministers have been invited to informal Council meetings on an *ad hoc* basis in recent years. However, national experts from the EFTA states participate in the more than 200 committees assisting the Commission in preparing new legislation. Being excluded from EU decision-making bodies, the inclusion in the preparatory phases of EU policy-making – 'decision-shaping' – becomes a key channel through which the EFTA states can influence EU policy that will eventually become binding on them. However, this participation in decision-shaping is becoming less significant. Since the EEA was negotiated in the early 1990s, the balance between the EU institutions has shifted, with a strengthening of the Council of Ministers and the European Parliament at the expense of the Commission and national parliaments. The Council and its working groups play an increasingly important role in shaping EEA relevant legislation, and the European Parliament has become an increasingly important actor in the process of EU decision-making.

The EEA states are also engaged in more traditional types of international cooperation with the EU through the EEA Agreement, participating in dozens of EU-led programmes and initiatives. They also participate – as full participants, associates, or observers – in the work of the growing number of Community autonomous agencies, either through their principal association agreements, or through separate bilateral arrangements. The ENP Strategy paper calls for increased participation in EU programmes and expansion of programmes on and including the countries of the new EU Neighbourhood Policy, for instance through opening the European Research Area (ERA) which is now being established. The ENP Strategy Paper is hesitant towards the idea of participation in Community agencies, but envisages a 'gradual opening of certain Community programmes' to the ENP countries.

One of the main slogans of the Prodi Commission on the ENP has been 'Everything but institutions'. According to the 2003 Communication, the neighbours are not to have 'a role in the Union's institutions' along the lines of the various models of participation accorded to the EEA countries. Combined with the relatively limited economic integration envisaged, the ENP that emerges falls far short of the EEA agreement. Many proponents of an EEA-model want this to be supplemented by a 'political component'. While the ENP Strategy Paper calls for strengthening political dialogue, it does not provide any specific proposals. In the EEA, political dialogue takes place in the ministerial-level EEA Council, which meets biannually, with the EU represented by the 'Troika'. Political dialogue with some of the ENP countries, for instance with Ukraine in annual summit meetings, is however already more extensive than the EU-EFTA dialogue.

Beyond the EEA: Justice and Home Affairs and the Common Foreign and Security Policy

Norway and Iceland are increasingly integrating with the EU in areas not covered by the EEA, notably in the fields of Justice and Home Affairs (JHA) and foreign security and defence policy (CFSP and ESDP). In the JHA area, this takes place principally through agreements of association with the Schengen regime on external borders, and the Dublin Convention on asylum. The Schengen association agreement is probably the third country agreement that goes the furthest in including non-member states in the decision-making process of the EU. Through the so-called Mixed Committee, established by the Schengen association agreement,[3] the associated states participate in what are, in effect, the Justice and Home Affairs Council, COREPER and the Council working groups relating to the Schengen agreement, including the right to make proposals. However, the Schengen associates do not have a vote, and the adoption of new acts is reserved to the competent institutions of the EU. If the Schengen associates decide not to accept new legislation, the entire agreement could be terminated.

Border management is, according to the ENP Strategy Paper, likely to be a priority, although the proposals on the movement of persons are limited to considering the possibilities for facilitating travel for select groups such as participants in EU programmes and diplomats. This could be followed by an examination of the 'wider application of visa free regimes' if the 'necessary conditions are in place', notably readmission agreements. The idea of a visa-free regime, currently being discussed bilaterally with Russia, is not mentioned, reflecting the great difference between the current level of cooperation and integration with the EFTA states in the JHA area and the more modest proposals of the ENP.

As part of the recently developed European Security and Defence Policy (ESDP), various non-legally binding arrangements for dialogue and participation on security and defence issues with third countries have been created. This includes dialogue at the ministerial level in a 15+6 and 15+15 format, with non-EU NATO members and EU candidates, respectively. As members of NATO, Norway and Iceland participate in both configurations. Closer dialogue on CFSP and ESDP is also envisaged in the ENP, with 'burden-sharing and joint responsibility for addressing the threats to stability created by conflict and insecurity'. This is to include a more active EU role in the conflicts of the new neighbours, although the EU's role is to be primarily in the post-conflict stages, with a role in conflict resolution limited to support of the OSCE and other mediators. The ENP Strategy Paper also proposes 'the possible involvement of partner countries in aspects of CFSP and ESDP'. While the specific content of this is uncertain as of August 2004, the proposals for enhanced cooperation in CFSP and ESDP again appear to fall short of the close relationship the EFTA states enjoy in these areas.

---

[3]   The Mixed Committee operates at the level of senior officials and ministers. It is comprised of the Justice and Home Affairs Council of EU Ministers plus the ministers of the associated states, minus ministers of EU member states that are not parties to Schengen cooperation (Britain and Ireland). The Mixed Committee meets either just before or just after meetings of the JHA Council.

Neighbourhood Policy as Enlargement Ersatz

The EEA did not turn out as Jacques Delors proposed in January 1989. His idea of a 'common European economic space' was intended as an alternative to full EU membership. However, three of the six EFTA states that negotiated the EEA – Austria, Finland and Sweden – opted instead for full membership, and were parts of the EEA as EFTA members for only one year before entering the Union as full members in 1995.

In contrast with most EU associates, none of the three EFTA countries in the EEA seek EU membership, and the EEA Agreement is thus to be regarded as a permanent alternative to membership. However, and in contrast to all other EU neighbours, the Northern European members of EFTA could easily fulfill the criteria for EU membership, and accession remains a strategic option available to both Norway and Iceland at their discretion.

A Polish non-paper on the 'Eastern Dimension' in late 2002 suggested that the EU should hold out the prospect of EU membership for Belarus, Moldova and Ukraine. However, according to Commission proposals, the ENP is 'distinct from membership' and the medium-term goal is 'not...to include a perspective of membership'. Instead the aim of the ENP is, in the words of Commission President Prodi, to create a 'ring of friends' around the Union (Prodi, 2002). The exclusion of membership has dominated discussion on the ENP in countries such as Moldova and Ukraine. This should not come as a surprise. Although the EU recently was enlarged for the fifth time, the EU itself has in fact been consistently reluctant to reciprocate expressions of interest in membership with acknowledgement of their EU prospects.

The British government filed its first application for membership in the then European Economic Community (EEC) in 1961. Following the two famous rejections of British membership by French President de Gaulle, Britain became a member in 1973, twelve years after its first application. Greece concluded an association agreement with the EEC in 1961, but had to wait for twenty years until it became a full member in 1981. Spain and Portugal requested association arrangements from the Community in 1962, and applied for membership soon after their 'democratic revolutions' in the mid-1970s. However, it took more than ten years before they joined the Community in 1986. In response to the events in Central and Eastern Europe in 1989, French President Mitterand proposed the creation of a European confederation. However, the states concerned opted instead for full membership, filing applications from 1994 onwards. In the end, these countries became members in May 2004, almost fifteen years after the fall of the Berlin Wall. The five countries of the Western Balkans were given the prospect of EU accession as a long-term goal by the EU in 1999. Apart, perhaps, from Croatia, it seems unlikely that any of these will become members during this decade, i.e., within ten years of being given EU 'perspectives'. Turkey's 'Europeanness', and thus in principle its eligibility for membership, was acknowledged by the Community upon the conclusion of an association agreement in 1963, although its prospects for eventual accession were not confirmed until 2002, almost 40 years later.

This brief survey of previous EU enlargements highlights the Union's general reluctance to enlarge. This reluctance manifests itself in various ways, from outright rejection to proposals for alternative arrangements such as the EEA, the European confederation and now the European Neighbourhood Policy, and only when these fail, attempting to draw out the process of accession as long as politically possible. While the creation of stricter conditions for membership through the elaboration of the Copenhagen criteria in 1993 was a natural consequence of deepening integration in the EU and the need to safeguard the credibility of the Single Market, these criteria also served to limit the speed and scope of enlargement, allowing the EU to undertake the necessary institutional changes to accommodate additional member states. However, the EU has now itself become constrained by the Copenhagen criteria: if a European country fulfills them there is, in the end, little the EU can do to prevent new applications for membership, and, eventually, new members of the EU.

Conclusions

Although the regional approach has played a limited role in confronting strategic challenges and resolving politically contentious issues in EU neighbourhood policies, it has become, however, an important albeit secondary element of EU 'structural diplomacy' (Keukeleire, 2000). An increasingly complex network of association and cooperation between the EU and its near abroad, with bilateralism the dominant mode of operation, has gradually emerged. The Northern Dimension is frequently referred to as a model for the ENP in official texts. The inclusive nature of the initiative is usually cited as the main lesson to be learnt from the Northern Dimension (European Commission, 2004). In contrast to the Baltic region, where the EU, following the 2004 enlargement, has one partner, Russia, the EU is faced with several partner countries in the Balkans and the Mediterranean region after the fifth enlargement. There is thus inherently a bigger role to play for multilateral mechanisms such as the Northern Dimension initiative. In many cases, such mechanisms are already in place, with the notable exception of the Eastern neighbours of the enlarged EU.

The Black Sea region stands out as an area where a regional approach could acquire more prominence, drawing on the lessons of the Northern Dimension. The inclusive nature associated with the regional approach seems increasingly relevant as relations with the EU's Eastern neighbours, such as Russia and Ukraine, are becoming increasingly difficult. In light of the existence of indigenously developed regional structures such as the Black Sea Economic Cooperation organisation (BSEC), the criticism that regional organisations in the North were not utilised sufficiently in the Northern Dimension initiative seems highly relevant. It may seem that this lesson is acknowledged in the Commission proposals for the ENP, stating that the EU 'is not seeking to establish new bodies or organizations, but rather to support existing entities and encourage their further development'.

The recent enlargements of the EU could be regarded as a result, in part, of the EU's inability to create association arrangements that are attractive enough to third countries in Europe when compared with full membership. The EEA stands out as the first, and the ENP perhaps the second, serious attempt to create such a 'neighbourhood policy'. Although the EEA is generally regarded as functioning well in a technical sense, there is widespread dissatisfaction with the arrangements in the EFTA states, which have recently been calling for an update or an upgrade of the Agreement. In spite of invocations of an 'EEA-model plus a political component' for EU neighbourhood policy, the initial proposals from the EU for its European Neighbourhood Policy fall far short of the sort of relations currently existing between the EU and the three EFTA states in the EEA. Given the state of political and economic reform in the ENP countries and the 3-5 year perspective of the ENP, this is understandable. But even in areas where it would be possible to approximate an 'EEA model', for instance concerning inclusion in EU programmes and agencies, participation in EU 'decision-shaping', and in the CFSP, the ENP official documents point towards a cautious approach on the side of the EU.

The ENP countries are faced with many of the same economic challenges of economic transition as those faced by the EU accession candidates of Central and Eastern Europe, and also the countries of South-East Europe, for whom EU membership is a more distant prospect. Although the ultimate aims for candidate states are the most far-reaching among the EU associates, the agreements themselves provide for less integration in the short- and the medium-term than the agreements between the EU and the non-candidate countries of EFTA. While the scope of the agreements is as broad as in the EEA, the commitments are less numerous and contain no evolutionary clause. The agreements contain rather limited commitments on the date of entry into force, and more ambitious aims to be achieved progressively and in the long-term, for instance the liberalisation of trade or participation in EU policies and programmes. From this perspective, the agreements that these countries have with the EU – Europe Agreements and Stability and Association Agreements, respectively – could appear to provide more suitable models for the ENP than the EEA.

However, the prospect of eventual EU membership is a fundamental premise underlying the Europe Agreements and the Stability and Association Agreements. For candidate countries, the underlying expectation is that full participation follows and depends on the introduction and implementation of all EU rules and policies. This asymmetry is acceptable to the associate countries because of the provision of assistance, because they are allowed certain derogations and exemptions, but mainly because it is temporary and will be followed by their full participation as members of the EU. The principal benefit of association with the EU is thus not to be found in the association agreement itself, but rather upon its termination. This fundamentally alters the incentives for the associated states in terms of what kind of provisions and institutional arrangements are deemed acceptable to them. The agreements with candidates for EU membership may thus not provide the most appropriate models for countries unless they are at the same time provided with the prospect of full EU membership. This conundrum is likely to dominate the debate on EU neighbourhood policies for years to come.

References

Bolkenstein, F. (2004), *The Limits of Europe*, Lannoo Press, Belgium.

Bonvincini, G., Vaahtoranta, T., and Wessels, W. (eds.) (2000), *The Northern EU – National Views on the Emerging Northern Dimension*, Programme on the Northern Dimension of the CFSP, Helsinki/Bonn, Ulkopoliittinen instituutti and Institut für Europäische Politik.

Brenton, P. and Machin, M. (2002), *Making EU Trade Agreements Work: The Role of Rules of Origin*, CEPS Working Document 183, Brussels.

Catellani, N. (2001), 'The Multilevel Implementation of the Northern Dimension', in Hanna Ojanen (ed.), *The Northern Dimension: Fuel for the EU?* Helsinki, Ulkopoliittinen Instituutti and Institut für Europäische Politik, pp. 54-77.

Cimoszewicz, W. (2002), *Speech at the inaugural Forum 'Together – on the future of Europe'*, Warsaw, February 18.

Council of the European Union (1999), *Presidency Conclusions*, Berlin European Council, March. Available at http://europe.eu.int.

Council of the European Union (2000), *Action Plan for the Northern Dimension with external and cross-border policies for the European Union 2000-2003*, 14 June 2000, 9401/00.

Emerson, M., Vahl, M., and Woolcock, S. (2002), *Navigating by the Stars: Norway, the European Economic Area and the European Union*, Brussels, CEPS.

European Commission (1999), *A Northern Dimension for the Policies of the Union: An Inventory of Current Activities*, Working Document.

European Commission (2003), *Wider Europe Neighbourhood: A New Framework for Relations with our Eastern and southern Neighbours*, COM (2003) 104 final, Brussels, 11.3.2003.

European Commission (2004), *European Neighbourhood Policy – Strategy Paper*, May 2004.

European Peoples Party (EPP) (2002), *A Constitution for a Strong Europe*, 18 October.

Haukkala, H. (2001), *Two Reluctant Regionalizers? The European Union and Russia in Europe's North*, Working Paper No. 7, Helsinki, Ulkopoliittinen instituutti.

Joenniemi, P. (1999), *Bridging the Iron Curtain? Co-operation Around the Baltic Rim*, Working Paper 22, Copenhagen, COPRI.

Keukeleire, S. (2000), *The EU as an International Actor*, Centre for Study of Diplomacy, University of Leicester, November.

Lipponen, P. (1997), *The European Union Needs a Policy for the Northern Dimension*, speech at Conference on the Barents Region Today, Rovaniemi, 15 September.

Moshes, A. and Haukkala, H. (2004), *Beyond the Big Bang: The Challenges of the EU's Neighbourhood policy in the East*, FIIA report 2004/9, Helsinki, Finnish Institute for International Affairs.

Nei til EU (2001), *Nei til EU's Motmelding en analyse av Norges muligheter utenfor EU og et kritisk blikk på EUs utvikling (Counter-report of the Norwegian 'No to the EU'- movement, an analysis of Norway's possibilities outside the EU and a critical view of the development of the EU)*, Oslo.

Ojanen, H. (1999), 'How to Customize Your Union: Finland and the Northern Dimension of the EU', *Northern Dimensions*, Helsinki, Finnish Institute of International Affairs, pp. 13-26.

Phinnemore, D. (1999), *Association: Stepping-Stone or Alternative to EU Membership?*, UACES/ Sheffield University Press.

Prodi, R. (2002), *A Wider Europe: A Proximity Policy as the Key to Stability*, speech at the 'Peace, Security and Stability, International Dialogue, and the Role of the EU,' Sixth ECSA-World Conference, Jean Monnet Project, Brussels, 5-6 December.

Selliaas, A. (2002), *EUs nordlige dimensjon – I Norges interesse?*, Den Norske Atlanterhavskomite, Det sikkerhetspolitiske bibliotek 6/2002.

Whyte, N. (2001), *Analysis of the Stabilisation and Association Agreement signed between the European Union and Macedonia on 9 April*, Europa South-East Monitor, Issue 21, March, Brussels, CEPS.

Chapter 5

Constitutionalising the European Union, Constructing EU Borders

Thomas Christiansen

Introduction

In the first few years of the 21st century, the EU has continued to develop at remarkable speed. 2004 stood out in particular as a year in which important decisions were taken which may in the future be regarded as historic. In particular, the accession of ten new member states to the Union, agreement among EU leaders to sign a Constitutional Treaty, and the decision to begin accession talks with Turkey in 2005, may come to define the kind of polity the EU is seeking to become. All these developments are 'constitutional' choices in the wider sense in which they reflect the underlying values of the integration project, while also seeking to provide the EU with a firmer and more lasting normative structure. However, both the Constitutional Treaty and the accession of Turkey are aims at this point, with the very real possibility that either or both may run into objections in one or more member states and be derailed as a result. Still, unless and until this happens, the decisions of 2004 constitute indicators of the likely normative direction of the European project.

Whereas the Constitutional Treaty, and the more formal process of constitutionalisation that led up to it, are about the legal-normative structure of the Union, the decisions concerning accession are not explicitly about normative choices. Indeed, past and future accessions to the Union imply the acceptance of acceding states of the *acquis* – the existing legal framework based on treaties and secondary legislation. However, the nature and the sheer size of the recent and possible future enlargements have a qualitative impact on the Union itself. They may come to define the Union in a territorial sense given that they significantly extend the border of the Union outwards, and that the new external border may indeed become the ultimate border of the Union.

In this way, in response to and in preparation for EU enlargement, two long-term processes – constitutionalisation and territorialisation – have come to a head (if not quite to a conclusion) in the early 21st century. The time is right to ask where that leaves the European Union and its relationship with the 'margins' or the 'periphery', in particular in the North of Europe, as is the aim of this volume. This chapter approaches the subject by first taking a closer look at the driving forces behind, and the consequences of, each of these two processes. The chapter then assesses the significance and the impact of these processes on the 'remaking' of Europe in the margins. By way of conclusion this chapter argues that the discourses more than the decisions, which have dominated the integration process in recent years, mark something of a departure from the previous 'post-Westphalian' path of European integration, and instead point towards a more statist conception of the European Union. It remains to be seen to what extent these discourses will subsequently have ramifications in normative, institutional and policy-terms, and what resistance to the choices implicit in these discourses will have to confront.

The New Discourse of Constitutionalism in Europe

From International Treaty to 'European Constitution'

While the formal – or officially sanctioned – debate about a European constitution began only after the Nice European Council in 2000, partially as a response to perceptions of failure given the limited decisions taken at that summit, the wider process of constitutionalisation has been going on for a long time (de Witte, 2002). The original legal framework underpinning the integration process was, of course, a set of international treaties, the Paris Treaty and the Rome Treaties. That these treaties and the institutionalised cooperation among member states were viewed as an issue of *foreign* policy was demonstrated by the fact that the key decision-making institution, the Council of Ministers, only met in the configuration of foreign ministers for the first decade of the EU. In the early years, European integration was foreign policy. In particular, it was about reconciliation between France and Germany and the anchoring of cooperative behaviour among states in war-torn Europe. It was also about the political and economic strengthening of Western Europe during the first Cold War. Thus, foreign policy objectives dominated the initial phase of integration, and economic concerns (which later came to dominate the process) were regarded as means towards the end of creating a lasting peace in Europe.

Over time, a number of factors eventually shattered this image of integration as foreign policy. First, the very nature of the issues under discussion demanded a kind of expertise from ministers and officials that could only be found outside foreign ministries, and soon the Council of Ministers developed into multiple fora with sectoral ministers given increasingly large rein in the decision-making process. Second, the growth of common institutions and the gradual increase in their competences, meant that the European Communities were increasingly involved in regulating the 'internal' affairs of the member states. It became evident, especially in the course of the 're-launch' of Europe in the 1980s, that through their membership in the European construction states were not only, and perhaps not even mainly, managing the relationship between themselves, but were in effect governing commonly an emerging polity in its own right.

The supranational institutions of the Commission, Parliament and, in particular, the Court of Justice (ECJ) all contributed to the formalisation of this process of polity-building. The European Commission was periodically instrumental in pushing forward the boundaries of defining what the integration project stands for, and the European Parliament, since the first direct elections in 1979, has been essential in democratising an institutional architecture that was originally essentially about diplomatic and bureaucratic decision-making. The ECJ has been the key factor in the creeping constitutionalising of the Union, not least through a case law in the 1970s and 1980s which recognised individuals as (European) citizens who had rights under the treaties, also *against* their own states. Through its fundamental rights jurisdiction the Court laid the foundations for the subsequent formalisation of these citizenship rights in the EU treaty, and through its willingness to introduce the 'C' word into the official language of the Union, by talking about the 'European constitutional order', the Court anticipated and prepared the eventual formal constitution-building process.

The process of constitutionalisation was a long and often slow road, and for a long time remained hidden behind the apparent stage of high politics on which statesmen and women fought pitched battles over national interests. However, once the spotlight turned on the formal constitution-building process it became apparent that the ground had been well-prepared, indeed that the house was pretty much built on it already. What remained was the task of knocking down a few walls and extensive re-decoration.

The Constitutional Convention: Europe's Philadelphia?

This task of giving formal expression to the constitutional nature of the European Union was handed to the Convention on the Future of Europe in 2001. Its life and impact is an interesting lesson in the potential of consultative politics, and the power of ideas: for the formal role of this convention, which was composed of national and EP parliamentarians and Commission and government representatives from all 25 old and new member states, was simply to 'prepare' the following Intergovernmental Conference (IGC) in which government representatives would actually take the decisions over treaty reform. In this sense, the Convention was formally little more than similar discussion fora, such as the Dooge Committee (preparing the Single European Act negotiations), the Delors Committee (preparing the Economic and Monetary Union Treaty negotiations) and the Reflection Group (preparing the Amsterdam Treaty negotiations), which previously had been used to explore national positions and search for possible compromise solutions.

However, under the chairmanship of Valery Giscard d'Estaing, the Convention turned out to be a much more important institution than its formal powers indicated, and perhaps than governments expected when they chose this format of preparing treaty reform. Several factors aided the impact of the Convention, but one important aspect was the changing discourse about European integration. Launched by German Foreign Minister Fischer's 2000 speech about the need for a debate about the *finalité politique* of the integration process (Fischer, 2000), and fuelled by the response from both the political class and the wider European public, the idea of discussing the future of Europe in constitutional terms gained steady momentum. Coming too late to make an impact on the Nice Treaty negotiations, the issue of constitutionalising Europe came to define the so-called post-Nice process, which was to deal with the 'left-overs' of Nice – key issues about institutional reform, simplification of the treaty and democratising the Union which had not been successfully concluded at Nice itself.

Envisaging a further instance of treaty reform to deal with such leftovers is common practice in the EU, as is the creation of reflection groups to prepare IGCs. What was special, indeed unique, in this case was the willingness of all key actors, European institutions but also national governments and parliaments, to debate European integration in *constitutional* terms (Walker, 2003). This was a discursive move which did not in itself imply any substantive choices. Indeed, as discussed above, it was largely the explicit recognition of implicit choices that had already been made in the course of European integration. However, the discourse of defining publicly and formally the choices facing Europe as being 'constitutional' did have a number of critical effects. It elevated the debate about institutional reform to greater public awareness, whilst it also bestowed greater significance and status on the Convention.

It was in this context that the Convention's President could then compare the European experience to the drafting of the US Constitution at Philadelphia, and describe the efforts of the Convention as a 'constitutional moment' for the European Union. This discourse, which aligned itself with the constitutional experience of the modern (federal) state, continued in the actual discussions in the Convention and the drafting of the treaty. Thus, there were proposals early on to change the name of the 'European Union' to the 'United States of Europe' and to create a 'Congress of the European People' – proposals which did not make it into the final draft agreed by the Convention.

But a sense of purpose and of occasion prevailed, and the Convention succeeded in maintaining a broad consensus in the drafting of a constitutional treaty, agreeing on a raft of reform proposals and effectively determining the agenda of the IGC. When the Convention came to a close, Giscard d'Estaing again emphasised the idea of a 'constitutional moment' by claiming that the draft treaty would lay down the institutional structure for decades to come. Regardless of the actual content of the treaty, and its relation to previous processes and existing provisions, the discursive construction of Europe's 'constitutional moment' was successful in a sense that the constitutional nature of the European construction is now recognised, and the need for broader public debate about the resultant choices is established.

Statist Imagery and Terminology in the Constitutional Treaty

The Constitutional Treaty was eventually agreed by governments in June 2004, after a previous attempt to conclude the IGC in December 2003 had failed. The treaty is to a large extent a revision of the existing treaties, changing certain provisions, spelling out existing ECJ case law in treaty articles and incorporating the Charter of Fundamental Rights. Despite the fact that compromises on long-standing issues such as the size of the Commission and Council voting were found, overall it remains a further step on the already existing path of integration, not a departure in a radically different direction. The existing institutional architecture, policy-making process and range of competences remain the basic building blocks of the Union, though there are several new and revised features. In substantive legal terms it remains a constitutional *treaty* rather than a European *constitution*.

However, the key change in this regard is *not* the substance of the new treaty, but the language which is used in it, and in which it is talked about. Just as the convention managed to elevate itself from a mere reflection group to the EU equivalent of Philadelphia, the significance of the treaty has been changed through the discursive choices made in and about it. Beyond the terminology of the 'constitution' itself, these concern above all the titles of key posts in the revised institutional arrangements. Under the 'constitution' there will be a President of the European Council and a European Union Minister for Foreign Affairs. The treaty also envisages the creation of a European External Action service, which sounds fairly similar to the diplomatic service known from the nation-state. The terminology for the key legal acts available to the EU is also set to change: what have been known as regulations and directives are now to be called European Laws and European Framework Laws.

The use of such statist language is presented under the banner of simplification, and it is true that it makes it easier to communicate to the public what European institutions are, and are doing. However, using the imagery and the terminology of the state in this way is a double-edged sword. What may be seen to encourage easier communication may also carry the risk of greater confusion. Giving the impression, purposefully or not, that the institutions and instruments of the EU are like those of the state, may lead to the perception that the EU *is* like a state, or is seeking to become a state. Depending on one's standpoint, that may be a blessing or a drawback, but either way it is a departure from the gradualist path which has characterised European integration so far. Convention members and observers have agreed that the language used in and about the Constitutional Treaty exceeds the substance contained in it, but have justified or explained this in terms of the heightened expectations which will subsequently have to lead to further changes that would then approximate political practice and legal form to the new language of constitutionalism. In other words, because we are speaking about a European Constitution, the people – the *people* – would push decision-makers and institutional actors to further reform the Union and thus lead the way to a genuine European constitution.

Constitutionalising the European Union: Implications for Future Developments

It remains to be seen whether this is a workable strategy. It certainly is high-risk, since it seems to confirm the scenarios of Euro-sceptics about the emergence of a European super-state, while at the same time pro-Europeans with high expectations about more effective, transparent and democratic governance at the European level are bound to be disappointed. Thus, the result may be threats to the legitimacy of the integration path from a number of different directions.

The discursive choices will nevertheless leave their mark, independent of the fate of the Constitutional Treaty in the course of ratification in 25 member states. The past process of constitutionalisation has been recognised and been made more visible, and large parts of the political class in Europe have participated in and contributed to a debate about the 'European Constitution'. The aim of providing the EU with its *finalité politique* remains, even if the treaty itself is hardly going to provide that. As a result of this debate, this discourse and this treaty, the EU has embraced the language of statehood. While still lacking key aspects of the modern state, this has been a significant turn for the EU.

The EU's constitutional discourse is not the only development that has pointed towards a more statist, and therefore less post-Westphalian, path of integration. For example, the rapid development of an EU military capacity, the identity politics connected to the issue of Christianity in the Constitutional Treaty, or the emergence of an internal security agenda for the EU in the wake of 9/11, are all signs that there is much less ambivalence about institutional and policy choices, which have traditionally remained off-limits to the EU precisely because they are seen to be closely connected to the core role of the state. But at the end of 2004 security and identity are not only firmly on the EU's agenda, they have also become important aspects of the Union's constitutional politics.

One attribute of the modern state, territoriality, has been another problematical issue for the EU. On the one hand, there has been a long-standing effort by the EU to achieve greater economic and social cohesion, a key policy that has essentially been defined in territorial terms and received much financial and institutional attention. On the other hand, the 'bordering' of the Union has remained elusive, precisely because enlargement has been a the long-term process. Eastward enlargement was preceded by partial policy-export and followed by lengthy transition periods, opt-out arrangements and differentiated integration (Friis and Murphy, 1999). The 'export' of integration towards the outside, and the numerous exemptions from integrative measures and policies on the inside, have created a polity with 'fuzzy borders' that has been better described in terms of concentric circles or 'neo-medieval empire' rather than clearly bordered space (Wæver, 1997; Christiansen, Tonra and Petito, 2001).

Yet, even in this respect recent developments have been interesting and to some extent contrary to past trends. With the achievement of Eastern enlargement and the landmark decision to open accession negotiations with Turkey, the culmination of the *process* of territorial expansion can be envisaged – the EU may then be reaching the point at which a definite border will (have to) be drawn. We may be 15-20 years away from that point, but the territorial shape of things to come may be visible much sooner. In other words, just as the process of defining a *finalité politique* is in full swing, we may be witnessing a separate, but related, process of establishing the *finalité territoriale* of the Union. The following section will look at this process of territorialisation in some greater depth, before the conclusions from the effects of both constitutionalisation and territorialisation can be drawn.

The Territorialisation of European Integration

Cohesion Policy and Territorial Politics in the European Union

The process of seeking to achieve *territorial* integration came relatively late to the European project. For most of its life the integration process had its emphasis on functional sectoral integration, geared towards greater mobility of goods, people and services in a common and single market. While this concerned the regulation of cross-border flows, there was considerable resistance to address the mobility goals in terms of the integration of the Community territory – in part precisely because of the sensitivity of member states, and indeed of the modern state as such, about territoriality. The EC/EU could regulate transborder flows and mobility issues *between* the territories of states, but it could not be seen to be governing territory itself.

Serious attempts at redressing the balance of functional and territorial integration only came in the 1980s with the reform of the structural funds. From 1988 onwards the EC devoted, for the first time, significant amounts of money to regional policy and centrally laid down fairly tight rules about the way in which this money could be spent. Institutional mechanisms were being developed, and through a mixture of competitive behaviour at the state and sub-state level, and subtle pressure from the centre, the reformed structural funds had an impact not only on the economic situations of the regions, but also on the territorial politics in the member states more generally.

The management of the structural funds required active cooperation and significant co-financing from national, regional and local authorities. This, in turn, was widely seen to require an institutional capacity at the sub-state level that would permit local and regional actors to apply for, prepare, co-finance, manage and evaluate substantive projects. In many cases, in particular in the traditionally more centralised member states, such institutional capacity at the sub-state level was lacking and only developed gradually during the 1980s and 1990s, in part due to ongoing domestic reforms in many member states, in part due to the pressures, incentives and opportunities at the European level.

This indirect, and in some ways unintended, impact of EU structural policies on the territorial politics of the member states has generally been seen as successful, because it strengthened the capacity of local and regional actors without threatening the territorial integrity of the member states. This can be seen as an achievement against a background of domestic territorial politics which are traditionally often seen in zero-sum terms: if the sub-state level gains, then the central government level must be losing. Or worse: if regions are being strengthened, then the unity of the state must be in danger – the 'break-up of Britain' scenario (which is not exclusive to the UK). The management of EU structural funds since the late 1980s, applying the principle of partnership between the various levels of government, has demonstrated that it could lead to regional policies being positive-sum games, where all levels would gain from the economic benefits arising, and where political power-sharing could be conceptualised as multi-level governance (Marks et al., 1996).

Thus, other EU policies with a more explicit territorial impact followed in the 1990s: the establishment of a Cohesion Fund, the development of a European Spatial Development Plan and the identification of a number of key infrastructure projects that would help to establish trans-European networks. All these policies developed in the 1990s began addressing the challenge of territorially integrating an expanding and increasingly diverse and disparate European Union. To some extent, it can even be said that territorial integration became mainstreamed in a sense that it entered into sectoral policies, for example research policy or, through territorial employment pacts, social policy.

The EU's Approach to Border Management

One dimension of the reformed structural funds that turned out to be particularly appealing to policy-makers was cross-border cooperation (CBC). This policy-instrument that was initially only a fairly limited Community initiative, turned out to be much in demand at the local and regional level, addressing precisely the issues of territorial integration at the borders of the member states that had been neglected by functional integration. The positive response from 'below' led to further promotion of CBC activities elsewhere, and CBC became an integral part of PHARE, TACIS, and pre-accession strategies more generally. CBC policies of the EU became more diverse and sophisticated, meaning that there was increasing recognition that different functional logics required solutions aimed at different territorial levels. Thus, CBC developed both at the micro- and meso-level, and both on the inside and the outside of the Union. Crucially for our purposes here, CBC policies tied in very well with attempts to manage the periphery of the Union, and in particular the Baltic, the Balkans and the Mediterranean became fertile areas for experimentation with policy-instruments that had initially been developed for overcoming problems at state borders on the inside of the Union.

In the process of designing, developing, mainstreaming and eventually exporting CBC policies the European Union established a particular approach to the management of its borders – an approach that was distinct from the way in which states manage their borders. The binary understanding of borders in the modern state has been that of a dividing line between inside and outside, and thus as an essential element in defining the political community and thereby also the identity of the state. In contrast, in the EU an approach has emerged that regards borders as spaces rather than lines, and that seeks to bring together rather than divide communities in the border area (Christiansen and Jørgensen, 2000). In this way the EU's CBC policies seek to ensure that the periphery of the EU is territorially better integrated.

The EU's particular approach to borders, together with the differentiated nature of integration, has created a kind of politics in the EU which have been described as 'concentric circles'. That is to say that even though membership is clearly defined, there are numerous ways in which member states, or parts of member states, may opt out of aspects of European integration. In turn, territories and states that are not members have ample opportunity to opt-in to EU policies and even into institutional structures. As a result, integration (as opposed to membership) is not a binary distinction between everything and nothing, of 'in' and 'out', but rather a question of more or less involvement in EU policy-making, institutional adaptation and social and economic orientation towards the EU centre.

This dimension of European integration is very much in line with the neo-medieval or post-Westphalian understanding of polity-building. Together with other aspects, such as the dispersion of sovereignty and the absence of internal hierarchies in the decision-making structure, the limits of territorial integration and the particular development of border management in the EU has contributed to a type of polity that is distinct from the modern state. However, as the previous discussion of the discursive turn in the process of constitutionalisation has shown, there have been developments to challenge the post-Westphalian nature of European integration in recent years. This is also true in the case of territorialisation, where over the past few years the trend towards providing the EU with a 'hard border' has become stronger. Two developments should illustrate this trend in particular and will be discussed below: first, the moves towards securitising the EU's border, and second, the nature of the discourse about Turkey's application for EU membership.

The Securitisation of the EU's Borders

While the EU has pursued a pro-active and innovative policy of encouraging cross-border cooperation, it has also experienced a number of counter-trends. These have contributed to EU borders becoming more divisive, and turning the EU's territory more into that of a bordered space of inclusion and exclusion. In part, this is a secular trend following logically from the growth of EU policy-competences and the repercussions this has in terms of the economic, social, and political Europeanisation of national domains. However, in addition to these indirect and perhaps unintended consequences of the integration process, specific policies have been developed to make the EU's borders more 'secure' and thus provide more of a hard shell for the EU. Given the developments of the past few years it may be fair to say that this process of the securitisation of the EU's borders has become more significant and effective than previous – and continuing – attempts to manage cross-border cooperation. Indeed, in a twist of irony, an increasingly important part of cross-border cooperation has been cooperation between customs officials and police forces on either side of the EU border to make this border more secure, i.e., to prevent illegal entry into EU territory from the outside.

The securitisation of the EU's borders goes back to the Schengen agreement and its subsequent incorporation into the EU's legal framework. As part of Schengen the abolition of border controls for private individuals in order to improve mobility inside the Union's territory, has been linked to tighter controls at the external borders. This, in turn, has required cooperation among EU states on issues such as immigration and visa controls, asylum policies, and border policing. It has been a process that has been largely successful in terms of achieving its stated aims: while those living inside the EU now can move freely across state borders without facing any regular checks, those seeking to enter the EU from the outside have to undergo more extensive controls and, in many cases, visa application procedures. Thus, Schengen has contributed to a greater divide between the inside and outside at the borders of the EU.

Two aspects have further fuelled this process: first, the concerns inside the EU about immigration, and; second, the EU's response to 9/11 and the global 'war on terror'. Both have had the impact of leading EU states to further tighten immigration policies, using existing measures to control movements across borders, whilst also developing new mechanisms to improve control. The issue of 'immigration' has in most EU countries been discursively linked to economic migration (and thus to a perceived threat to employment of EU citizens), but also to benefit fraud, organised crime, and human trafficking. Given the predominant discourse about immigration, the voices of those arguing that the EU in fact needs more immigration given its demographic prospects, and that immigration on the whole has a positive impact on labour markets and social systems, remain marginal.

And while the perception that immigration heralds instability and constitutes a threat to social and economic welfare is long-standing, the aftermath of 9/11 has contributed to further aggravate the situation. The EU has been drawn into a global 'war on terror' pitching 'the West' against 'Islamic extremists', and even though the European response has been distinct from the US approach, it has nevertheless also involved a further securitisation of immigration policies. The EU is agreed that it needs to protect itself from an external threat, and that it must do so *collectively*, this requiring member states to work together in the defence of the EU's territory. The 11 March 2004 bombings in Spain, and the realisation that these were carried out by an al-Qaeda cell based in Morocco – a territory from which Spain faces the regular influx of immigrants – has further linked the issues of immigration and security in the public mind.

The perception that this external threat is coming from the *Muslim* world has also had an impact on the process of identity-formation in the EU. As part of this process of identity formation there has been greater awareness and, by some, greater emphasis, on the religious heritage of Europe. In particular, there have been arguments about the way in which the EU ought to recognise a particular debt to *Christianity* in its cultural development. In fact, the debate as to whether such a statement should be part of the preamble to the Constitutional Treaty was one of the major divisive issues in the final stages of the negotiations (Norman, 2003, pp.83-4).

As a result of these developments the EU's borders have become securitised, and the EU has become more of an integrated territory. Based on these trends there are attempts to define the EU, not only as an economic and political space, but also as a space with a common identity that is distinct from other spaces outside that are different and must therefore be excluded. It is against this background of a more security-aware, territorially-integrated and identity-conscious EU that the question of Turkish EU membership has been discussed. It is a question that has long been on the table and has seen many attempts at postponing an answer, but which has not gone away. In 2004 the issue reached the top of the agenda, leading to debate in and across many EU member states, as well as in Turkey. The point had been reached where a principled decision on the prospect for membership had to be taken, a decision which was all the more difficult to address because beyond the immediate significance of Turkey's accession to the EU it would also define the nature and the extent of the borders of the EU in a much wider sense.

The 'Turkey Question' and the Construction of Europe

The question about the possibility of Turkish membership of the EU has been debated for some decades, but not always as the subject of front-page news. The EC/EU and Turkey have a long history of economic and trade cooperation, culminating in the 1990s with the agreement on a customs union. However, while on the Turkish side this has always been seen as a process that would ultimately lead towards full membership, on the EU side decision-makers have been more circumspect. Economic indicators, human rights problems, the lack of civilian control over the military and Turkish occupation of Northern Cyprus, for a long time excluded any serious consideration of the Turkish application for membership. Instead, the EU has sought to steer towards an arrangement that would tie Turkey politically and economically to Europe *without* offering full membership (Buzan and Diez, 1999). Bringing Turkey in as a full member would, among other things, also pose serious questions to both the redistributive policies and the institutional life of the Union.

Behind these issues of preparedness for Turkish EU membership, or rather the lack of it, on both sides, a broader question has been lingering all this time: to what extent is Turkey a 'European' state that could or should belong to a Union that defines itself in geographical and cultural terms? Ironically, perhaps, the 1989 fall of the Berlin wall and the subsequent process of 'Europe growing together again' complicated this picture further. Whereas previously the integration process was clearly a *West* European process of market integration, it now subsequently turned into a process of unification of the entire continent. As various studies of the process of enlargement towards Eastern Europe have shown, accession of the countries of Central and Eastern Europe was not really a question of a rational choice among the existing members (though such choices certainly affected the timing and the conditions of entry) – eventual accession of the CEECs was simply taken for granted and viewed as a question of time (Fierke and Wiener, 2001).

If Europe as a whole has been united in the post-Cold War phase, then a decision about the Turkish application was bound to become a defining issue for the territorial reach of the EU. Beyond that, the *taking* of such a decision, regardless of whether that decision would be favourable or negative, implied that integration would become territorialised in a way it had not been until that point. Deciding that Turkey could join would imply a 'greater EU' that was ready to expand towards the Middle East, the Caucasus and the Caspian Sea regions. A decision to reject Turkey as an EU member state, on the other hand, would limit the EU to a smaller core that sought to privilege homogeneity over diversity.

Following this logic, the decision to take a decision is almost as significant as the eventual decision itself. It is in this respect that 2004 appears to have been a watershed year. Pressure on both sides, in Turkey and in the EU, led a situation in which a decision had to be taken. Until then, the EU appeared to be content, and rather successful, at postponing the decision and achieving a situation in which eventual Turkish membership was always seen as possible, but ultimately remained elusive. Various strategies, including the customs union, the device of a 'European Conference' bringing all European states together, the Euro-Mediterranean partnership and the inclusion of Turkey in selected EU programmes and policies were used, not so much as *preparation* for accession, but as ways of delaying the taking of a decision on accession. Turkey thus became a territory on the fringes which was highly affected and influenced by the EU, and was partially included in its institutional structures, but which lacked the prospect of eventual membership. Turkey was a territory that by this nature of being both inside and outside the EU exemplified the fuzzy borders of the European construction (Christiansen, Tonra and Petito 2000).

With the debate shifting to questions of membership and the starting date, length and outcome of accession negotiations, the discourse has shifted to such an extent that it is almost exclusively about the question of 'in' or 'out', rather than the continuation of the 'in-between' status that had been the order of the day until then. This is not to say that for the duration of the accession negotiations there will not continue to be uncertainty about the final outcome, about when a decision about membership will be taken and when that may be. In any case, by general agreement that is at least a decade away. However, a process has been set in motion that requires a decision to be taken. In spite of all the uncertainties and the careful language applied in the Commission reports and Presidency conclusions, this is understood in the discourse which is about whether Turkey should join or not. While negotiations will be 'open-ended' and may lead to alternative solutions other than membership, the outcome has been discursively constructed, by advocates and opponents alike, as a decision about Turkey being 'in' or 'out'. The EU has set itself on a path which is bound to lead to the construction of a hard border and the creation of a European Union that will also be defined in territorial terms.

Conclusions: Implications for the Remaking of Europe at the Margins

Constitutionalisation and Territorialisation: Developing the Hard Core and the Hard Shell of Europe?

It is on this issue that we can also observe how the processes of constitutionalisation and territorialisation, which we have so far observed in isolation, have become linked. The question of Turkey's potential EU membership is seen to define the Union not only in terms of fixing a lasting territorial border, but also as a crucial test of the development of a polity based on values, culture and, in the views of some, identity. The presence of democratic values and respect for human rights in the Turkish state has been a crucial issue in the process of approaching the question of membership. But beyond that, as the Turkish state has succeeded in addressing these issues and otherwise made progress in meeting the Copenhagen criteria, other concerns have come to the surface: the question of whether Turkey fits into the EU culturally, and whether the identity of the EU is compatible with a member state that is both as different from the existing members, and as large and populous as Turkey. In other words, a decision on Turkish EU membership raises cultural and ideational issues in a way that a Norwegian or Polish application does not.

Religion plays a central role here. In the constitutionalisation process, the question of whether Europe's Christian heritage, or indeed a reference to God, should be mentioned in the preamble was a highly divisive issue. Apart from the power politics issues of voting weights in the Council, the inclusion or otherwise of such a 'Christian reference' was one of the unresolved items at the Brussels December 2003 European Council that failed to conclude the Constitutional IGC. And while this dispute was eventually resolved in favour of a more general reference to 'the cultural, religious and humanist inheritance of Europe' in the preamble of the Constitutional Treaty, the discourse as to whether the EU is defined as a *Christian* polity is alive.

Here, it links up with the discourse about Turkish EU accession, where some opponents reject the possibility of membership on the grounds that a state with a large Muslim population cannot have a place in the European Union. It is an argument that is presented in different degrees and intensities, but it does feature increasingly in the debate about Turkey and Europe. Thus, a discourse about the identity of the EU as a polity based not only on economic interest, functional interdependence, efficiency of governance, or on the development of a legal and institutional framework, but also on *Christian* values, has had a significant place in both the process of constitutionalisation and in the process of territorialisation.

Together these twin processes, and the policy and institutional developments they encompass, have led to a hardening of the 'core' of the European Union. They have contributed to an image of the EU that is more statist, in that it has a clearer sense of its underlying norms and values, as well as in having a more clearly defined outer boundary. And each of these attributes also come with the aspiration towards greater permanence – a 'constitution' that should not require frequent reform, a border that will be closer to the 'final' boundary of the Union – that is traditionally the hallmark of the modern state. Thus, the *process* of European integration, which has been in flux both constitutionally and territorially during most of its history, is moving close to becoming a *state*.

The EU's Neighbourhood Policy: Maintaining Fuzzy Borders

It would be misleading, however, to present these recent developments as pointing only in one – a more statist – direction. Whilst there have been these developments there have also been counter-trends, or rather, some of the underlying, non-statist aspects of the EU have been hard to eradicate and continue to work away within the institutionalised structure of the Union. Several examples could be given related to both the constitutionalisation and the territorialisation processes. Compare, for example, the willingness of the drafters of the Constitutional Treaty to include a provision for the withdrawal of member states from the EU, with the way in which West European states have responded to even moderate moves towards greater autonomy from territorial minorities. Such a withdrawal provision, and the resultant uncertainty about territorial integrity, is not something that one would expect to be written into a state constitution.

A similar observation can be made about the emerging EU policy on developing a special relationship with its neighbours. The 'European Neighbourhood Policy' (ENP) demonstrates the willingness of the EU to continue a policy of managing its outer borders and maintaining special relationships with countries and territories bordering on the Union (European Commission, 2003). While being based on several long-standing instruments of EU policy-making, namely the instances of cross-border cooperation such as the Northern Dimension and the Euro-Mediterranean Partnership, the ENP is also clearly and explicitly connected to the mainstream foreign policy of the European Union, and in particular to the security strategy (Council, 2004). It is a classic case of a policy that cuts across several domains (internal and external, political and economic) and indeed across the institutional boundaries between the Commission and Council Secretariat. Even inside the Commission it spans across the DGs for Enlargement and External Relations, being managed by a joint task force made up of members of both services.

While the EU makes it clear that this is *not* an enlargement policy, it constitutes a policy that brings together numerous instruments, combines several objectives and involves almost all the sectoral policies of the Union. Its territorial target is clearly twofold – on the one hand, being aimed at Russia and the countries of Eastern Europe that have no prospect of EU membership, and on the other hand, looking to the South Mediterranean and the Near East. While the security and economic concerns the EU has with regard to these countries are fairly obvious, the idea of developing an integrated approach bringing together sectoral policies and applying these selectively in neighbouring territories is an innovative way of making policy. Or rather, it would be innovative from a statist perspective, but in the EU this approach of addressing territorial issues in such a way is long established. Indeed, in the EU this has been the *traditional* way of doing things.

The ENP, which has received a boost in the course of the appointment of the Barroso Commission and the institutional changes that came with it, is a sign that the EU is still able to develop, promote and execute policies which look for new and unconventional ways of managing territory, and that as such distinguish the EU from the standard practices of the modern state. Thus, the ENP is one, albeit small and limited, example of the kind of elements in the integration process that make the EU a polity remaining distinct from the idea of modern statehood.

For the governance of the North of Europe these developments spell both opportunity and constraint. To the extent to which the statist claims have an impact on discourses, policies and institutions, the kind of post-modern governance that many have identified in the North of Europe, and around the Baltic Sea in particular, may have a more difficult time in sustaining themselves. Even if the statist discourses in the constitutional debate and in the territorialisation process will take time to filter through, they would be expected to have an effect there just as they will elsewhere. A special regime, if that is what has developed around the Baltic, may sustain itself in the face of a European centre developing in a different direction, but that would in any case weaken its ability to provide inspiration for the European project as a whole. The North of Europe would therefore continue to live in the margins, and perhaps even more so. Of course, this may also mean that further experimentation would be possible there, given that it would be considered a part of the Union (if not the world) that is simply different.

Such a distinctive development in the North of Europe, a post-Westphalian part of a more statist European Union, may still have significant support to expect from the centre, in particular in the form of the ENP which may provide instruments, resources and legitimacy to continue a particular kind of policymaking in this area. Thus, there may well be strong grounds for a North European *Sonderweg* in the EU, even if global, i.e., EU-wide trends are pointing in a different direction.

In any case, the most likely development is that European integration continues to be an open-ended and to some extent contradictory process. The statist claims that have come with the twin processes of constitutionalisation and territorialisation point in one direction of future development, whereas other aspects of the EU, such as the ENP, point in the opposite direction. And while the EU remains a polity best characterised as *sui generis*, constitutionalisation and territorialisation have pushed its developmental path away from the kind of post-

Westphalian construction that it has been identified with by many scholars in the past, towards a more statist development. What this demonstrates is that the conceptual dichotomy between a more statist and a more post-national trajectory remains a valid and useful analytical tool, but also that we need to re-assess continuously how discourses, policies and institutions develop in order to be able to better understand the nature and the direction of European integration.

References

Buzan, Barry and Diez, Thomas (1999), 'Turkey and the European Union: Where to From Here?', *Survival*, Vol. 41(1), pp. 41-57.

Christiansen, Thomas and Jørgensen, Knud Erik (2000), 'Transnational Governance 'above' and 'below' the state: The changing nature of borders in Europe', *Regional and Federal Studies*, Vol. 10(2), pp. 62-77.

Christiansen, Thomas, Tonra, Ben and Petito, Fabio (2000), 'Fuzzy Politics Around Fuzzy Borders: The European Union's "Near Abroad"', *Cooperation and Conflict*, Vol. 35(4), pp. 389-416.

Council of the European Union (2004), *Conclusions of 14 June 2004 on the ENP and the Conclusions of the European Council on the ENP*, 17/18, Luxembourg.

De Witte, B. (2002), 'The Closet Thing to a Constitutional Conversation in Europe: the Semi-Permanent Treaty Revision Process', in Paul Beaumont, Carole Lyons and Neil Walker (eds.), *Convergence and Divergence in European Public Law*, Oxford, Hart, pp. 39-57.

European Commission (2003), *Paving the way for a New Neighbourhood Instrument*, Communication, Brussels.

Fierke, Karin and Wiener, Antje (2001), 'Constructing Institutional Interests: EU and NATO Enlargement', in Thomas Christiansen, Knud Erik Jørgensen and Antje Wiener (eds.), *The Social Construction of Europe*, London, Sage, pp. 121-39.

Fischer, J. (2000), *From Confederacy to Federation: Thoughts on the Finality of European Integration*, speech given at the Humboldt University (Berlin).

Friis, Lykke and Murphy, Anna (1999), 'The European Union and Central and Eastern Europe: Governance and Boundaries', *Journal of Common Market Studies*, Vol. 37(2), pp. 211-32.

Marks, Gary., Hooghe, Liesbet and Blank, Kermit (1996), 'European Integration from the 1980s: State-Centric v. Multilevel Governance', *Journal of Common Market Studies*, Vol. 34(3), pp. 341-79.

Norman, Peter (2003), *The Accidental Constitution*, Brussels, EuroComment.

Walker, Neil (2003), 'After the Constitutional Moment', *The Federal Trust Constitutional Online Paper Series*, No. 32(3). Available at http://ssrn.com/abstract=516783.

Wæver, Ole (1997), 'Imperial Metaphors: Emerging European Analogies to Pre-Nation-State Imperial Systems', in Ola Tunander, Pavel Baev and Einagel, Victoria I. (eds.), *Geopolitics in Post-Wall Europe: Security, Territory and Identity*, London, Sage, pp. 59-93.

Chapter 6

Westphalian, Imperial, Neomedieval: The Geopolitics of Europe and the Role of the North

Christopher S. Browning

Introduction

Since the creation of the European Union (then the European Community) in 1957 discussion regarding the future trajectory and model of governance aspired for by the Union has been lively. At stake has been the issue of what the Union is about, and what its 'final' geopolitical identity should be. In geopolitical terms two metaphors have been particularly prominent, especially in recent years.

First, there is the idea that the EU is developing in statist terms, the goal being to turn the EU into a traditional unitary actor akin to a modernist Westphalian nation-state (Ginsburg, 1999). Evidence for this is usually drawn from the Union's desire to develop a unified subjectivity through such things as the Common Foreign and Security Policy (CFSP) and the common European Security and Defence Identity (ESDI). Likewise, the creation of a post for an EU foreign minister and discussions regarding the Constitutional Convention that call for more majority voting also seem to support this view. Finally, the Schengen border regime has also been understood in traditional terms as a statist-type border aimed at preserving and re-instituting the Union's territorial sovereignty *vis-à-vis* its neighbours and where political space is necessarily seen as divided into exclusive and clearly demarcated political units (Grabbe, 2000). For many people this vision of the EU's future trajectory is considered highly undesirable, as was evident, for example, in the UK's European election debates in 2004 where it seemed repeating a mantra of 'reclaiming sovereignty from Brussels' was a prerequisite for electoral success. For others, however, the continued political and economic unification of Europe through enhanced integration is seen as a positive development and the natural course for the Union.[1]

---

[1]   For example, a report written by a 50-strong group of commentators and politicians that was commissioned by Romano Prodi and released at the end of May 2004 called for a

The second metaphor depicts the EU as increasingly exhibiting Empire-type features (e.g., Cooper, 2003). According to this model EU governance should be conceptualised as a series of concentric circles with power located at the centre in Brussels and being dispersed outwards to varying and declining degrees (Zielonka, 2001, p.509; Wæver, 1997a). Central here are ideas of the EU as a peace project with the mission to increasingly extend peace beyond its borders, an aspiration requiring the EU to take an interest in political and economic developments beyond its borders and to try to order the space of neighbouring regions. This has been a central motivation of the enlargement process and of the principles of conditionality. However, it is also apparent in the Barcelona Process which aims to disseminate EU values to Mediterranean countries that have little hope or desire of joining the EU in the future. At the same time, and as we will see below, there are also more traditional neo-colonialist notions of empire evident in EU understandings. What is important for now, however, is that the Empire metaphor entails consequences for how the EU's political space and its borders are understood, with the EU's borders conceptualised as fuzzier, with the start and end of EU space less clear than in Westphalian conceptualisations.

Both metaphors have been proposed either as a description of what the EU is like now, or as teleological idealisations of how it should develop. This chapter aims to contribute to this debate on the future geopolitical configuration of Europe. The starting point, however, is that in general the Westphalia and Empire metaphors are centrist discourses told from the perspective of Brussels, the Commission or the larger member states. Consequently, the opinions and experiences of those in the EU's margins and border regions have been largely ignored. This is a mistake since as was argued in the book's Introduction the margins can actually exert considerable influence on how the EU/Europe will develop in the future. Using the experience of the Northern Dimension Initiative the chapter illustrates how actors in the margins have been able to impact on European governance such that an alternative metaphor of a 'neomedieval' Europe has also entered the debate. This metaphor depicts a different understanding of European governance, political space and borders and shows that other, non-centrist ways of conducting policy and being an international actor may also be available to the EU.

At the same time, interpretations of the Northern Dimension Initiative are contested, so whilst neomedieval stories can be identified concerning its impact on European geopolitics, so too can more Westphalian and Imperial perspectives. Therefore, whilst the margins can impact back on the constitution of the whole, using the competing discourses and interpretations of the Northern Dimension as an example, the chapter seeks to explore what happens when these different visions collide and what this might mean for the future of Europe more generally. Will one

---

fully-fledged 'political union' as the next step for the EU once the constitution was fully ratified (Hennessy, 2004, p.2).

of the metaphors triumph over the others, or is a hybrid version more likely to emerge?

Neomedievalism, Olympic Rings and the Northern Dimension

The Northern Dimension Initiative was proposed by Finland in September 1997 as a broad policy framework for cooperative projects of an environmental, economic, social, cultural and political nature, aimed at stabilising Northern Europe by integrating the Baltic States and Russia into the Western democratic community. Drawing on the principles of liberal democratic peace theory it has been presented as an alternative way to tackle the security problems of the Baltic Sea Region. Rather than relying on traditional military strategies it is claimed security will be better provided by integrating Russia and the Baltic States into European security structures and international norms of acceptable behaviour. As Archer has put it, through promoting welfare it has been assumed warfare will be prevented (Archer, 2001, pp.202-3). In June 2000 the Northern Dimension firmly reached the EU agenda when it received its first Action Plan, which was renewed in 2003 for the period 2004-2006.

Positive interpretations of the Northern Dimension have championed it as a chance to overcome the previous dividing lines of the Cold War East-West conflict. Such notions have been captured well in the re-designation of the old East-West border as a *frontier*, a motivational metaphor that encourages engaging with whatever exists across the boundary (Parker, 2000, p.7). This emotive rhetoric has been utilised by academics and policy-makers alike. For example, in 1999 Finland's Secretary of State for political affairs, Jukka Valtasaari, proclaimed that the Finnish-Russian border had become 'an innovative meeting place – a frontier – instead of the dividing line that it used to be' (Valtasaari, 1999). On the academic front, Sergei Medvedev has declared the 'North as the Last Frontier', a largely blank space that blurs the East-West divide and that provides space for new stories of European identity emphasising commonality and cooperation, not difference (Medvedev, 2001; 1998, p.8; Joenniemi, 2000a, p.128).

In this respect the Northern frontier is presented as an opportunity for adventure to explore, and in the same process constitute, a new type of regional politics. At times this has been made explicit, particularly in the case of Finland where the Northern Dimension has been tied to notions of the Finns as innovators and pioneers in the new regional cooperation.[2] More generally notions of adventure and exploration have been aroused through the emotive call to turn the Baltic Sea

---

[2]   For example see the following article by Ole Norrback (1998), the then Minister for Europe. A similar discourse of adventurism was also used in the early 1990s when the Norwegians set about gaining support for the construction of the Barents Euro-Arctic Region (see Tunander, 1994, pp.31, 39).

Region into a modern day neo-liberal version of the medieval Hanseatic trade regime.

Importantly, such visions appeal within the EU as they play on ideas of the EU as having a mission to extend peace throughout Europe through the dissemination of its values beyond its borders, a role which Antola (1999, p.126) notes 'is very much at the heart of the Northern Dimension'. However, regional cooperation in the Northern Dimension is not simply about exporting European values and Europeanness across the boundary, but is actually a process in which the boundary is given new meaning and Europe and the EU in turn are re-invented. Indeed, through the Northern Dimension the focus to some extent even moves beyond a concern with linear borders to the construction of a border region, an intermediary space in the North between (EU) Europe and Russia.

The Northern Dimension's aim of engaging with Russia in regional and local forums blurs clear distinctions between the inside and outside of the Union, which consequently affects how we conceptualise the subjectivity and nature of the EU and Europe. To repeat a growing dogma of the social sciences, the discursive construction of boundaries is usually a central element in constituting identity. As Paasi (1998, p.75) reminds us, boundaries are not simply lines on the ground, but are also 'manifestations of social practice and discourse'. Boundary discourses carry symbols of meaning that differentiate social groups from each other, establishing one group's identity in reference (and sometimes negation) to the presumed nature and identity of those on the other side of the boundary. With identity understood as a boundary producing practice differentiating the self from others the way in which difference is narrated, and the boundary between self and otherness constructed, in turn affects the character of relations that become possible across the boundary (Paasi, 1998, pp.80-1).

For example, during the Cold War when both East and West were widely constructed in antithesis to each other the border between the two became conceptualised as impermeable (an Iron Curtain), with East-West contacts consequently being highly regulated and limited. With the end of the Cold War, identity narratives differentiating East and West ameliorated, opening space for more active and cooperative relations. For its part, at its most visionary the Northern Dimension does not simply call for a further amelioration of the East-West boundary, but its total eradication in favour of a 'Northern' regional signifier encompassing all. The implications of such rhetoric behind the Northern Dimension are significant. If the borders between inside and outside are blurring, then so too is a European identity traditionally centred on a clearly bounded EU with a defined decision-making centre. If the Northern Dimension aims at Russia's inclusion in European norms and structures through promoting ever-increasing levels of cross-border cooperation, then patterns of EU/European subjectivity and governance tomorrow will be unlike those of yesterday or today. For example, reflecting on the future of regional cooperation following EU and NATO enlargement Erkki Tuomioja (2004), Finland's Foreign Minister, has stated that in the future cooperation will be driven by grassroots endeavours with central authorities largely excluded.

Although the ultimate consequences of this view of the Northern Dimension remain to be seen, two points are worth mentioning to highlight the case. First, if the goal really is the breaking of previous dividing lines, then the implication behind the Northern Dimension is that the EU needs to find ways to accommodate the views of outsiders such as Russia and its regions in EU decision-making in regard to the European north (Haukkala, 2001b, p.18). The pressures for this have been apparent from the start with Russia being occasionally critical of their exclusion from decision-making, despite statements within the Northern Dimension Action Plans that they would be included.[3]

Second, it is important to note that the Northern Dimension is actually an instance where the margins of Europe have asserted themselves in order to set the agenda of European integration. As Joenniemi (2003, pp.234-7) has argued, the emergence of the Northern Dimension can be seen precisely as an instance where a peripheral actor (Finland) has capitalised on its marginality by orienting the EU to its concerns. Whereas traditionally the north has been understood as entailing isolation, in this case the 'North' has been understood as a place from which to speak and act. Instead of running from the North, as might be expected given the peripherality usually associated with the concept, the 'North' has been utilised as a resource to position Finland in Europe and in the EU game, and at the same time to impact on the nature of the whole.

In particular, the North is presented as a signifier and space for transcending East-West boundaries and for building a new relationship with Russia. Arguably, Finland's power has derived from its location on the EU's edge and border with Russia. Instead of letting the EU and Russia define that border, the marginality and 'edginess' of Finland's position has been seen as a resource. Utilising the Northern signifier has undermined centrist understandings of what Europe is about, and instead a more decentralised Europe is envisaged where the North is no longer seen as the end of the road, but as a road going somewhere. From being an edge, the North is depicted as a meeting place and a resource – not just a problem – not only for Finland, but also for the EU and Russia.

Importantly, such de-centralisation has gone beyond the nation-state as local actors have begun to engage extensively in cross-border cooperation. This development is giving traditionally exclusive state borders new meaning as they become more porous, but which in the case of the Finnish-Russian border also contributes to dissolving the EU's external border. Most emblematic of the role of local actors in such agenda setting in Northern Europe is the existence of a Regional Council that provides a forum for non-state regional and local actors to exercise subjectivity in the context of the Barents Euro-Arctic Council (Joenniemi, 1994, p.216).

---

[3]   In particular, this has been the case with Kaliningrad, where Moscow has clearly felt left outside the loop in the EU's policy formation towards the exclave.

When projected into an idealised future vision, this aspect of the Northern Dimension suggests the possibility of reconstituting Europe away from centralism towards a new 'postmodern' or 'neomedieval' regionality in which governance and the figure of Europe become altogether more flexible. Although this is a development yet to be fully realised, Medvedev (1998, p.8) does suggest that in Northern Europe one can identify 'a sort of "future territory"...an experiment in post-modern territoriality', where the formerly clear territorial picture of the EU is no longer identifiable as a fixed single space, but is better represented by a series of overlapping transparencies. Elsewhere, this vision has been seen as presaging the emergence of a *Europe of Olympic Rings*, the notion of variable interlocking rings, each representing various regional formations in Europe, emphasising a move away from a hierarchically ordered Europe centred on Brussels to a more equitable one where governance, authority and decision-making is dispersed and brought closer to the people (Joenniemi, 2000a, pp.129-31; Medvedev, 2000, p.100).

When viewed this way the Northern Dimension implies giving both those on the periphery, and those across the border, a constitutive voice in the construction of Europe and Europeanness – or at least giving them a chance to contribute to the European debate. Therefore, although EU documents give the impression that all the Northern Dimension entails is the export of European values across the border, the fact that local and regional (state and non-state) actors in Northern Europe see the Northern Dimension as a vehicle for enhancing their own interests, has meant a *de facto* process in which the de-centralisation of EU governance has become valued as a goal for many. In this process EU borders are not simply blurring, but our traditional understandings of EU and European subjectivity and governance are challenged. In this process, from being *the* hierarchical central actor of Europe, the EU is re-conceptualised in Northern Europe as one actor amongst others, each connected through various networks and regional forums.

Westphalia Bites Back

This neomedieval/postmodern reading of the impact of the Northern Dimension on EU governance, subjectivity and territoriality is, however, not the only interpretation available. Indeed, despite the rhetoric of breaking borders arguably the postmodern promise has been somewhat marginalised by the dominance of another discourse surrounding the Northern Dimension that threatens to leave Northern Europe and the EU trapped in traditional Westphalian understandings of subjectivity, borders and political space.

This discourse envisages the development of the EU into an increasingly unified global actor with its own government and ministers that participates at the negotiating tables of the world's major forums. Attempts to provide the EU with a unified subjectivity, whether through the CFSP, ESDI, Economic and Monetary Union, or the extension of qualified majority voting contribute to a traditional modern discourse that sees the world and political space as clearly divided between exclusive political units. Indeed, Wæver (1996, pp.121-3) argues that the continued unification of Europe has become securitised such that any move towards de-centralisation or fragmentation is easily presented as an existential threat to the EU and to European security that threatens a return to the fractious politics of the 1930s – precisely what the EU was designed to overcome.

This drive for centrality is also supported by the dominant theoretical models of European integration: federalism, functionalism, neo-functionalism. These classical integration theories, rather than simply trying to explain European integration, have also sought to enhance the process. Underlying them is a 'unitarist thesis' constituting the philosophical heart of the EU and that holds that European integration is (or at least should be) driving towards ever greater cultural, economic and political unity (Parker, 2000, p.18).

Given these elements it is unsurprising that the neomedievalist visions of the Northern Dimension can appear problematic for the EU. For federalist idealists 'Europe' remains something still to be fully achieved, an ordered modernist utopia characterised by political, cultural, economic and social unity. Consequently, proposals such as the Northern Dimension that call for de-centralisation and regionality across the EU's borders may in fact be understood as threatening when seen through the lens of a modern Westphalian discourse.

In Wæver's (1996, p.128) terms, the securitised discourse of integration has taken on an existential quality 'because integration/fragmentation is not a question of *how* Europe will be, but *whether* Europe will be' (emphasis added). Another aspect, however, is that from the perspective of the centre the EU's external borders should not be blurred or the authority of the core challenged. Rather than welcoming input from the peripheries, the 'noise' coming from the North has therefore been understood as disrupting the construction of a common European space. As Joenniemi (2003, p.223) argues, from the perspective of the core power and influence should flow in one direction, from the core outwards.

It is notable, therefore, that the EU has been cautious concerning the neomedieval elements of the Northern Dimension and initially adopted a guarded approach towards it. Indeed, the EU has appeared keen to purge the de-centralising notions from the initiative, whilst in other respects it has turned the Northern Dimension into an initiative that actually supports the development of the Union's actor status. Consequently, the focus of the Northern Dimension has shifted somewhat from what the EU can do for Northern Europe, to what the Northern Dimension can do for the EU.

For example, the EU's lack of enthusiasm for the Northern Dimension's visionary elements is apparent in that the original Finnish initiative of 1997 was much more ambitious than the subsequent EU Action Plan of 2000. Whilst the Finnish initiative advocated the creation of a distinct EU policy towards the North, the Action Plan consigned it to a role of co-ordinating existing programmes (Heininen, 2001, pp.37-8). As the Commission put it, the Northern Dimension should not be understood as a new regional initiative, but as an additional element to existing instruments and frameworks of EU-Russian relations, like the

Partnership and Cooperation Agreement (PCA) and the pre-accession Europe Agreements made with the Baltic States and Poland. In the Commission's first communication on the Northern Dimension in 1998 its links with existing frameworks and instruments were stressed many times and enhanced an impression that the Commission was unsettled and confused by it and wanted to downplay its significance (Commission of the European Communities, 1998). In Moisio's (2003, pp.91-2) opinion, this indicated the Commission's desire to control new developments and to prevent the formation of a new spatial framework in Northern Europe, and in particular to prevent the emergence of a new regionality that would hinder the development of the EU into a modern state-type actor.

However, the Finnish proposal was not rejected and the initiative has made steady, if unexceptional, progress onto the EU agenda. One explanation is that the one thing that seems to have resonated with the EU is precisely the initiative's promotion of greater coherence within the Union. Arguably, the most championed aspect of the Northern Dimension in EU discourse (the 'added value' in EU jargon) is that it promotes enhanced *synergies* and *efficiencies* by promoting co-ordination between the EU's various directorates and policy instruments – and as such may improve the Union's actorness.[4] Indeed, the Finnish government actively played on the EU desire for greater coherence in external affairs when initially trying to sell the initiative (Ojanen, 2001, p.219). Finnish Prime Minister, Paavo Lipponen (1997), stressed it would help make 'the Union a more effective global actor'. Particularly indicative of how the EU has generally viewed the Northern Dimension was its statement at the Cologne European Council in 1999, that the Northern Dimension is 'a suitable basis for raising the European Union's profile in the region' (Presidency Conclusions, 1999). Thus, the Northern Dimension was valued for enhancing the EU's actorness, profile and power in Northern Europe, with the question of what the North might gain from this becoming secondary. Put another way, the development of a coherent and powerful EU actor appears to have become an end in itself to which regional questions have been partially subordinated.

Also indicative is the EU's attitude to other actors in Northern Europe. As Catellani notes, despite initial protestations that regional actors like the Council of Baltic Sea States (CBSS) and the Barents Euro-Arctic Council (BEAC) would be treated as equal partners in identifying and implementing Northern Dimension priorities, the reality has been different. The role assigned to regional actors has been limited, with the first Action Plan simply stating that they *may* be consulted (Council of the European Union, 2000, p.7). Instead, the EU Council and the Commission 'have claimed for themselves the role of sole decision-maker when it comes to implementing the Action Plan' (Catellani, 2001, pp.58, 65-6). Consequently, for some the first Action Plan created an impression that the

---

[4]   'Synergy' has become a buzzword of Northern Dimension discourse. For example, an article on the Northern Dimension by External Affairs Commissioner, Chris Patten, and the Swedish Foreign Minister, Anna Lindh, in the *Financial Times* used it 4 times (Patten and Lindh, 2000).

Northern Dimension was an initiative to be imposed top-down on Northern Europe, with the inclusion of regional voices dependent on the magnanimity of the EU Council and the Commission. Similarly, although the regional organisations were asked for their views regarding the drafting of the Second Action Plan, the impression that the Commission has not prioritised its relations with these organisations and rather finds the multiplicity of actors in the North a problem, not a resource, is easily gained.

Importantly, the division of labour between the EU and the regional organisations is not simply a question of decision-making and implementation (Ojanen, 2000, p.374), but also concerns the construction of Europe and the EU. In this respect, giving the regional organisations an equal role would significantly pluralise EU governance in Northern Europe. However, with the Commission generally valuing the Northern Dimension as something that could enhance the EU's coherence and actorness, there is a desire to avoid this. As Ojanen (2001, p.233) notes, a rather traditional power politics frame is evident where any promotion of pluralisation may be understood as strengthening the EU's neighbours and regional organisations at the expense of the EU's authority. When interpreted in modern Westphalian terms, therefore, giving other organisations a constitutive voice is seen as detrimental to the construction of EU subjectivity.

This hierarchical approach to regional questions was also emphasised by the Northern Dimension's initial subordination to two other EU policy instruments for dealing with EU-Russian relations – the Partnership and Cooperation Agreement (PCA) and the Common Strategy on Russia (CSR) – both of which have served as attempts to create a unified EU strategy towards Russia and to enhance the coherence of the CFSP.[5] The effect has been two-fold.

First, the CSR and PCA have undermined the emergence of a new neomedieval regionality as both policies treat Russia as a homogeneous whole (Joenniemi, 2000b, pp.164-5). In other words, they envisage dealing with Russia *bilaterally* through Brussels-Moscow negotiations, and imply the EU to be a unified actor with centralised decision-making akin to a modern nation-state. With EU-Russian relations in the PCA and CSR conducted through high-level consultations, summits and regular committees an institutional framework has been established of mutual recognition that re-enforces each other's geopolitical subjectivity in modern terms (Aalto, 2002). Notably with the formulation of the CSR in 1999, EU-Russian relations were re-conceptualised as a 'strategic partnership' (Common Strategy of the European Union on Russia, 1999), a metaphor that implies the existence of two distinct actors, but also presupposes that relations between these actors will be premised on shared (rational, strategic) interests, as opposed to shared identities.

Second, is that in this 'strategic partnership' Russia remains treated as an outsider, a point further inscribed by the sharp boundaries of selfhood of the Schengen border regime (Leshukov, 2001, p.135). Russia's exclusion from the EU 'us' has been highlighted by Javier Solana, the EU's Mr CFSP, who has argued that

---

5   On the CSR see Haukkala and Medvedev (2001).

the EU's Common Strategies should not be published in order to prevent others (outsiders) from influencing them (Ojanen, 2001, p.226). This significantly contradicts the Northern Dimension's visionary rhetoric that sees it as breaking down (East-West) borders, as de-centralising governance, and as giving an equal voice to non-EU members in the formulation of Northern Dimension priorities. Subsumed within the PCA and CSR, the localised and regionalising aspects of the Northern Dimension are marginalised as the EU has sought to assert itself as an international actor on the world stage.

Moreover, these Westphalian 'modernist' discursive proclivities have had real effects. This has been illustrated by Tarja Cronberg (2001), formerly the Executive Director of the Regional Council of North Karelia in Finland, whose job involved developing cooperation across the Finnish-Russian border as a part of the EU's EuregioKarelia. Despite such cooperation being championed at a rhetorical level in the Northern Dimension Action Plans, her experience was that in practice this rhetoric was largely empty and never intended to develop into anything substantial. Instead of overcoming it, she suggests Russia's otherness was actually re-enforced in the Euregio process.

The Northern Dimension and the EU Empire

Given the prevalence of modern discourse promoting the development of the EU into an international actor and the Northern Dimension's gradual co-option into this, it can appear that the initiative has become part of a process reconstructing Europe in Westphalian form. On this reading, the regionality of a Europe of Olympic Rings of neomedieval/postmodern visions has been superseded by a modern Westphalian metaphor that indicates the continued division of European political space into clearly delineated sovereign territorial units, and in which the EU is a kind of super-state in the making.

An alternative view, however, is that current developments are better described by the metaphor of an emerging EU Empire. Central to the notion of Empire are two important points. First, contra neomedieval/postmodern visions, the Empire notion maintains the preservation of borders between self and others to be crucial in constructing and protecting subjectivity. Second, however, and contra the modern Westphalian metaphor, the Empire notion also illustrates how borders are not as clearly defined as before and that the centre's control of the periphery has been undermined, resulting in a certain de-centralisation of power and governance.

Central is to understand that two interests stand out for the EU in regard to Russia. First, with Finland's membership in 1995 the EU acquired an external border that is viewed as entailing several potential serious security threats for the Union. The Baltic States' and Poland's accession has exacerbated this perception. These threats are listed as including environmental pollution, nuclear safety, the spread of disease, immigration, and organised crime. These threats occupy a considerable portion of EU comment on the Northern Dimension, particularly in respect of Russia's Kaliningrad exclave (e.g., Commission of the European Communities, 2001). In this respect, the Northern Dimension is explicitly understood as an alternative security policy designed to combat these threats in cooperation with Russia. However, whilst cooperation implies opening the border somewhat, understood as threatening the Northern Dimension very much remains a border strategy.

What emerges is a traditional discourse in which Russia is again understood as a constituting other of Europe. For example, in the Northern Dimension Russia is presented as a potential site of contamination, disorder and chaos, in contrast to EU rationality, order and cosmos. This is well illustrated in Swedish Prime Minister, Goran Persson's, comment on Kaliningrad as a site of pollution, diseases like HIV and tuberculosis, and nuclear waste. In short, 'Almost every problem you can find you have there' (quoted in Grajewski, 2001). As such, the EU self is reified with threats seen to reside on the fringes and threatening to undermine internal unity. Whilst internally processes of integration and debordering are valued as producing a Deutschian-esque security community, external borders need to be preserved to pre-empt contamination from external threats. However, the fear of the instability presumed to be resident in Russia's north-west has also become a motivation for EU engagement in these regions, to counteract these 'security' problems, and in the process to control and order Russian political, social and environmental space. Therefore, although the boundary between 'us' and 'them' is to be preserved, the boundary is transformed and extended into something of a zone as the EU attempts to extend its influence beyond its official borders.

This approach is supported by the EU's second principal interest in Russia's north-west, the need to secure access to the region's abundant natural resources. When reading EU documents, speeches and articles on the Northern Dimension the impression is easily gained that the EU's only real concern is in opening up resource-rich Northern Russia for exploitation by European capital. For example, at a conference in May 2000, Jan-Peter Paul, the head of DG-10 at the European Commission, completely ignored the Northern Dimension as a policy designed to promote regionality and to democratise EU governance and instead declared that:

> The Northern Dimension should be seen in the context of the strategic importance of Russia for the energy sector of the European Union. The resources of north-western Russia including gas, oil, coal, forest and minerals are vast and can hopefully be harnessed for European use as well (Paul, 2000, p.58).[6]

Instructively, EU reports on the Northern Dimension have devoted significant attention to emphasising the importance of the implementation of a liberal democratic market economy in Russia and the extension and improvement of

---

[6] Likewise, one can note the 1998 report of the Commission which stressed that 'The strategic importance of the North's natural resources is foremost to both the region and the Community' (Commission of the European Communities, 1998).

transport networks. It is legitimate to ask whether this is for the locals' benefit, or more part of the EU's economic agenda. Key, however, is that although the EU wishes to retain its external border, once again it has an interest in the development of Russian economic space. Notably, the EU presents continued access as a security prerogative (especially regarding energy resources (Council of the European Union, 2003, p.5)), which ultimately requires the preservation of stable and cooperative relations with Russia. However, understood as a security issue the EU has constructed a discourse that also rationalises active participation in north-western Russia to foster the development of Western structures there, in order to combat the assumed endemic instability. Combined, what these two points illustrate is that the EU is using the Northern Dimension, not necessarily to overcome the border between 'us' and 'them', but to provide an opportunity for the EU to engage in ordering Russian space.

More broadly, however, these issues have consequences for the construction of European political space and European identity that are quite distinct from those of a Westphalian or Neomedieval/Olympic Rings understanding. To utilise the rhetoric of Christiansen et al., (2000, p.393), from this perspective what emerges is an EU Empire where power and subjectivity are focused on the centre, but the borders of which are becoming increasingly fuzzy as the EU seeks to assert its presence in its near abroad.

In one respect, the Empire metaphor highlights how the EU has become focused on the concerns of its centre. This is evident in the Northern Dimension where its re-orientation to questions of EU 'security' and 'actorness' indicate how the initiative's original concerns with establishing a new regional/European politics focused on the needs of the peripheries, have partially been marginalised. As such, a hierarchy is identifiable in which the concerns and needs of the periphery are subsumed to the ambitions of Brussels.

At the same time, through the Northern Dimension the EU is exerting its power of governance beyond its external border to Russia's north-west in order to provide for security and access to vital Russian resources. Through holding out rewards for the instigation of Western norms based on the asymmetric dependence of Russia's north-west on the EU, Russia's north-west periphery has been partially drawn into the realm of EU governance, whilst the EU itself is left free of responsibility for developments there.[7] In another respect, however, the Empire metaphor indicates that EU governance in Northern Europe is not total and that space exists in the periphery for independent subjectivity, even if this is constricted by the centre's concerns and its desire to maintain a border, however porous, between 'us' and 'them'.

---

[7]   This draws on Wæver (1997a, pp.69-71, 81).

Conclusion

Having laid out three interpretations regarding the regional initiative of the Northern Dimension, in conclusion we are left with the question of which metaphor (Westphalia, Empire, Neomedieval) best describes the particular trajectory of European geopolitical development. First, it is necessary to stress that this is a political issue and consequently the metaphors identified here are not mutually exclusive – each metaphor surely grasps some of the picture. However, certain predictions regarding the future configuration of European geopolitics are possible.

First, the emergence of a Westphalian super-state is unlikely. Even if the Northern Dimension has to some degree become co-opted and imbued with modernist EU discourse, what the Northern Dimension experience does illustrate is the extent to which regional actors have emerged claiming their own subjectivity. As noted, the 'North' has become a location from which to speak and by which different actors can take a stance *vis-à-vis* the rest of Europe. Importantly, although Finland coined the initiative others have also tried to utilise the signifier to their own benefit, as for example when Denmark emphasised more Arctic notions of Northernness during its EU presidency. At times, therefore, a marginal location has been embraced as entailing certain resources of power and influence. Arguably, the recent round of EU enlargement may enhance such processes, since in a larger Union building regional coalitions and playing on one's own distinctiveness may turn out to be a better strategy than simply aspiring for the core.

De facto, therefore, the future shape of Europe and the EU remains open for negotiation and is a process in which voices at the periphery are playing a crucial role. With the EU's enlargement into the peripheral North the peripheries have become hard for the EU to ignore and the EU no longer has full control over the agenda of European integration. Since the end of the Cold War localities, regional organisations and states in Northern Europe have got used to interacting with each other across borders, including the EU's external border with Russia: whether they will tolerate being continually thwarted by the modernist concerns of Brussels (and Moscow) is therefore debatable. Instructive, however, is that there are signs of frustration in Northern Europe at the EU's perceived increasing reluctance to engage in the multilevel implementation of the Northern Dimension and to foster greater levels of cross-border cooperation and de-centralisation (Haukkala, 2001a, p.111). This can be seen, for example, in Cronberg's critique of the EU's approach to Northern Dimension decision-making, which has left local sub-national actors somewhat disaffected with the EU. Similarly, it is also questionable whether the Northern European states are prepared to let the EU dominate the Northern Dimension agenda. Notably, and unlike the Commission, Finland, Sweden and Norway have been rather supportive of giving regional actors an active role in identifying and implementing Northern Dimension priorities (Catellani, 2001, p.66). Such attitudes are crucially important because the EU's capacity to act is largely dependent on the member states' willingness to let it do so.

What this highlights is that despite Westphalian aspirations the Northern Dimension is unlikely to support the EU's development in traditional state form. Consequently, it appears the future configuration of Europe will lie somewhere in the debate between Imperial and Neomedieval notions of Europe. Importantly, these models are not necessarily antithetical to each other. This is because, to the extent that an Empire model of the EU emerges, a certain freedom of action for the Union's peripheries is also envisaged. However, an undeniable tension between the models is apparent. Like the Westphalia metaphor, the Empire metaphor understands sovereignty over territory and governance to be centred at a single decision-making pole. In contrast, the regionality of the Neomedieval model calls for the de-centralisation of decision-making to multiple regional and local bodies and networks. This is not so much a dispersal of sovereignty as the conduct of politics outside of sovereign governance (Wæver, 1997b, pp.301-3, 312). In short, although the Empire model opens space for regionality, as regionality is strengthened and regional actors claim and build distinct subjectivities, the ability of the Imperial centre to project its power and preferences into the periphery is likely to decrease. It is precisely this tension that is evident in centre-periphery relations in Northern Europe.

References

Aalto, Pami (2002), 'A European Geopolitical Subject in the Making? EU, Russia and the Kaliningrad Question', *Geopolitics*, Vol. 7(3), pp. 142-174.

Antola, Esko (1999), 'The Presence of the European Union in the North', in Hiski Haukkala (ed.), *Dynamic Aspects of the Northern Dimension*, Turku, Jean Monnet Unit, University of Turku, pp. 115-32.

Archer, Clive (2001), 'The Northern Dimension as a soft-Soft Option for the Baltic States' Security', in Hanna Ojanen (ed.), *The Northern Dimension: Fuel for the EU?* Helsinki, Ulkopoliittinen instituutti and Institut für Europäische Politik, pp. 188-208.

Catellani, Nicola (2001), 'The Multilevel Implementation of the Northern Dimension', in Hanna Ojanen (ed.), *The Northern Dimension: Fuel for the EU?* Helsinki, Ulkopoliittinen instituutti and Institut für Europäische Politik, pp. 54-77.

Christiansen, Thomas; Petito, Fabio and Tonra, Ben (2000), 'Fuzzy Politics Around Fuzzy Borders: The European Union's Near Abroad', *Cooperation and Conflict*, Vol. 35(4), pp. 417-31.

Commission of the European Communities (1998), *A Northern Dimension for the Policies of the Union*, Brussels, 25.11.1998 COM 589 Final.

Commission of the European Communities (2001), Communication from the Commission to the Council, *The EU and Kaliningrad*, Brussels, 17.01.2001, COM 26 Final.

Common Strategy of the European Union on Russia, 4 June 1999, (1999/414/CFSP).

Cooper, Robert (2003), *The Breaking of Nations: Order and Chaos in the Twenty-First Century*, London, Atlantic Books.

Council of the European Union (2000), *Action Plan for the Northern Dimension with external and cross-border policies of the European Union 2000-2003*, Brussels, 14 June 2000, 9401/00.

Council of the European Union (2003), *The Second Northern Dimension Action Plan, 2004-2006*, Brussels, 16-17 October 2003. Available at http://europa.eu.int/comm/external_relations/north_dim/ndap/ap2.pdf.

Cronberg, Tarja (2001), 'Europe Making in Action: Euregio Karelia and the Construction of EU-Russian Partnership', presented at the Think Tank Seminar on the Northern Dimension and the Future of Barents Euro-Arctic Cooperation, Kiruna Sweden, 14-17 June 2001.

Ginsberg, Roy H. (1999), 'Conceptualizing the European Union as an International Actor: Narrowing the Theoretical Capability-Expectations Gap', *Journal of Common Market Studies*, Vol. 37(3), pp. 429-54.

Grabbe, Heather (2000), 'The sharp edges of Europe: extending Schengen eastwards', *International Affairs*, Vol. 76(3), pp. 519-36.

Grajewski, Marcin (2001), 'Russian Enclave a Crossroads before EU Expansion', *Reuters*, 15 January 2001. Available at http://virtual.finland.fi/reuters/.

Haukkala, Hiski (2001a), 'Comment: National Interests *versus* Solidarity Towards Common Policies', in Hanna Ojanen (ed.), *The Northern Dimension: Fuel for the EU?* Helsinki, Ulkopoliittinen instituutti and Institut für Europäische Politik.

Haukkala, Hiski (2001b), *Two Reluctant Regionalizers? The European Union and Russia in Europe's North*, (UPI Working Papers 32), Helsinki, The Finnish Institute of International Affairs.

Haukkala, Hiski and Medvedev, Sergei (eds.), (2001), *The EU Common Strategy on Russia: Learning the Grammar of the CFSP*, Helsinki, Ulkopoliittinen instituutti and Institut für Europäische Politik.

Heininen, Lassi (2001), 'Ideas and Outcomes: Finding a Concrete Form for the Northern Dimension Initiative', in Hanna Ojanen (ed.), *The Northern Dimension: Fuel for the EU?* Helsinki, Ulkopoliittinen instituutti and Institut für Europäische Politik, pp. 20-53.

Hennessy, Patrick (2004), 'Prodi wants Europe-wide vote on EU constitution', *The Sunday Telegraph*, 30 May 2004.

Joenniemi, Pertti (1994), 'Region-Building as Europe-Building', in Olav Schram Stokke and Ola Tunander (eds.), *The Barents Region: Cooperation in Arctic Europe*, London, Sage Publications, pp. 213-26.

Joenniemi, Pertti (2000a), 'Changing Politics along Finland's Borders: From Norden to the Northern Dimension', in Pirkkoliisa Ahponen and Pirjo Jukarainen (eds.), *Tearing Down the Curtain, Opening the Gates: Northern Boundaries in Change*, Jyväskylä, SoPhi, pp. 114-32.

Joenniemi, Pertti (2000b), 'Kaliningrad, Borders and the Figure of Europe', in James Baxendale, Stephen Dewar and David Gowan (eds.), *The EU and Kaliningrad: Kaliningrad and the Impact of EU Enlargement*, London, Federal Trust, pp. 157-71.

Joenniemi, Pertti (2003), 'Can Europe Be Told from the North? Tapping into the EU's Northern Dimension', in Frank Möller and Samu Pehkonen (eds.), *Encountering the*

North: Cultural Geography, International Relations and Northern Landscapes, Aldershot, Ashgate, pp. 221-60.

Leshukov, Igor (2001), 'Can the Northern Dimension Break the Vicious Circle of Russia-EU Relations?', in Hanna Ojanen (ed.), *The Northern Dimension: Fuel for the EU?* Helsinki, Ulkopoliittinen instituutti and Institut für Europäische Politik, pp. 118-41.

Lipponen, Paavo (1997), 'The European Union Needs a Policy for the Northern Dimension', speech presented at the 'Barents Region Today' conference, Rovaniemi, Finland. 15.09.1997.

Medvedev, Sergei (1998), 'Tertium datur est: North as the Third', *OSCE Review. Special Issue on the Northern Dimension*, Vol. 6(2), p. 8.

Medvedev, Sergei (2000), *Russia's Futures: Implications for the EU, the North and the Baltic Region*, Helsinki, Ulkopoliittinen instituutti and Institut für Europäische Politik.

Medvedev, Sergei (2001), 'North and the Politics of Emptiness', Paper presented at the workshop, 'Identity Politics, Security and the Making of the Geopolitical Order in the Baltic Region', in Kuusamo, Finland, 14-17 June 2001.

Moisio, Sami (2003), 'Back to Baltoscandia? European Union and geo-conceptual remaking of the European north', *Geopolitics*, Vol. 8(1), pp. 72-100.

Norrback, Ole (1998), 'Small States and European Security', *Irish Studies in International Affairs*, Vol. 9, pp. 5-9.

Ojanen, Hanna (2000), 'The EU and Its 'Northern Dimension': An Actor in Search of a Policy, or a Policy in Search of an Actor?', *European Foreign Affairs Review*, Vol. 5, pp. 359-76.

Ojanen, Hanna (2001), 'Conclusions: Northern Dimension – Fuel for the EU's External Relations?', in Hanna Ojanen (ed) *The Northern Dimension: Fuel for the EU?* Helsinki, Ulkopoliittinen instituutti and Institut für Europäische Politik, pp. 217-37.

Paasi, Anssi (1998), 'Boundaries as Social Processes: Territoriality in a World of Flows', *Geopolitics*, Vol. 3(2), pp. 69-88.

Parker, Noel (2000), 'Integrated Europe and its 'Margins': Action and Reaction', in Noel Parker and Bill Armstrong (eds.), *Margins in European Integration*, Houndmills, Macmillan, pp. 3-27.

Patten, Chris and Lindh, Anna (2000), 'The Northern Dimension of EU Foreign Policy: From Words to Action', *Financial Times* 20 December 2000.

Paul, Jan-Peter (2000), Text of speech delivered in Copenhagen on 17-18 May 2000 in *Conference on The Northern Dimension and Kaliningrad: European and Regional Integration*, Copenhagen, Royal Danish Ministry of Foreign Affairs, pp. 58-64.

Presidency Conclusions (1999), Cologne European Council, 03-04 June 1999, Cologne (04-06-1999) - Document 150/99 (Presse 0).

Tunander, Ola (1994), 'Inventing the Barents Region: Overcoming the East-West Divide in the North', in Olav Schram Stokke and Ola Tunander (eds.), *The Barents Region: Cooperation in Arctic Europe*, London, Sage Publications, pp. 31-44.

Tuomioja, Erkki (2004), 'New Opportunities to be Opened for the Baltic Countries', Address to the Baltic Ports Organization General Assembly, Helsinki 3 June 2004.

Valtasaari, Jukka (1999), Secretary of State, Address at the Parliamentary Evening of the State Representation of Mecklenburg-West Pomerania in the German Reichstag, Berlin, 14 September 1999.

Wæver, Ole (1996), 'European Security Identities', *Journal of Common Market Studies*, Vol. 34(1), pp. 103-32.

Waever, Ole (1997a), 'Imperial Metaphors: Emerging European Analogies to Pre-Nation-State Imperial Systems', in Ola Tunander, Pavel Baev and Victoria Ingrid Einagel (eds.), *Geopolitics in Post-Wall Europe: Security, Territory and Identity*, London, Sage Publications, pp. 59-93.

Wæver, Ole (1997b), 'The Baltic Sea: A Region after Post-Modernity', in Pertti Joenniemi (ed.), *Neo-Nationalism or Regionality: The Restructuring of Political Space Around the Baltic Rim*, Stockholm, NordREFO, pp. 293-342.

Zielonka, Jan (2001), 'How New Enlarged Borders will Reshape the European Union', *Journal of Common Market Studies*, Vol. 39(3), pp. 507-36.

PART III

RUSSIAN PERSPECTIVES

Chapter 7

Russia and the Challenges of Regional Cooperation in Northern Europe

Alexander Sergounin

Introduction[1]

Russian perceptions of Northern Europe in the post-Cold War era have been rather contradictory and embracing a more post-sovereign agenda of regional cooperation has been a particularly difficult task. On the one hand, regional developments – NATO and EU enlargements, tensions with the Baltic States, degradation of the socio-economic and environmental systems in North-Western Russia and so on – have posed new challenges for Russia. On the other hand, the region (where Russia has its only border with the EU) has offered numerous opportunities for international cooperation. Russia's North-Western regions such as Kaliningrad, Karelia, Novgorod and St. Petersburg belong to the most advanced sub-national units in terms of market reforms and integration into the European economy. The EU has indicated its interest in cooperation with the Russian North-West in areas such as energy, transportation, health care and the environment. To provide such cooperation with a proper institutional framework, the EU launched the Northern Dimension (ND) initiative. In fact, the Northern Dimension has turned into a rather significant venue for collaboration between the EU and Russia in Europe's North. Other subregional organisations, such as the Council of the Baltic Sea States (CBSS), the Barents Euro-Arctic Council (BEAC), the Nordic Council, and the Nordic Council of Ministers have also participated actively in collaborative projects with Russia. Even the United States has been engaged, launching the so-called Northern European Initiative (NEI) – now transformed into the enhanced Partnership in Northern Europe (e-PINE) – to cope with the region's problems.[2]

---

[1] This study has been prepared with the support of fellowship research grants from the Local Government Initiative and International Policy Fellowship programmes. Both are part of the Open Society Institute (Budapest) and INFO-Centre (Moscow).

[2] NEI was initiated the same year as the ND (1997). The United States' official goal was to demonstrate that integration and cooperation in Northern Europe will benefit Russia and its Baltic neighbours. The NEI had six articulated specific priorities: trade and business promotion, law enforcement, civil society building, energy,

This chapter seeks to broaden understanding of Russian policies in Northern Europe by considering the following research questions: First, how have Russian policies changed with regard to the region? Second, what major problems/challenges does Russia face in the region? And, finally, what are the possible (and best) solutions to these problems?

Changing Perceptions

Russia's political and academic communities were basically taken by surprise by regional initiatives such as the Northern Dimension project and the NEI. For example, it took almost two years to formulate Moscow's official strategy towards the ND (Strategiya razvitiya otnosheniy Rossiyskoi Federatsii s Evropeiskim Soyuzom na srednesrochnuyu perspectivu (2000-2010), 1999, pp.22, 26) and to produce more or less thorough academic analyses of the issue (Leshukov, 1999, pp.30-1). At the same time, it is also notable that America's NEI has never received an official response from the Russian side. However, five main challenges to traditional Russian thinking were posed by these initiatives of regional cooperation.

First, the ND entails a shift from 'hard' to 'soft' security domains. This was unusual for Russian strategy planners because the 'High North' and North-West Russia have always been perceived as a zone of confrontation with the West (from the Teutonic Order in the Middle Ages to NATO during the Cold War period). In particular, there has been a high concentration of Russia's armed forces – both nuclear and conventional – in the region and the Russian military has always had a major say in defining the future of the region. With the advent of the ND, however, the 'hard' security issues lost part of their former importance and in essence a new agenda has emerged. The regional agenda has been desecuritised as 'normal' non-security issues have increasingly started to influence the regional agenda of cooperation. 'Grand' policy has retreated to the shadows and so-called 'low politics' (economy, trade, societal issues, ecology, border infrastructure, migration, etc.) have dominated the scene. This 'soft' security agenda has questioned the role and capabilities of more traditional actors (NATO, OSCE, etc.,) in dealing with the new set of challenges. Instead, it seems that newly created institutions (CBSS, BEAC, Arctic Council) are better attuned to cope with the new problems. However, it took some time for Russian policies to become accommodated to this new reality.

Second, the Northern Dimension project challenges the core principles underlying Europe's Cold War security architecture, that of European security

---

environment, and public health. In reality, the NEI was focused on the Baltic States rather than on Russia. It turned out that the NEI's record in the case of Russia was quite modest and incomparable with the more impressive ND experience. On the NEI, see Browning (2001), (2003) and Sergounin (2001).

being seen as indivisible. Now, security may also be comprehended in more region-specific terms with a region (such as Northern Europe) turning increasingly secure, and this without the creation of a security regime that spans the whole continent. This, then, shakes the role of the traditional security organisations (OSCE and NATO) as the major security providers in Europe. If seen against this background, the ND and NEI hence tend to undermine a core pillar of the traditional security policy pursued by Russia in Europe, one that aimed at elevating the OSCE into the principal pan-European security institution.

Third, the regional initiatives (especially the ND) for the first time in Russia's relations with the West, have provided Moscow with a degree of choice and initiative. Usually, Russia has had to play by rules defined by the West from the very start. In contrast, the Northern Dimension has been premised on a rather loose frame for cooperation, implying that each partner acts on an equal footing and decides himself how to contribute to the cooperative process. The ND has invited, in some of its aspects, Russia itself to define what should become a priority for cooperation – energy, environment, societal issues, fighting organised crime, and so on. Clearly, Moscow has not been accustomed to such a situation and consequently it remained for a while unable to pursue the options opened. Russian traditionalists preferred to see the failure of the ND as an opportunity to blame Brussels for the lack of cooperation and good will, rather than as a chance to take the initiative in designing a new political course.

Fourth, the Northern Dimension also revealed that Moscow underestimated the role of regionalism/transregionalism, both domestically and internationally. Internally, Moscow viewed regionalism as a continuation or an extension of the highly centralised federal policies at the local level. Internationally, Russia saw regional cooperation as either a low priority (compared to 'grand policy') or as an additional room for diplomatic manoeuvring (if 'grand strategy' failed). Moscow was hence quite suspicious about the regional nature of the Northern Dimension and the NEI. The Federal government worried about a possible strengthening of separatist tendencies in Russia's North-Western regions (especially in Kaliningrad and Karelia) as a result of their deep involvement in regional cooperation. Only with time has Moscow realised that regionalism brings more positive than negative results and has started to think of the Russian North-West as an exception or 'pilot' region.[3]

Finally, regional cooperation in the North has challenged Russia's traditional conception of national sovereignty. Moscow's original position was that all of Russia's regions constitute an integral part of the Russian Federation, and thereby have an equal status. It was strongly felt, therefore, that international cooperation should not raise questions about the belonging of any region to Russia and it should not cause disparities between different regions by involving particular territories in more profound cooperation while excluding others. Initially, Moscow feared that regional projects would strengthen such disparities and evoke an

---

[3]   On the change of Russian thinking on regionalism, see Sergounin (1999).

unhealthy competition between Russia's regions. In consequence, Russia insisted that it was able to solve the regions' problems (even in the case of Kaliningrad) by itself.

However, with time Moscow has understood that nobody is trying to challenge Russia's territorial integrity and that by engaging Russia's North-Western regions in cross-border and transregional cooperation the regional actors simply aim to create a zone of stability and economic prosperity, rather than to foster the disintegration of the country. In particular, the need to link up, in one way or another, with European integration and various economic incentives has been crucial. Russia needs to be engaged and not excluded from the new Europe. Moves of debordering and fragmented sovereignty are not designed to further marginalise Russia in European affairs, whilst regionalisation might actually help Russia to consolidate its space and place in Europe. Moscow's preferences have thus gradually shifted from semi-isolationist, unilateral options to a more cooperative model that favours multilateral solutions (as best demonstrated by the cases of Kaliningrad and Karelia).

It should nonetheless be noted that many elements of traditional thinking still remain and current Russian perceptions of regional cooperation in Northern Europe represent a mixture of different schools and approaches. Much of this modern discourse is premised in geopolitical and realist understandings that sanctify the boundaries of the state and privilege the core in relation to the margins. According to this view, Russian national identity has been intimately bound up with the Russian state, which as such leaves little space for regions or an emphasis on regionality. There is, therefore, sensitivity about the status of the state's borders, which from this perspective remain seen as sites of exclusion rather than of integration and cross-border cooperation.

Regional Cooperation: An Institutional Framework

To better understand what is going on in the North and to understand some of the rather fundamental challenges Russia faces there, it is useful to elaborate somewhat on the various and multiple cooperative policy initiatives and institutional mechanisms that have been instigated since the end of the Cold War. All of this has added considerable complexity and has provided Russia with multiple avenues for engagement at the regional level, and all of which has challenged traditional modernist discourses regarding Russian identity and its understanding of its borders. First, it can be noted that in order to provide regional cooperation with proper institutional support numerous mechanisms and procedures have been established in Northern Europe. The EU has certainly been the most important actor in this regard and in the 1990s the EU launched a number of programmes (INTERREG, TACIS and PHARE) that aimed at promoting trans- and cross-border cooperation, and which were to varying degrees also inclusive of Russia.

One of the EU programmes aimed at regional cooperation is INTERREG. Through INTERREG Finland and Sweden have been able to involve Norwegian and Russian regions in cross-border cooperation if this is in the interest of their own border regions and if the partners are able to provide fifty per cent in matching funds. At present two out of four INTERREG programmes cover the Russian North. INTERREG Barents includes Nordland, Troms and Finnmark in Norway, Lapland in Finland, Nordbotten in Sweden, and the Murmansk *Oblast* in Russia. INTERREG Karelen includes Finnish Karelia and the Karelian Republic in Russia.

TACIS[4] has been another important instrument for intensifying cross-border contacts. The ND has envisaged the following priorities for cross-border cooperation under the TACIS programme:

- Assisting border regions in overcoming their specific development problems (with special emphasis on cooperation and business development between communities);
- Encouraging the linking of networks and assistance on both sides of the border, e.g., in regard to border crossings and training (especially crossings located in the Crete Corridors);
- Reducing tranboundary environmental risks and pollution as a major goal of cross-border activities;
- Promoting more effective administration and law enforcement;
- Promoting institution building and the development of civil society (Commission of the European Communities, 2000, p.25; Council of the European Union, 2001, p.7).

Kaliningrad is of the highest importance for the TACIS programme. According to EU data, TACIS has so far spent €40 million on various projects in the region (Commission of the European Communities, 2002). A new TACIS office was opened in Kaliningrad at the beginning of 2001, whilst the 2004-2006 National Indicative Programme for Russia (March 2003) contains a special programme for Kaliningrad (worth €25 million) with the following priorities:

- To develop the administrative capacity of the region, with particular emphasis on the improvement of overall conditions for business development;
- To improve the quality of primary and preventive health care services;
- To promote the intellectual potential of the region;
- To induce a positive culture of cooperation across its borders (Commission of the European Communities, 2003b, p.37).

Russia has been generally positive about such EU-led regionalising initiatives, although for its part, Russia has argued that the financial resources from the EU's

---

[4] Technical assistance to the CIS countries.

different programmes should be combined in order to better foster cross-border cooperation. As Foreign Minister Ivanov (2000, p.8) stated a few years ago:

> We agree that the resources of the European Union's existing programmes and private corporations and banks have a role to play. However, these are not sufficient to carry out major infrastructure projects, say, in the energy and transport sectors. New solutions will be required, including expansion of the operations of the European Investment Bank to cover Russia. Also, it will be logical to pool a part of the funds of TACIS, PHARE and INTERREG into a single 'financial window'.

In this regard, Moscow has also suggested a number of changes for the EU's existing programmes. First, it has been suggested that the EU's technical assistance programme (PHARE), and not least its investment component, should be extended to the whole territory of the ND, i.e., so that it would also include Russia. Second, it has been argued that the possibility of partial financing of cooperation projects from the EU's structural funds should also be opened up. Third, and finally, it has been argued that Russian enterprises should be able to bid for contracts related to the implementation of ND projects financed by the European Investment Bank, PHARE, INTERREG and EU Structural Funds that take place in the territory of other countries in the ND area.

However, with the introduction of the European Neighbourhood Policy (ENP, May 2004) the future of the ND (like other regional 'dimensions') is unclear. As Vahl notes in his chapter in this volume, the question is one of how much flexibility will be entailed in the ENP to allow specific regional approaches like the ND to continue to operate, or if instead the ENP will develop as a 'one-size-fits-all' policy by which the EU approaches its neighbours, thereby leaving little room for flexibility and heterogeneity for cross-border and regional cooperation. Likewise, after 2006 TACIS, INTERREG and other EU instruments will be replaced by new mechanisms, which are still under consideration. Will the new instruments be more generous to Russia? Will they be more coherent and better co-ordinated than existing ones? Will they retain the regional focus or be more centralised? These questions remain to be answered, but how they are answered will obviously impact on the character of regional cooperation in Northern Europe and the nature of Russia's engagement in it.

However, along with the EU, other regional organisations can and have also contributed to the development of trans- and cross-border cooperation in Northern Europe. For example, the CBSS (established in 1992) has an ambitious programme aimed at regional cooperation in areas such as the economy, trade, finance, transportation, communications, conversion, ecology, border and customs control, fighting organised crime, etc., (Diplomaticheskiy Vestnik, 1996, pp.8-11). A Northern eDimension Action Plan (NeDAP) is also being developed by the CBSS in partnership with the European Commission. NeDAP aims at developing information technology standards in the region in order that they would reach EU and world standards. Similarly, public health issues are dealt with by the CBSS

Task Force on Communicable Disease Control (Council of the Baltic Sea States, 2002).

The BEAC also pays great attention to regional cooperation. The Barents cooperation regime has a two-level decision-making structure. On the national level, the Barents Council, consisting of the foreign ministers (or other ministers, e.g., ministers of environment or transportation) from the four founding states (Finland, Norway, Russia and Sweden) as well as representatives from other interested nations, makes strategic decisions. The leaders of regional governments, however, meet in the Regional Council to discuss more concrete problems, such as economic cooperation, the environment, regional infrastructure, science, technology, education, tourism, health care, culture and matters related to the indigenous peoples of the region. National secretariats in each state coordinate the activities of these two bodies.

The Arctic Council (AC) also provides the regional actors with some opportunities for intensive trans- and cross-border cooperation. The European Commission's participation in the ministerial meetings of the Arctic Council signalled its increased attention to Arctic issues (the so-called 'Arctic Window') within the Northern Dimension. The EU has already supported a number of Arctic initiatives in the areas of information society, ecology and sustainable use of natural resources, support for indigenous peoples, research, economic development of scarcely populated areas and the development of human resources (Council of the European Union, 2001, p.10).

The Euroregion concept is another opportunity for regional cooperation. For example, Kaliningrad belongs to the Baltic Euroregion, which was set up in 1998. It was established as an international lobbying group of local governments from Poland, Sweden, Denmark, Lithuania, Latvia and Russia. The President of the Baltic Euroregion has stated that the most important task for cooperation between communes from the various countries is subregional economic planning and the construction of transport routes (Fairlie, 2000, p.97). Since 1999 a new Euroregion, named Saule, has been under consideration, involving Slavsk, Sovetsk and Neman in the Kaliningrad *Oblast*, along with participants from Lithuania, Latvia and Sweden (Fairlie, 2000, p.97).

Kaliningrad can also participate in the Neman Euroregion, which is designed to link Kaliningrad, Lithuania and Belarus. There was reportedly some Russian reluctance to the Neman project because of a perception that Poland did not want the chairmanship of the Euroregion to rotate. Moreover, Moscow believes that the current charter of the Neman Euroregion does not reflect Russian national interests and as such has so far blocked the signing of the documents needed to bring it into operation (Deryabin, 2000, p.46).

As noted, the point of this brief overview of the variety of regional cooperation initiatives and instruments underway in the North is to indicate the extent to which the North has become a site of considerable activity, innovation and opportunity for Russia to become engaged with some of its neighbours at a regional level. In other words, in the North it seems Russia has been presented with a space where it can become engaged in broader European processes. These institutional mechanisms are not only important venues for regional cooperation, but also provide helpful experiences for the further development of the collaborative schemes in the area. However, whilst the North has begun to stand out as a site of opportunity for Russia it is important to ask the following question, which is: to what extent do the various mechanisms, initiatives and policies meet the real needs of the region, and how should/could they be better coordinated? It is to this issue we now turn.

Regional Cooperation: A Future Agenda

Although it has been argued that Russia has increasingly embraced the growing number of cooperative projects in the North, there have also been a number of limitations restricting Russia's engagement and the success of different projects *per se*. Therefore, when thinking about the future of regional cooperation in the North it is important to note that in the current situation both challenges and opportunities for regional cooperation can be identified. In the following, therefore, the aim is to highlight a number of the more serious challenges and obstacles that exist to enhancing effective regional cooperation, whilst in turn also suggesting a number of possible solutions to those problems.

Problems and obstacles to regional cooperation can be identified on both the EU and Russian side. Starting with the Russian aspect, one of the major sources of concern relates to the economic and political hardships in Russia. For example, some experts have pointed out that some of the key arguments about the economic importance of Russia to Europe, which were initially seen as a factor likely to promote regional projects, have in fact been undermined by Russia's continued economic and political problems. The reason is that Russia's ability to shoulder the responsibility of becoming a major partner of the Union in Northernmost Europe is rather weak, although there have been recent improvements in this regard.

Another obstacle to regional cooperation has been Russia's pursuit of the second Chechen war, which provoked EU concerns about Russia's excessive and indiscriminate use of military power, as well as about the human rights situation in the area. This led, for some time, to a worsening of the Russia-EU relationship. For example, after the EU Helsinki summit in December 1999, as a penalty for its actions in Chechnya, the Russian part of TACIS aid was reduced from $130 to $40 million (Fairlie, 2000, p.88). According to a speech made by External Affairs Commissioner, Chris Patten, in May 2002 at a plenary session of the European Parliament: 'The situation in Chechnya remains hugely worrying and reports of human rights violations during so-called "mopping up" operations have not stopped' (Patten, 2002). Today, however, it may also be observed that in practice the issue has been to some extent pushed to the sidelines.

In addition, however, Moscow is very suspicious of any attempt to put the Northern Dimension, NEI and other regional initiatives in the context of a

Baltic/Nordic region-in-the-making and has been keen to ensure its control over those Russian regional authorities involved. This reflects Moscow's concerns over regional separatism and the possible disintegration of the Russian Federation noted above. However, such actions may well have an adverse impact on the very spirit of regional cooperation projects.

Notably, however, on the EU side of things similar obstacles exist relating to the fear of decentralisation. For example, the Brussels' bureaucracy has also been unenthusiastic about the decentralising impact of regional collaborative initiatives as well. Thus, Hiski Haukkala, a Finnish researcher, has found reason to explore whether the EU also belongs to the camp of 'the reluctant regionalisers' (Haukkala, 2001). In this regard, the EU Commission appears to be unwilling to delegate responsibility to any particular group of countries for region-specific policies. When it comes to the ND, for instance, Haukkala therefore notes that 'The Dimension should not be seen as a new regional initiative, which in the Commission's view is not necessary'. It is instead stressed that the ND is a matter of joint concern for all the EU member countries. In 2000 the then Finnish Prime Minister, Paavo Lipponen, also stressed that 'The Northern Dimension of the EU is not a regional initiative but refers to a policy of the whole Union' (Lipponen, 2000, p.3). Also notable is that the EU's recent ENP initiative is basically centralist in nature. As such, if it is understood in a narrow manner this may also restrict region-to-region and cross-border cooperation in other contexts as well, by indicating that there are limits for such developments. The emphasis in the ENP is clearly on the involvement of the EU at large, and in a similar fashion Russian representatives have underlined that the partnership is constituted by Russia as a whole and not just only the North-Western regions (Deryabin, 2000).

In this context, it is important to note that North European regional cooperation precisely should not be interpreted as an artificial top-down project. Instead, it should be understood as a bottom-up process with very lively grass roots and it is this that centralising tendencies in Russia and the EU threaten to undermine. In contrast, therefore, it can be argued that the best way to make a contribution to regional cooperation in the North is precisely to use the potential of the existing international networks of subnational and non-governmental actors – rather than to bypass them via centralising initiatives such as the ENP. Instead, bottom-up actors should thus have access to decision-making processes in the regional context and be treated in inclusive terms. For example, according to a report of the Council of the European Union, civil society organisations should be involved throughout the launching, implementation, monitoring and continued development of ND activities, and authorities at all levels should cooperate to this end (Council of the European Union, 2001, p.14). Whether the ENP will continue to support such proclamations is a matter for debate.

However, it is also suggested that to maintain the regionalist nature of the project Moscow and Brussels should give their local and regional entities the necessary leverage and means in order to enable their full-fledged participation in interregional and cross-border activities. These should not be seen as hampering, but as enriching national foreign policies. On the positive side, it seems that to some extent Moscow recognises the need to further encourage Russia's regional authorities to actively participate in collaborative regional projects. According to former Foreign Minister Ivanov (2000, p.8):

> An important, proactive role in the implementation of the Northern Dimension is to be played by the entities of the Russian Federation located in the North and Northwest of our country. Participation in these activities will help revive the real sector of their economies, and solve social and environment protection issues, as well as problems of [the] indigenous population of the Arctic.

Notably, therefore, in the course of the drafting of a Russian position paper on the Northern Dimension, the Foreign Ministry requested that the region's authorities prepare a list of their suggestions and concerns. At the May 2000 Conference on the Northern Dimension and Kaliningrad in Copenhagen, the Kaliningrad delegation even delivered a list of concrete recommendations to be included in the Northern Dimension Action Plan (Romanovsky, 2000b). At the same time, along with providing the regions with a certain amount of autonomy, Moscow should be assured that regional initiatives – in creating stability and well-being by mobilising resources across borders and in previously somewhat isolated regions – will not entail Russia's disintegration.

In contrast to Russia's concerns about some elements of regional cooperation that it sees as potentially undermining Russia's territorial sovereignty, it is notable that Moscow is also unhappy with the universalist approach of the ENP concept in the way the EU is now thinking about cooperation with its neighbours. The point is that Russia does not want to be treated in the same way as Belarus or Morocco and rather claims a special status and special relationship with Brussels. Likewise, Moscow is also discontented with the ENP concept in that – in contrast with the ND – it leaves almost no room for Russia in setting the bilateral cooperative agenda. The concept is rather based on the assumption that the EU's neighbours should simply accept its rules of the game and upgrade their legislation in accordance with European standards, rather than the EU developing specific models for each country. To overcome these shortcomings it can be suggested that the ENP should be made more differentiated in order to take into account the peculiarities of each neighbouring country (including Russia) and also of particular regions (e.g., Northern Europe). In short, in putting forward the ENP, the rather innovative elements of the ND should not be discarded. As far as the practical aspects are concerned, the EU should also emphasise technical assistance and investment rather than credits and loans, whilst priority should also be given to long-term projects with positive effects on the local economy and society.

In particular, both Moscow and Brussels should give priority to actually making Kaliningrad a pilot region, rather than simply proclaiming it to be one. A number of suggestions can be made here. First, the Kaliningrad region could be the first (among Russia's regions) put into the context of the Common European

Economic Space (CEES) initiative recently launched by the EU with Russia. The CEES itself should be developed to set out a deeper and broader timetable for legislative approximation between the EU and Russia. Participation in selected EU activities and programmes, including aspects such as consumer protection, standards, environmental matters and research bodies, could be opened to Kaliningrad and then to the rest of Russia (Commission of the European Communities, 2003a).[5] For example, EU standards should be established for Kaliningrad-produced goods. A joint EU/Russia Standardisation Committee should also be created and efforts to support the further development of enterprise policy by Kaliningrad/Russia should accompany regulatory approximation.

Another step forward could be the creation of an EU-Russia Free Trade Area (FTA). This could be done both in parallel with and as a follow up to CEES activities. A Free Trade Area is envisaged in the EU-Russia Partnership and Cooperation Agreement (PCA), but no timetable has ever been attached to this. To implement this idea objectives and benchmarks should be developed. In particular, this process could be started by concluding a free trade agreement with the Kaliningrad region and then replicating this experience to the rest of Russia. However, some Russian experts feel uneasy about this idea because it could lead to the erection of customs barriers between the *Oblast* and the rest of Russia, at least in the transitional period (Fyodorov and Zverev, 2004).

Over the long run, upon the implementation of the CEES and FTA projects the EU and Russia could think of creating a European Economic Area-type arrangement that aims at the further harmonisation of European and Russian regulatory regimes. Again, Kaliningrad could be a pilot region in implementing such an ambitious project.

One more problem that exists for the future of regional cooperation in Northern Europe has been the shift in the EU's regional priorities since the late 1990s. Many specialists have noted that the war in Kosovo and the need to deal with the Balkans in the aftermath of the war gained such a high priority, was so demanding and

---

5   In the Concept Paper on the CEES prepared by the EU-Russia joint High-Level Group the CEES is defined in the following way: 'The CEES means an open and integrated market between the EU and Russia, based on the implementation of common or compatible rules and regulations, including compatible administrative practices, as a basis for synergies and economies of scale associated with a higher degree of competition in bigger markets. It shall ultimately cover substantially all sectors of economy'. The paper sets up three major goals within the CEES: (1) promoting trade and investment between the EU and Russia, based on well-functioning market economies, aiming at sustainable development, taking into account internationally recognised principles, such as, *inter alia*, non-discrimination and transparency and good governance; (2) creating opportunities for business operators through common, harmonised or compatible rules and regulations, as well as through inter-connected infrastructure networks; and (3) enhancing the competitiveness of the EU and Russian economies worldwide (EU-Russia Joint High-Level Group 2003, pp.2-3).

turned out to be so costly that there is little energy left for Northern issues. The crisis in the Middle East, the need to deal with problematic neighbours such as Northern Africa, Belarus, Moldova and Ukraine, the Union's enlargement and the new emphasis on security-related matters within the Union might have a similar impact.

In consequence of such challenges, there is no unity among the EU member states regarding the pace and scale of regional cooperation in Northern Europe. While Finland, Sweden, and to some extent Denmark, are enthusiastic about it and perceive it in terms of a long-term strategy, other – and more powerful players – have favoured other priorities such as enlargement, the Balkans, European Monetary Union, the European army and so on. These countries tend to perceive the Northern Europe problematique more in terms of an extension of the Union's own programmes and approaches (the universalist ENP concept), and their time frame and attention span is much shorter, thereby limiting regional initiatives (such as the ND) to short- or medium-term endeavours.

Another disputable question for EU member states consists of the possible involvement and participation of non-European countries, such as the US and Canada, in regional projects. While many European countries favour such an inclusion, in particular France wants to keep this activity as a purely European exercise. The position tends to be that the US and Canada may take part in carrying out individual projects, but this must not lead to a possible acknowledgement of their institutional position (Heikkinnen, 2000, p.32).

Similarly, the EU has also been wrought by differences of opinion on the Union's visa and border regimes. While some Nordic/Baltic countries and Italy have suggested liberalising the visa and customs regimes and improving border crossings (particularly in the Kaliningrad zone), Brussels and some other EU member states (e.g., France and Spain) have favoured strengthening the Schengen system. Notably, Poland and the Baltic countries were forced to introduce Schengen-like visa rules at an early stage, even before formally joining the EU, actions which left a sour taste in the North and not least in Kaliningrad (Janicki-Rola, 2000; De Miguel, 2000, pp.65-66; Slepavicius, 2000; Usackas, 2000, p.83).

To support regional activities in Northern Europe, therefore, the interoperability of various EU cooperative programmes should be improved in the new institutional framework of the ENP. In short, it is essential that flexibility remains a central tenet of the EU approach. It is therefore positive to note that steps have already been taken by the European Commission in 2000-2001 to ensure better coordination between the different programmes. The PHARE and INTERREG regulations have been aligned to a great extent with Joint Programming Documents established by the 'PHARE 2000 review – Strengthening Preparations for Membership'. In April 2001 the Commission also prepared a 'Guide to bringing INTERREG and TACIS funding together' (Commission of the European Communities, 2001b). This work should be completed by the time of the formal introduction of the Wider Europe/ENP strategy.

Yet, in addition to increased coordination between the various EU-instruments, the North European region also seems to require special financial facilities of its own. The aim should not just be one of creating synergies between existing EU policies, but to create specific Northern Europe related projects. For example, some specialists have suggested establishing a special sub-programme on North-West Russia within the TACIS programme (Fairlie, 2000, p.88).

EU projects within the ND area should be coordinated with activities of other regional institutions (CBSS, BEAC, AC, Nordic Council, etc.) and the Commission should be granted with sufficient powers to be able to cooperate with such bodies. As the former Russian Foreign Minister, Igor Ivanov (2000, pp.8-9), noted in 2000:

> we should not forget about the existing plans which have not been fully implemented yet due to the lack of funds and resources. They include, in particular, the projects of the Council of the Baltic Sea States, Barents Euro-Arctic Council and Arctic Council. Let the priority projects agreed upon within those institutions become a tentative step for the Northern Dimension.

EU documents also emphasise the need to use the experience and know-how of regional bodies as well as to establish an efficient division of labour among them, building on their respective competencies and geographical coverage (Council of the European Union, 2001, p.13), although in practice the implementation of such a stance has turned out to be difficult. Instead of contributing to discord between the Nordic countries (as was the case with the BEAC), new regional projects need to function as a unifying element among the Nordic countries. A division of labour is called for among these countries as well as between the EU member-states more generally with regard to Russia. It is also obvious that financial conditions surrounding projects and administrative procedures should be transparent.

Finally, it is important that attention should be paid not only to the 'reformist' Russian regions (such as St. Petersburg, Novgorod, Karelia and Kaliningrad), but also to regions with a relatively poor democratic record (Pskov, Murmansk, Archangel, Yamalo-Nenets Autonomous District, Komi Republic, etc.).

Conclusion

The post-Cold War period brought fundamental changes both in Russian foreign policy thinking and strategies towards the North European region. Although the realist/geopolitical paradigm still dominates Russian security discourse, the mainstream of Russian political thought no longer perceives Northern Europe as a zone of military confrontation with the West and rather favours opening up Russia's North-Western regions for international cooperation.

In this respect, the ND has made Northernness an attractive concept and a concept that is now used by those within its sphere in unifying terms. No longer is the concept simply used by outsiders in a negative sense as a representation of otherness, as has historically been the case.[6] Put otherwise, Russia with a Nordic/Northern element to it is nowadays much more attractive to the European common space than a Russia without this element. Being part of the regionalising 'North' has made it much easier to 'sell' policy initiatives than if Russia is simply conceptualised as a traditional state-type actor.

These are arguably rather profound developments. Reflections about Northernness/'Nordicity' once again lead Russia to introspect somewhat about its identity and relations with Europe. Ultimately, regionalising developments underway in the North raise rather fundamental questions about the very nature of Russia, the nature of the North, the nature of the EU and the nature of EU-Russian relations. In the North, the perennial question of whether Russia is a unique entity, or whether it shares something in common with Europe, appears to point to the latter answer where Northernness stands out as a unifying and mediating space. At the same time, the chapter has raised some questions about how far cooperation in the North is possible. Important questions exist as to how 'correctly' the EU and Russia understand each other's natures, and as such whether the 'Russian' and 'European' projects are compatible. Arguably, these questions are far from being properly addressed. In this chapter a number of solutions to various identifiable obstacles to regional cooperation have been noted, however, it should also be noted that accepting these proposals and suggestions also entails buying into a particular conception of Russia, the EU and European space more generally that prioritises regionalisation, decentralisation and a certain way of thinking about borders and sovereignty. Despite this, however, it needs to be emphasised that Russia has a lot to gain from Northern developments, and it is arguably here where Russia may be best able to consolidate its space and place in Europe.

In this regard, an important aspect of the regional cooperative process in the North is that Russia is treated in inclusive terms. It is invited to join and change emphasis from a traditional political-military agenda ('hard' security) to an economic-human ('soft' security) one. It is encouraged to develop its Northern parts as a resource for partaking in European policies rather than merely becoming a source of cheap energy for Europe. In contrast with the past when the Russian North-West was perceived as only a Russian problem, now there is a growing feeling among the regional actors (including the EU) that it should be a sphere of shared responsibility. This means that not only Russian, but also EU policy towards North-Western Russia should be radically revised, and this also calls for international rather than unilateral efforts and solutions that provide Russia with an avenue and voice into debates about European governance more generally.

Russia and Brussels agree in principle that EU enlargement should not entail the creation of dividing lines in Europe and that the four freedoms (movement of people, goods, services and capital) in the region should be ensured. They support

---

[6]   On the development of more positive readings of Northernness, see Joenniemi and Lehti (2003).

various collaborative projects, including in the areas of economy, trade, energy security, social system, health care, environment, and the improvement of border and transport infrastructures. They also favour concluding a special agreement on Kaliningrad to facilitate its deeper integration into the European economic and legal space. As noted, though, there are still numerous barriers to reaching such an agreement stemming from the inflexibility of the EU and Russian bureaucracies and legislation, as well as from differences in economic, political and security interests. However, the positive dynamics in the EU-Russian relationship are obvious.

More generally, one of the most important lessons to draw from the North European case is that regional cooperation is increasingly becoming an important positive factor in Northern Europe. Regionalism offers opportunities for developing Russian democracy and civil society and it need not result in the further disintegration of the country. Instead, it can serve as a catalyst for successful reforms and international integration. Regional cooperation facilitates the rise of a mechanism of interdependence in Northern Europe and promotes mutual trust and understanding among nations there. By doing this regionalism helps to solve local problems and to prevent the rise of new threats and challenges. If Russia and the EU are able to use the opportunities of subregionalism in full then Northern Europe will become a 'success story' of Russia/Europe cooperation.

References

Browning, Christopher S. (2001), 'A Multidimensional Approach to Regional Cooperation: the United States and the Northern European Initiative', *European Security*, Vol. 10(4), pp. 84-108.

Browning, Christopher S. (2003), 'Complementarities and Differences in EU and US Policies in Northern Europe', *Journal of International Relations and Development*, Vol. 6(1), pp. 23-50.

Commission of the European Communities (2000), *Action Plan for the Northern Dimension in the external and cross-border policies of the European Union 2000-2003*, Commission Working Document, Draft, 28 February 2000, Brussels.

Commission of the European Communities (2001b), *Guide to bringing INTERREG and TACIS funding together*. Available at http://europa.eu.int/comm/external_relations/north_dim/conf/ formin2/intreg_TACIS.pdf.

Commission of the European Communities (2002), *EU Support to Kaliningrad*. Available at http://europa.eu.int/comm/external_relations/north_dim/kalin/ index.htm.

Commission of the European Communities (2003a), Communication from the European Commission to the Council and the European Parliament, *Wider Europe. Neighbourhood: A New Framework for Relations with our Eastern and Southern neighbours*. Available at http://europa.eu.int/comm/external_relations /we/intro/.

Commission of the European Communities (2003b), *National Indicative Programme. Russian Federation, 2004-2006. 21 May 2003.* Available at http://europa.eu.int/comm/external_relations/russia/csp/04-06_en.pdf.

Council of the Baltic Sea States (2002), 11th Ministerial Session of the Council of the Baltic Sea States, Svetlogorsk, Kaliningrad *Oblast*, 5-6 March 2002. Available at http://europa.eu.int/comm/external_relations/north_dim/doc/11cbss.htm.

Council of the European Union (2000), A*ction plan for the Northern Dimension with external and cross-border policies of the European Union 2000-2003*, 9401/00, June 14. Brussels, Council of the European Union, 2000. Available at http://europa.eu.int/comm/external_relations/north_dim/ndap/06_00_fr.pdf.

Council of the European Union (2001), *Full report on Northern Dimension policies*, 9804/01, 12 June. Available at http://europa.eu.int/comm/external_relations/north_dim/doc/full_report.pdf.

Deryabin, Yuri (2000), 'Severnoye izmerenie politiki Evropeiskogo Soyuza i interesy Rossii' [The EU Northern Dimension and Russia's interests], Moscow, Institute of Europe, Russian Academy of Sciences.

EU-Russia Joint High-Level Group (2003), *The Common European Economic Space (CEES)*. Concept Paper. Available at http://europa.eu.int/comm/external_relations/russia/summit11_03/1concl.pdf.

Fairlie, Lyndelle (2000), 'Will the EU use the Northern Dimension to solve its Kaliningrad dilemma?', in Tuomas Forsberg (ed.), *Northern Dimensions 2000: The Yearbook of Finnish Foreign Policy*, Helsinki: The Finnish Institute of International Affairs, pp. 85-101.

Fyodorov, Gennady and Zverev, Yuri (2004), *Personal communication*, April 30.

Haukkala, Hiski (2001), *Two Reluctant Regionalizers? The European Union and Russia in Europe's North*, Working Papers 32, Helsinki, The Finnish Institute of International Affairs.

Heikkinen, Ari (2000), *EU's Northern Dimension Action Plan – challenges for implementation*, speech at the King's College, London, 11 November.

Ivanov, Igor (2000), 'Cooperation between the EU and Russia in the European North', in Marja Nissinen (ed.), *Foreign Ministers' Conference on the Northern Dimension, Helsinki, 11-12 November 1999. A Compilation of Speeches*, Unit for the Northern Dimension in the Ministry for Foreign Affairs, Helsinki, Finland, pp. 7-9.

Janicki-Rola, Andjei (2000), *Interview with Mr Andjei Janicki-Rola*, Polish Consular General in Kaliningrad, 9 June.

Joenniemi, Pertti and Lehti, Marko (2003), 'The Encounter between the Nordic and the Northern: Torn Apart but Meeting Again?', in Marko Lehti and David J. Smith (eds.), *Post-Cold War Identity Politics: Northern and Baltic Experiences*, London, Frank Cass, pp. 128-56.

Leshukov, Igor (1999), 'Severnoye izmerenie ishet koordinaty tselei' [The Northern Dimension defines the co-ordinates of its targets], *Euro* (Moscow), no. 11, pp. 30-1.

Lipponen, Paavo (2000), 'Opening address', in Marja Nissinen (ed.), *Foreign Ministers' Conference on the Northern Dimension, Helsinki, 11-12 November 1999. A Compilation of Speeches*. Unit for the Northern Dimension in the Ministry for Foreign Affairs, Helsinki, Finland, pp. 3-6.

de Miguel, Ramon (2000), 'The answer to Europe's important challenges in trans-border matters: cooperation in Justice and Home Affairs', in Marja Nissinen (ed.), *Foreign Ministers' Conference on the Northern Dimension, Helsinki, 11-12 November 1999. A Compilation of Speeches*. Unit for the Northern Dimension in the Ministry for Foreign Affairs, Helsinki, Finland, pp. 65-7.

Patten, Christopher (2002), *EU-Russia Summit and Hoff Report on Kaliningrad*, Speech by The Rt Hon Chris Patten, European Parliament - Plenary session. Strasbourg, 14 May. Available at http://europa.eu.int/comm/ external_relations/news/patten/sp02_201.htm.

Romanovsky, Victor (2000b), *Report of the Head of the Kaliningrad Delegation at the Conference 'The Northern Dimension and Kaliningrad: European and Regional Integration'*, 17-18 May 2000, Copenhagen, unpublished paper.

Sergounin, Alexander (1999), 'The bright side of Russia's regionalisation', Cambridge, Ma., Davis Centre for Russian Studies, Harvard University, Programme on New Approaches to Russian Security Policy Memo Series, No. 59.

Sergounin, Alexander (2001), 'The United States' Northern Dimension? Prospects for a U.S.-Russian Cooperative Agenda in Northern Europe', in Program on New Approaches to Russian Security Policy Conference, *Policy Memo Nos. 210-242*. Washington, DC, Jan. 25, 2002. Washington: Centre for Strategic and International Studies, Policy Memo 232, pp. 127-132.

Slepavicius, Ricardas (2000), *Interview with Ricardas Slepavicius*, Consul, Consulate General of Lithuania in Kaliningrad, 8 June.

Strategiya razvitiya otnosheniy Rossiyskoi Federatsii s Evropeiskim Soyuzom na srednesrochnuyu perspectivu (2000-2010) [Medium term strategy for development of relations between the Russian Federation and the European Union] (1999), *Diplomaticheskiy Vestnik*, no. 11.

Usackas, Vygaudas (2000), 'The speech of Mr Vygaudas Usackas, Vice-Minister of Foreign Affairs, Lithuania', in Marja Nissinen (ed.), *Foreign Ministers' Conference on the Northern Dimension, Helsinki, 11-12 November 1999. A Compilation of Speeches*, Unit for the Northern Dimension in the Ministry for Foreign Affairs, Helsinki, Finland, pp. 83-4.

Chapter 8

EU-Russian Regional Cooperation: Logics of Regionalisation and the Challenge of the Exception

Sergei Prozorov

Introduction

The development of EU-Russian relations since the early 1990s, while conventionally international in the sense of being a treaty-based partnership, has also been marked by a phenomenon of relative novelty: the active formation of transboundary regional linkages. This international regionalisation is an obvious novelty for Russia, whose Soviet-era foreign policy was limited to exclusive and elitist state diplomacy, but is also approached as a landmark phenomenon within Europe, where it is frequently cast as a 'postmodern' challenge to sovereign statehood and modern territoriality. However accurate the 'postmodern diagnosis' may be, the process of regionalisation does pose important questions about the relation of cross-border regional cooperation to sovereign statehood. It is the contention of this article that this relation is markedly different in the case of the EU and post-communist Russia, which may account for the problems and contradictions in EU-Russian relations. The chapter first briefly outlines the key features of EU-Russian regional cooperation and critically addresses existing interpretations of the problematic aspects of this cooperation. It then argues that regionalisation processes in the EU and post-communist Russia follow substantively divergent logics. Proceeding from the problematic of the 'vertical displacement' of statehood in Russian politics during the 1990s, the chapter attempts to reconstruct a (more properly 'postmodern') logic of post-Soviet regionalisation in Russia. Finally, the chapter outlines the significance and the potential positive implications of the federal reforms of the Putin presidency for EU-Russian regional cooperation.

Common Strategies and Points of Contention in EU-Russian Regional Cooperation

It is notable that Russian-EU inter-regional cooperation is geographically limited to Northern Europe. This area is arguably the most advanced in the creation of multiple regional institutional arrangements, such as the Barents Euro-Arctic Region (BEAR) and the Council of the Baltic Sea States (CBSS), etc. It is this multiplicity that permits us to speak of the area as a *regionalised network*, in which the multiperspectival reconstruction of political space displaces the strict divide between the domestic and the international (Haukkala, 2001; Joenniemi, 2003). On the other side of the border, in Northwest Russia, the situation in the 1990s was marked by a similar, albeit less ordered and more spontaneous 'autonomisation' of the regions, a process whose political justification made frequent reference to European practices. While never at the forefront of the quest for regional autonomy, the regions of Northwest Russia have succeeded in accumulating greater authority internally and undertaking relatively independent policies in their external relations[1] – an opportunity made possible by the antagonistic politics of the 1990s, in which regional leaders were powerful 'balance holders' in the struggle between the Presidency and the oppositional legislature.

Concrete forms of EU-Russian cooperation at the regional level in the Russian Northwest range from city-twinning activities, to more ambitious projects such as EuregioKarelia (Cronberg, 2003; Prozorov, 2004a). We may also note the Russian proposal to make Kaliningrad *Oblast'* a 'pilot region' in which new forms of EU-Russian cooperation could be experimented with, or the Northern Dimension initiative that is in part advanced as an umbrella concept for EU-Russian regional cooperation. These, and other forms of cooperation, clearly exemplify productive experiments of emulating the 'intra-EU' (and more specifically Nordic) experience, which succeeded in 'pluralizing' foreign relations at concrete local sites and opening formerly absent avenues of direct socio-economic interactions. On the other hand, these activities face obvious challenges, including the deep socio-economic and structural asymmetries existing between Russia and the EU, their incommensurable bureaucracies, and the complex EU funding procedures for regional cooperation (e.g., the impossibility of combining the funds of Tacis and Interreg programmes for projects such as Euregios). A more fundamental challenge, particularly regarding the Putin presidency, may nonetheless lie in the political dimension and concerns the divergence of Russian and European perspectives on regionalisation (and, as will be argued in detail below, in the two *processes* of regionalisation). This difference is hardly discernible in the official discourse of the two parties, since the official 'common strategies' of Russia and the EU with regard to each other appear to encourage and facilitate regional cooperation (*pace* the caricaturised view of the Putin presidency as bent on curtailing regional autonomy).

---

[1]   See Aleksandrov (2001); Makarychev (2000); Cronberg (2003).

The 1999 EU Common Strategy on Russia advocates 'strengthening cross-border and regional cooperation'. This was concretely elaborated in the framework of the Northern Dimension initiative, which became an official part of the EU's 'external relations' in 1998. While being neither institutionalised nor endowed with an independent budget, the Northern Dimension is important as a delimitation of the EU's interest in Russia, singling out the Russian Northwest as a priority area. This delimitation was anticipated in Europe as liable to misconstrual on the part of the Russian authorities as possibly contributing to further fragmentation and disintegration of the Federation (Haukkala, 2001). However, Russia's initial restrained response was rather motivated by the absence of any substantive content in the Initiative, aside from its focus on natural resources. Indeed, the 1999 Russian Midterm Strategy on the EU, the only official framework document on Russian policy towards the EU, emphasises 'substantializing by joint efforts the initiative of the Northern Dimension in European cooperation [...] to ensure that the implementation of this initiative is directed not only at the promotion of exploration and exportation of raw materials but also at the integrated development of Northern and Northwestern Russia' (Russia's Midterm Strategy towards the EU).

One of the concrete substantive proposals made by Russia in this context is for the abolition of the visa and passport control regime, which during Putin's presidency has become a primary object of problematisation in EU-Russian relations. Indeed, the extension of the Schengen regime in the enlarged EU entails the imposition of a visa regime that far exceeds in its strictness the bilateral visa practices that previously existed between Russia and the new EU members. The problem is particularly critical with regard to Kaliningrad *Oblast'*, which has now become an enclave within the enlarged EU. This not merely complicates its socio-economic relations with the rest of Russia, but also serves to complicate cross-border cooperation arrangements between the *Oblast'* and its neighbours in Poland and Lithuania (Fairlie and Sergounin, 2001). In contrast to standard EU policy discourse with its valorisation of inclusion, integration and regional cooperation, the unequivocal extension of the Schengen regime draws a clear line of exclusion from the 'area of freedom, prosperity and justice'. Moreover, and what is less often articulated, it actually destroys the various *ad hoc* cooperative arrangements, from shuttle-trading to cultural exchanges, that *already exist* and were made possible by the relaxed border control regimes agreed on bilaterally by Russia with Poland and Lithuania.

It appears that the almost exclusive academic and political focus on the *development* (through administrative practices) of cooperative regional arrangements reflects a certain *programmatic a priori* (Rose, 1996) that prejudices governmentally constructed, and hence *sanctioned*, practices to the detriment of spontaneous and *ad hoc* arrangements, not subject to governmental disposition. In other words, the speculative discourses on the possibilities of developing *new* forms of cooperation silence the question of whether present or potential future governmental efforts in this direction might not in fact be squarely antagonistic and detrimental to *antecedent* cooperative practices, as the insistence on the uniform application of the Schengen regime clearly seems to be.

The EU-Russian debate on the problem of Kaliningrad illuminates a broader conceptual problematic in EU-Russian relations. It is frequently argued that Russia's opposition to the EU's stance on Kaliningrad reflects a misunderstanding of the formal and rule-governed character of EU policies, in contrast to Russia's persistent emphasis on 'traditional' diplomacy, which is particularly evident in its tactic of relocating contentious issues to the domain of bilateral or multilateral relations with individual EU member-states (Haukkala, 2003; Bordachev, 2003). With regard to these claims, we may suggest that Russia's 'non-appreciation' of the formal and rule-governed character of EU policies reflects the greater attunement of the former to the *exceptional* nature of such issues as Kaliningrad and, more broadly, the exception itself as an integral feature of political life.[2] This attunement may be grasped with the help of a reading of post-communism as a political moment of *emergence* of a new order, logically marked by the absence of *foundations* thereof (Prozorov, 2004b; cf., Mau and Starodubrovskaya, 2001; Magun, 2003). This notion attunes us to the specificity of post-communist politics, a specificity irreducible to either the institutional defects on the path of 'transition to democracy' or the determinants of culture and tradition.[3] Instead, the sources of this specificity are immanent to the *exceptional* character of political practice, whereby the foundations of the emergent social order are to be instituted in the condition of the 'dissolution of markers of certainty' (Lefort, 1988, p.19) that accompanies the demise of the Soviet order. The literally limitless possibilities of socio-political construction are aligned with the disappearance of all stable foundations that could ground a founding decision. In Carl Schmitt's famous dictum, a constitutive decision logically 'emanates from nothingness' (Schmitt, 1985, p. 12), since it is by definition limited by neither that which it displaces nor by that which it founds.

The consequence of the decisionism of the Russian 'politics of emergence' for the policy process in EU-Russian relations is the perception of the radical openness of the strategic field of political possibilities, i.e., the tactical *negotiability* of every decision. Easily misconstrued as 'unprincipled' and adventurist opportunism, when contrasted with the law- and value- governed practices of the EU, this stance is indeed *unprincipled*, albeit in an ontological sense, i.e., lacking all recourse to more fundamental principles, simply because the latter are presently absent or being instituted in a decisionist manner. Concretely, in the case of Kaliningrad, this stance posits the manifestly exceptional character of the existence of a Russian enclave within the EU and proposes to deal with this issue as literally unprecedented, and hence amenable to an unlimited range of possible political

---

[2]   The affirmation of the exception as the constitutive principle of the political is central to the work of Carl Schmitt. See Schmitt (1976; 1985).

[3]   See Prozorov (2004b), chapter 1 for the criticism of the continuum between 'transitionalism' and 'traditionalism' in Russian studies.

(rather than technical) solutions. In contrast, the EU's insistence on the sanctitude of the Schengen principles is marked by the effacement of the exceptional character of the Kaliningrad enclave, which forms a *gap* in the EU's common socio-political, economic and legal space, and therefore functions as its *internal outside*. While the Russian government and the *Oblast'* administration emphasise that Kaliningrad ought to be treated as an exceptional case, to which general regimes must not apply, the EU's insistence on the non-amendability of Schengen effaces but, to recall Schmitt (1976, pp.21-22), does not thereby *annul* the exception, the result being that the innovative possibilities of managing Kaliningrad *as an exception* remain foregone.

The example of Kaliningrad demonstrates that problems in EU-Russian regional cooperation do not necessarily emanate from Russia's wariness of regional autonomy in foreign relations. In fact, the Midterm Strategy explicitly mentions the need to 'encourage contacts among Russian and EU regions [...] with a view to fostering humanitarian and economic ties and sharing experiences of local self-government and business administration' (Russia's Midterm Strategy towards the EU). This positive assessment of the foreign relations of the regions clearly contrasts with the frequently mentioned negative Russian attitude to regionalisation that has allegedly intensified during the Putin presidency. Hiski Haukkala has posited a binary opposition between Russian and European foreign policy discourses, which may be summed up in terms of three distinctions. First, the EU discourse is taken to be 'value-based', centred on the affirmation of human rights and humanitarian principles, while Russia 'approaches international relations, and thus its relations with the EU, through the prism of realist thinking, where concepts such as balance of power and geopolitics are more important than references to common values' (Haukkala, 2001, p.8). Second, 'whereas the EU can be seen as moving towards a post-modern and post-sovereign political system, the Russian project is still very modern in its essence' (Ibid., p.9). Third, while the EU is taken to embrace a positive stance towards the dual processes of globalisation and regionalisation, Russia is perceived as wary of globalisation, seeing it as a form of US hegemony, and regionalisation, which is depicted as a negative force of fragmentation that threatens Russia's very territorial integrity.

This is not the place to argue extensively against these rather general and facile distinctions, yet a number of points deserve to be elaborated. First, the opposition between liberal-humanitarian and realist-geopolitical policies ignores the way in which the former concerns are necessarily supplemented by the latter considerations: the 'politics of principle' (Campbell, 1993) is always contaminated by the 'principle of the political', in the Schmittian sense of the friend-enemy distinction. Second, the grand dichotomy of modern/postmodern politics (itself deserving a longer critique[4]) ignores that the EU governmental practices of

---

[4]   In Prozorov (2004b) (chapter 3) I attempted to demonstrate how such features of what is frequently referred to as 'postmodernity', as decentralisation and dissemination of authority, multi-level and multi-lateral governance, liaisons between the state and the

'pooling sovereignty' *are*, in the strict sense, *acts* of sovereignty, in which its statist *form* may be amended, but its decisionist *principle* is reaffirmed rather than abandoned. Moreover, the very distinction of 'modern' and 'postmodern' *policy projects* between which a state might *choose* appears to rest on an ultimately 'modern' instrumental governmental rationality.

Finally, the distinction between negative and positive attitudes to regionalisation presupposes the essential *identity* of regionalising processes in Russia and the EU, making different policy orientations towards them a matter of *reception*. Let us suggest that in this case we might rather be dealing with a case of two distinct *logics* of regionalisation, which may account for the different relation of the EU and the Russian Federation to these processes. To elucidate this difference we must first pose the basic question: in response to *what* does the Putin presidency presently assert sovereignty? What has been the positivity of the mode of centre-region relations in the 1990s that is presently problematised and reformed in Russia? Answering these questions in detail would require extensive empirical research of post-communist political practices, unhampered by theoretical postulates so abundant in the 'transitionalist' paradigm in Russian studies. For now, let us advance five theses about post-Soviet regionalisation in Russia and its fate during the Putin presidency.

The Logic of Post-Communist Regionalisation: The End and the Beginning of Russian Statehood

Russia as a 'New State'

The 'traditionalist' prejudice in Russian studies, that tends to view post-communist Russia as the 'remainder' of the Russian empire, obscures the evident fact that the Russian Federation is a new state, that never existed in its present borders, and was born in December 1991 as a result of thoroughly contingent political events that led to the dissolution of the USSR. Unlike the states of Central and Eastern Europe or the Soviet republics, which were endowed with ceremonial attributes of statehood, Russian statehood was dispersed in the Soviet power structures and had to be created *entirely* anew and simultaneously with the liberalising and democratising project. Furthermore, aside from the vacuous reference to federalism in the official title of the RSFSR, Russia never existed as a *federation*, hence the novelty of the specific *type* of the state-building project embarked on in the 1990s. In the early 1990s the Russian Federation had therefore to be built from scratch

---

private sector, are in fact inherent features of a reconfiguration of liberal governmentality towards the 'neo-liberal' mode. See also Rose (1996) and Dean (1999) for a discussion of this transformation. While certainly significant, this reconfiguration is considerably more modest and specific than the epochal shift that the 'postmodern' transformation is presented to be.

within the uncomfortably contingent post-Soviet borders and within the highly unstable political configuration of 'dual power', a confrontation between the Yeltsin presidency and the Congress of People's Deputies that was dominated by forces rejecting the post-Soviet settlement.

In contrast to the contingency of the emergence of Russia as a new state, its internal administrative-territorial division (ATD) was inherited from the RSFSR and largely remained intact in the post-Soviet period. Thus, while in the moment of the dissolution of the USSR Russia faced the problem of its *self-creation* as a state, the retention of the Soviet-era ATD resulted in the existence in the post-communist state of stable 'ready-made' political units: *oblast's*, republics, *krais* and *okrugs*. Consequently, from the outset of post-communist transformation, as products of the Soviet-era ATD, the regions were in a stronger political position than the newly emergent and politically fragmented 'federal centre' and were able to appropriate substantial authority at the expense of the latter.

Regionalisation as a Vertical Displacement of Statehood

This situation is described by Vladimir Kagansky (1995) as the '*regionalisation* of post-Soviet space', in contrast to the prevailing European discourse of *regionalism* as a conscious affirmation of regional identity and the policy design of regional autonomisation. Regionalisation is rather conceived as an 'anarchic', 'by-default' process of the displacement of upper levels of authority by lower ones, marked by the immanent logic of fragmentation. The most marked contrast between (simplistically conceived) 'Russian' and 'European' logics of regionalisation is thus between *fragmentation* as a consequence of the demise of the Soviet order, and *decentralisation* as a policy innovation undertaken by governmental design.

This logic of fragmentation may be elaborated within the context of the Russian politics that surrounded the emergence of the new state. The foundational practices of the Yeltsin presidency, culminating in the 1993 institution of a new constitutional order after the violent resolution of the problem of 'dual power', have, throughout the 1990s, been marred by the failure of attempts at a depoliticising sedimentation of the new 'political principle' of statehood into the *grounds* of a *system of politics*. In concrete terms, this condition may be summed up as the *displacement* of statehood by a complex web of decentred practices along horizontal and vertical axes.

Along the horizontal axis, the crumbling of the Soviet economy and the radical economic reforms of the early 1990s have led to a reconfiguration of the boundary between the *private* and the *public* and an erosion of the distinction between the two realms. The rejection of statism in the course of liberal reforms in the 1990s entailed the *reversal* of the elite hierarchy, whereby the economic elite assumed primacy over the political elite and redefined the latter's conditions of functioning. The quintessentially public institution of the state, according to many accounts of Russian politics, has become *privatised* by quasi-oligarchic financial-political groups – a tendency that we may refer to as a *horizontal displacement of statehood*.

In this process the logic of privatisation (integral to liberal reforms) was radicalised to embrace the very *agent* of privatisation and dissolved the very distinction between state and society that is crucial to modern liberalism.

Along the vertical axis, the influence exercised by the regional authorities on federal policy has led to the reconstruction of the image of the Russian state as a secondary figure, derivative from mobile tactical configurations and alliances with and between the regional leaders. This situation can be described quite accurately in terms of 'neofeudalism', a heteronomous patchwork of multiple overlapping and interpenetrating authorities. This tendency, frequently discussed in benign or neutral terms of 'regionalisation', may be referred to as a *vertical displacement of statehood*. In other words, the logic of regionalisation, central to federalist reforms, was radicalised to embrace the very *agent* of regionalisation, whereby the space of the state turned into a site of negotiation and competition between various coalitions of regional leaders, frequently articulated with financial-political groups.

The practices of horizontal and vertical displacement of the state took place partly as a result of tactical alliances between the presidency, business and regional elites and, rather than working to consolidate the constitutional order, were in themselves *para-constitutional*. The effect was to make every aspect of politics tactically negotiable, contingent on the decision and therefore chronically unstable. We may refer to this situation as the 'lingering of the political' (Prozorov, 2004b, pp.332-338), which refers to the failure to complete the double movement of the appearance of a founding decision and its occultation through its reinscription as a stable foundation delimiting the positive socio-political order. In Richard Sakwa's remark from 1999, 'in an ironic perversion of Frederik Engels's idea, the [Russian] state is indeed withering away' (Sakwa, 1999, p.24).

The obverse side of the lingering of the political on the federal level was the phenomenon of the *depoliticisation of regional politics*: the consolidation of the authority of regional elites (frequently retaining key positions from the late-Soviet period) under the aegis of a discourse of 'managerialism'. Self-portrayed as technocratic managers (*hozyaistvenniki*) as opposed to 'Moscow' politicians, regional leaders accumulated disproportionate political power, all the while depoliticising their own activities as neutral, business-like and common-sense, and hence not subject to political contestation. As a result of this depoliticisation regional political spaces have, with few exceptions, been substantially narrower and more exclusionary than the space of federal politics.

Neo-medievalism and Russian 'Postmodernity'

The description provided above brings us to a paradoxical conclusion. The Russian political constellation of the 1990s, the patchwork of overlapping authorities and loyalties coexisting in the decentred, subjectless, segmentary and heteronomous political space, bears an uncanny resemblance to contemporary European discourses of neo-medievalism and 'postmodernity'. Let us venture that what we observe in the Russian displacement of statehood, is neither an aberration of the

European logic of postmodern regionalisation, nor a phenomenon entirely heterogeneous to this logic, but ironically, the ultimate *fulfilment* of the 'European model', the extreme limit of the 'neomedieval project'. If anything, Russia is *more* advanced and consistent than the EU in this project: unlike the EU, Russian 'postmodernity' is not conditioned by stable and decidedly modern statehood *coexisting* with new regional innovations, but is rather constituted by the radical generalisation of the logic of regionalisation. The key difference between the displacement of Russian statehood in the 1990s and the 'postmodern' turn in European governance is that the latter developments have been undertaken by political *design*, while the displacement of statehood in post-communist Russia has manifestly occurred by *default*, as a result of the weakness and incapacity of state authority. While European regionalisation unfolds *as part of* the governmental strategy and *within* a single governmental rationality, the Russian experience of the displacement of the state was marked by the decentring of governmental rationality itself and is far more in accordance with the dispersed and disseminative logic of what is conventionally understood by postmodernism. Rather than half-heartedly attempting and failing to imitate European postmodern practices, the Russia of the 1990s exemplifies the logical conclusion of the postmodern project taken to its extremity.

While this experience of the displacement of statehood was marked by undeniable pluralism, it was hardly conducive to the success of the liberal reforms proclaimed by the state. The incapacitation of state authority has been problematised as the disappearance of the very agent of liberal reforms, and thus the main reason for their stagnation in the 1990s. More specifically, with regard to the vertical displacement, liberal reforms have been disabled by the lack of a common economic space, which is instead punctured by unconstitutional regional legislation, and which in turn has created various barriers to the free movement of goods and capital. The problematisation of the 'neomedieval situation' by Russian liberals (see e.g., Ulykaev, 1999; Gaidar, 2001) is nonetheless not only pragmatic, but also follows logically from the liberal denial of heteronomous pluralism that cages the individual in the network of segmented communities and ascribed identities (see Hall, 1995).

The Putin Presidency and the Reconstitution of the State

Within this framework of conceptualising the Russian politics of emergence, the Putin presidency may be interpreted as a clear successor to Yeltsin's project of liberal reforms that is nonetheless discontinuous with and antagonistic to the vertical and horizontal displacements of the state of the Yeltsin presidency. Putin's project of the 'reconstitution of the state' (Sakwa, 2000) is manifested in the enactment of the discourse of 'strong statehood' in the practices of restoring a degree of Federal control over the regions by 'establishing the vertical of power', and reconstructing political space 'horizontally' by consolidating the state's capacity of agency *vis-à-vis* 'oligarchic' financial-political groups. The reassertion of statehood is advocated as a necessary condition for the project of liberal socio-economic reforms that have been reactivated and radicalised during Putin's presidency.[5]

> The answer to [present] challenges cannot be given without the strengthening of the state first. *Not a single national task can be fulfilled without it.* [...] Our key task is to *learn to use the instruments of the state for ensuring freedom.* [...] *Only a strong, effective - if someone does not like the word 'strong', we will say that only an effective and democratic state can uphold civil, political and economic freedoms* (Putin, 2000).

The question of the relation between freedom and state-strengthening is beyond the scope of this article.[6] We may only suggest that Putin's stance is indeed confirmed by the experience of the 1990s, in which neither 'regionalisation' nor the 'privatisation' of the state did anything to enhance individual and social freedoms, but rather enabled new modes of exercising power. In a more theoretical sense, this position recalls the Foucauldian thesis on the immanence of power relations to the social domain, which disables the facile anti-statism that characterises much of 'critical' thought (Foucault, 1990, 1991). If the manifest weakness of the state in the 1990s did not 'liberate', and if the vacuum left by the ineffective state was filled by a multiplicity of non-state agents of power relations, the facile opposition between statism and liberalism appears wholly untenable.

Vertical Reconstitution and Proper Federalism

Furthermore, the criticism of Putin's 'statism' confuses the *quantitative* expansion of state powers (which, as the governmental policies of socio-economic deregulation illustrate well, is entirely contrary to the President's policy) with the *qualitative* delineation of a distinct domain of statehood *as* such. What is at stake in the 'reconstitution of the state' is not the *specific* question of strengthening state authority in particular domains, but the *general* question of the state's *effective presence as a self-identical positivity*. The much-maligned metaphor of the 'single vertical of power' and the notion of *mono-centrism* (Bunin et al., 2001; Zudin, 2003), that has been developed in Russian political science as a designator of 'Putin's regime' in contrast to the 'poly-centric' Yeltsin presidency, must therefore be qualified. While it is undeniable that the political autonomy of regional and business leaders has decreased since 2000, one can hardly speak of an increasing concentration of power solely in the figure of the president at the expense of legislative and judicial branches of power. Instead, a Putinian 'mono-centrism'

---

[5]   For a discussion of the socio-economic reforms of the Putin presidency, see Sakwa (2000); Bunin et al., (2001); Tompson (2002); Nicholson (2001); Zudin (2003); Prozorov (2004b) chapter 4.

[6]   See Prozorov (2004b) chapter 4 for a more detailed analysis of this relation in President Putin's policy discourse.

may be defined as the elimination of the *para-constitutional excesses* of the politics of the 1990s, which serves to depoliticise and consolidate as a foundation the constitutional order established in 1993. Thus, the term 'single vertical of power', applied with regard to the 'vertical reconstitution' of the state, is unfortunate since it connotes the hierarchical subordination of the lower levels of government to upper ones, which in contemporary Russia is made impossible by the federative constitutional structure.

Putin's federal reforms of spring-summer 2000 proceed from precisely this imperative to consolidate state autonomy within the constitutional domain and to install the very *distinction* between the federal and the regional that has been obscured in the vertical displacement of statehood.[7] The formation of seven Federal Districts, headed by presidential plenipotentiary envoys, serves to restore control over the activities of federal governmental institutions in the regions, which in the 1990s became subordinated to regional governments, whose very activities they were supposed to monitor and supervise. The reform of the composition of the Council of the Federation seeks to break down the nexus of legislative and executive power that the former system created and thus restores the constitutional principle of the separation of powers. Finally, the introduction of the legal procedure of federal intervention, that gives the president a highly restricted right to dismiss regional governors accused of constitutional violations, similarly does little more than provide for the enforcement of the principle of the superiority of the Russian constitution over regional legislation. For all their political radicalism, Putin's reforms have unfolded strictly within the constitutional space and hence exemplify by no means an abandonment of federalism, but rather its ordering and structuration. Exemplary in this regard is the President's refusal to extend the power-sharing treaties between the Federation and the regions, a practice prevalent between 1996-1999 during the period of utmost weakness of the federal centre. The treaties, whose content was contingent on the political weight of the regional leader in question, manifestly contradicted the constitutional equality of the subjects of the Federation. This made the distribution of power between the centre and the regions permanently (re)negotiable and resulted in structurally built-in political instability.

Putin's federal reforms are thus simultaneously modest and radical, unfolding strictly within the constitutional space, but creating a new socio-political reality by restoring state autonomy and introducing new patterns of identification. Even according to observers opposed to Putin's reforms (Smirnyagin, 2001), these decisions, whatever their alleged 'authoritarian' intent, have actually strengthened Russian federalism by eliminating its most notorious quasi-feudalist excesses without, as it were, throwing the baby out with the bathwater. The inability of the federal centre to dominate regional politics by 'converting' Putin's high approval rating into support for challengers to incumbents in regional elections demonstrates

---

[7] See e.g., Nicholson (2000); Hyde (2000); Smirnyagin (2001).

the continued existence of regional diversity and the irreducibility of regional politics to the nationwide political arena (see Makarychev, 2004).

To conclude, we may claim that Putin's reconstitution of the state and re-assertion of sovereignty have not been undertaken as 'conservative' attempts to *ward off* 'postmodern' regionalisation, but are rather responses to the 'triumphant march' of the latter in the 1990s. Putin's state-centric 'modernism' may thus be ironically redefined as 'post-postmodern'. Second, these practices, rather than undermining Russia's fragile federalism, are conducive to its proper emergence in the form prescribed by the 1993 Constitution. The installation of the clear legal federal-regional distinction and the elimination of para-constitutional excesses are thus in principle entirely compatible with the encouragement of regional cooperation within the context of EU-Russian relations, as stipulated in the Russian Midterm Strategy.

New Sites of Regionalism: The Northwestern Federal District as a Subject in EU-Russian Relations?

Even though, as we have argued, the Putin presidency is not in itself antagonistic to federalism and regionalism, there arises the question of whether Putin's reforms have also introduced *new* sites of regionalism that may supplant the 'region', understood in the conventional sense of the 'subject of the Federation', as potential partners in EU-Russian cooperation.

Let us begin by noting that the discussion of Russian regionalisation has tended to obscure the fact that during the 1990s the regions not only appropriated excessive authority at the expense of the federal centre, but also dominated the space of local government. Meanwhile, the value of regionalism in European discourse is located precisely in the local, bottom-up or grassroots character of regional politics. These features are of course difficult to conceive of in Russian 'regions' such as Krasnoyarsk *krai*, the territory of which exceeds that of the entire Western Europe. On the other hand, such objectives of regionalisation as an innovative response to the 'challenge of globalisation' are severely disabled by the existence of autonomous development strategies of 89 Russian regions, whose relations with each other may frequently be substantively weaker than with their outside partners. The automatic focus in the discourse of regionalisation on the subject of the federation as the 'middle' level of authority in Russia obscures what appears to be evident: the subject of the federation as the product of the Soviet ATD is *an increasingly unfit unit for regionalisation* and an obstacle to the development of more innovative forms of regional cooperation. Rather than hindering international regional cooperation, Putin's policy of containing and constraining the power of regional governments, actually opens *new* possibilities for EU-Russian relations.

Of particular interest in this regard is the problematic of *macro-regionalism*, which entered political discourse with the establishment of the federal districts.

During Putin's first presidential term, the Northwestern Federal District (NWFD) was particularly active in promoting a macro-regional identity, divorced from the regional delimitation of political space. This activity was concretely exemplified by the formation of the Northwestern department of the Strategic Designs Centre (SDC), a major expert institution, in which the federal government's programme of socio-economic reforms (the 'Gref Programme') was originally designed. In 2001-2002 the SDC 'North-West', led by the Muscovite cultural philosopher Petr Shedrovitsky, prepared the Doctrine for the Development of Northwest Russia, which seeks to supplement, if not override, the development strategies of individual regions.[8] The Doctrine proceeds by problematising the *deficit of strategic thinking* on the macro-regional level that has resulted in Russia's failure to successfully adapt to the new international environment. The second point of departure in the SDC's discourse is the sharp problematisation of the existing administrative-territorial division of Russia, which has led to the relative autonomy of the strategic development plans of the subjects of the Federation and the consequent *fragmentation of the macro-regional space of strategic planning*. A potentially important function of Federal Districts may therefore be the development of macro-regional integration *within* Russia, which of course need not be viewed as exclusive of regional cooperation with the EU.

The solution envisioned by the Doctrine consists in a 'new assembly' of the Northwest tied into a macro-regional project based on the institutional structure of the Federal District. The Doctrine explicitly problematises the formation of a new kind of *political subjectivity* on the macro-regional level. The Centre thus presents itself as a new site for the coordination of the activities of various subjects of development in the macro-region, 'offering a common language' for addressing the problematic of reform on a new level. However, this move must not be interpreted in terms of a facile understanding of the slogan of the 'unitary vertical of power'. What is problematised in the SDC discourse is rather the introduction of new *horizontal technologies of governance*, 'the system of strategic interaction', between the regional authorities as well as between regions and other actors in the area, including business corporations and civil society actors (see Shedrovitsky et al., 2001). The SDC also presents itself as not merely an organising structure for improved inter-regional interaction, but as a locus of 'discursive innovations' that may rupture the depoliticised consensus in regional politics and offer a more ambitious political vision for the Northwest.

Even in its terminology, novel and unusual in Russian regional political discourse, the Doctrine corresponds more to 'postmodern', network-based European regionalisation projects than narrow, problem-solving or 'survival-oriented' strategies of particular regions that lack in innovative potential and render the regions in question passive objects of external policies. Moreover, the 'mega-projects' proposed by SDC-NW for the Northwestern macro-region accord with

---

[8] The discussion below draws on my more detailed analysis of the discourse of SDC 'Northwest' in Prozorov (2004c).

EU interests in the area, particularly in their focus on human resource development, multicultural communications and innovational development (see Prozorov, 2004c). Yet, what is conspicuous by its absence in the text is any reference to the 'promotion of democracy' that the EU has increasingly prioritised in its relations with Russia. Integration with Europe is similarly not advanced in terms of Russia's *unilateral* adoption of EU practices in political, socio-economic or cultural spheres. Instead, there is an emphasis on joint *inter-subjective* efforts by Russia and the EU in the Northwestern space (Perelygin et al., 2001).

> The most significant among these fundamental [EU-Russian] disagreements, which entail frustration in many practical aspects of cooperation, is the difference between Russia's self-evaluation and the image of Russia widespread among the EU officials. *The European Union regards Russia primarily as an object of policy, not as a subject* (Kaveshnikov and Potemkina, 2003; see also Cronberg, 2003a, pp.286-7).

We may therefore suggest that the obstacles to more ambitious efforts in regional cooperation between Russia and the EU do not consist in substantive policy divergences, but rather are grounded in the *problematisation of interactional asymmetry* and the demand for 'strategic intersubjectivity' in EU-Russian relations that would transcend the 'subject-object relationship' characteristic of the 1990s.

The interface of the SDC-NW programme with the Northern Dimension initiative would radically reorient EU-Russian regional cooperation away from largely tactical, problem-solving projects undertaken on EU terms and on the basis of the EU's interest in minimising so-called 'soft security' threats. This development would be a fundamental policy shift that abandons the facile dichotomy of 'regional autonomy' vs. 'federal control'. The Northwestern Federal District may then become the proper 'pilot project' for EU-Russian relations, instead of Kaliningrad, which as an exceptional case is not fit for the pilot status *by definition*, insofar as we take the concept of 'pilot' to refer to an experiment with potentially generalisable results (cf., Khudolei, 2003, p.27). Such a project, grounded in the interface of strategic visions, could endow with concrete content the principles of 'complementarity, subsidiarity and synergy' proclaimed in the Second Northern Dimension Action Plan, and substantialise the long-term project of cooperation that has been stipulated in the EU initiative of the 'Wider Europe'.

However, just as we have discussed above with reference to the case of Kaliningrad, the potential for EU-Russian cooperation in the Northwestern region ultimately depends on the degree to which the EU is able to accommodate the exception (which is an integral element of the Russian politics of emergence), rather than merely insist on the unamendability of its rules or attempt to extend their application to the territory of the 'neighbourhood' of the enlarged Union. As the prospect of Russia's EU membership is increasingly perceived, even by liberal political forces, as substantively unattractive (Baunov, 2003; Chubais, 2003), and as Russia's foreign policy becomes more assertive due to the political consolidation in Putin's presidency, it appears unrealistic to anticipate that Russia will embark on a course of unilaterally approximating its legislation and practices with those of the EU *acquis communautaire*. On the other hand, the very overcoming of the protracted crisis of the 1990s enhances the potential for EU-Russian cooperation to be something more than 'crisis management' or a 'firefighting' *response* to 'new security threats'. Thus, the innovative potential of EU-Russian regional cooperation appears to depend on the EU's willingness to recognise Russia as a *sovereign subject* rather than a passive object of the implementation of a Common Strategy, and hence accept the legitimacy of Russia's *taking exception* from the constitutive normative principles operative within the EU.

In short, it appears necessary to move beyond the dichotomies of inclusion/exclusion and self/other in the assessment of EU-Russian relations. As a state with a newly gained appreciation of sovereignty Russia appears not merely as an object of 'exclusion' from EU space, but as an active subject of 'self-exclusion' keen to retain its freedom of manoeuvre in domestic reforms and foreign policy. Both normatively and institutionally, Russia is thus likely to remain the 'outside' or the 'other' of the EU, and in the case of Kaliningrad, as the other within. However, it is hardly warranted to infer from political and institutional *divergences* between Russia and the EU that a dubious 'cultural', let alone 'civilisational' *difference* exists. The potential for EU-Russian cooperation may rather be enhanced by the recognition of 'the other' as a legitimate political subject, endowed with its interests that need not automatically be aligned with EU values or principles, but which might offer productive sites of EU-Russian interface. Ironically, the affirmation of the need for such recognition of *legitimate difference* entails a clear return to the pluralistic political ontology of classical realism (Schmitt, 1976, 1985), which is allegedly outdated and discredited in the discourses of postmodernity and globalisation. Such a return need not take the shape of facile state-centrism, but rather relates to the problematic of managing the space of EU-Russian relations as a *pluriverse of intersubjectivity* rather than a *universe of values*, i.e., a space of properly *international* relations.

References

Aleksandrov, Oleg (2001), *The Role of the Republic of Karelia in Russia's Foreign and Security Policy*, Working Paper no. 5, Eidgenössische Technische Hochschule Zurich.

Baunov, Alexander (2003), 'Kak Voiti v Evropu. Chast' Pervaja: Put', Zakryty dlya Rossii', *Grazhdanskie Debaty*. Available at http://www.globalrus.ru/opinions/134780/.

Bordachev, Timofei (2003), "Strategiya' i Strategii', in Arkady Moshes (ed.), *Rossiya i Evropeisky Soyuz: Pereosmyslivaja Strategiju Vzaimootnosheniy*, Moskva, Gendalf, pp. 79-114.

Bunin, Igor et al. (2001), 'Karnavala Ne Budet: Politicheskie Budni Bolshoi Reformy', *NG-Stsenarii*, No. 6 (62).

Campbell, David (1993), *Politics Without Principle: Sovereignty, Ethics and the Narratives of the Gulf War*, Boulder, Lynne Rienner.

Chubais, Anatoly (2003), 'Missiya Rossii v 21-m Veke', *Nezavisimaya Gazeta*, No. 209 (3041).

Cronberg, Tarja (2003), 'Euregio Karelia: In Search of a Relevant Space for Action', in Lars Hedegaard and Bjarne Lindström (eds.), *The NEBI Yearbook 2003: North European and Baltic Sea Integration*, Berlin, Springer, pp. 223-39.

Dean, Mitchell (1999), *Governmentality: Power and Rule in Modern Society*, London, Sage.

Doctrine of the Development of the Northwest of Russia, Tsentr Strategicheskih Razrabotok 'Severo-Zapad', Sankt-Peterburg. Available at http://www.csr-nw.ru.

Fairlie, Lyndelle D. and Sergounin, Alexander (2001), *Are Borders Barriers? EU Enlargement and the Russian Region of Kaliningrad*, Helsinki, Ulkopoliittinen Instituutti and Institut fur Europäische Politik.

Foucault, Michel (1990), *History of Sexuality. Volume One: An Introduction*, Harmondsworth, Penguin.

Foucault, Michel (1991), 'Governmentality', in Burchell, Graham et al. (eds.), *The Foucault Effect: Studies in Governmentality*, London, Harvester Wheatsheaf, pp. 87-104.

Gaidar, Yegor (2001), 'Revolutsiya Ostalas' v 20-m Veke; Reformy Prodolzhayutsa v 21-m', *Izvestia*, No. 6 (25844).

Hall, John (ed.), *Civil Society: Theory, History, Comparison*, Cambridge, Cambridge University Press.

Haukkala, Hiski (2001), *Two Reluctant Regionalisers? The European Union and Russia in Europe's North*, Working Paper no. 32, Helsinki, Finnish Institute of International Affairs.

Haukkala, Hiski (2003), 'Polozhitelnye Aspecty Realizatsii Obshey Strategii ES po Rossii', in Arkady Moshes (ed.), *Rossiya i Evropeisky Soyuz: Pereosmyslivaja Strategiju Vzaimootnosheniy*, Moskva, Gendalf, pp. 35-78.

Hyde, Matthew (2001), 'Putin's Federal Reforms and their Implications for Presidential Power in Russia', *Europe-Asia Studies*, Vol. 53(5), pp. 245-74.

Joenniemi, Pertti (2003), *The European Union and Border Conflicts: the EU's and Russia's North*, Paper presented at the CEEISA/ISA International Convention, Budapest, Hungary, June 26-28.

Kagansky, Vladimir (1995), 'Sovetskoye Prostranstvo: Konstruktsiya i Destruktsiya', in *Inoe: Antologia Novogo Rossijskogo Samosoznania*, Moskva, Argus, Available at http://www.russ.ru/antolog/inoe.

Kaveshnikov, Nikolai and Potemkina, Olga (2003), 'Rational Insight or Political Kitsch? Dividing Lines Existing or Imaginary, EU-Russia: Cooperation or...?' Paper presented at the Second RISA Convent 'Managing the Recreation of Divisions in Europe', Moscow.

Khudolei, Konstantin (2003), 'Otnoshenia Rossii i Evropejskogo Soyuza: Novye Vozmozhnosti, Novye Problemy', in Arkady Moshes (ed.), *Rossiya i Evropeisky Soyuz: Pereosmyslivaja Strategiju Vzaimootnosheniy*, Moskva, Gendalf, pp. 13-35.

Lefort, Claude (1988), *Democracy and Political Theory*, Cambridge, Polity Press.

Magun, Artemiy (2003), 'Opyt i Ponyatie Revolutsii', *Novoye Literaturnoje Obozrenie*, Vol. 64.

Makarychev, Andrei (2000), *Islands of Globalization: Regional Russia and the Outside World*, Working Paper no.2, Eidgenössische Technische Hochschule Zurich.

Makarychev, Andrei (2004), 'Adapting to the Power Vertical: The Experience of Nizhny Novgorod Oblast 2003', *Russian Expert Review*. Available at http://www.rusrev.org.

Mau, Vladimir and Starodubrovskaya, Irina (2001), *The Challenge of Revolution*, Oxford, Oxford University Press.

Nicholson, Martin (2001), 'Putin's Russia: Slowing the Pendulum Without Stopping the Clock', *International Affairs*, Vol. 77(3), pp. 867-84.

Perelygin, Yuri et al (2002), *Vstrecha s Zhurnalistami*. Available at http://www.csr-nw.ru/doings.php?code=44.

Prozorov, Sergei (2004a), 'Border Regions and the Politics of EU-Russian Relations: The Role of the EU in Tempering and Producing Border Conflicts', Copenhagen, Danish Institute of International Studies, *Working Paper Series in EU Border Conflict Studies*, no. 3. Available at http://www.euborderconf.bham.ac.uk.

Prozorov, Sergei (2004b), *Political Pedagogy of Technical Assistance: A Study in Historical Ontology of Russian Post-communism*, Tampere, Studia Politica Tamperensis.

Prozorov, Sergei (2004c), *The Russian Northwestern Federal District and the EU's Northern Dimension*, Working Paper No.4, Copenhagen, Danish Institute of International Studies. Available at http://www.diis.dk.

Putin, Vladimir (2000), *State of the Nation Address to the Federal Assembly*. Available at http://www.russiaeurope.mid.ru/RussiaEurope/speech6.html.

Rose, Nikolas (1996), 'Governing 'Advanced' Liberal Democracies', in Andrew Barry, Thomas Osborne and Nikolas Rose (eds.), *Foucault and Political Reason: Liberalism, Neoliberalism and Rationalities of Government*, London, UCL Press, pp. 37-64.

Russia's Midterm Strategy towards the EU. Available at http://www.eur.ru/eng/neweur/user_eng.php?func=rae_rae_common_strategy.

Sakwa, Richard (1999), *Russia's Crisis and Yeltsin's Leadership*, Gateway Papers Vol. 4, Tampere, International School of Social Sciences, University of Tampere.

Sakwa, Richard (2000), 'Crisis and Reconstitution of the State in Russia', in Helena Rytövuori-Apunen (ed.), *Russian-European Interfaces in the Northern Dimension of the European Union*, Tampere, Studia Politica Tamperensis, pp. 11-42.

Schmitt, Carl (1976), *The Concept of the Political*, New Brunswick, Rutgers University Press.

Schmitt, Carl (1985), *Political Theology: Four Chapters on the Concept of Sovereignty*, Cambridge, The MIT Press.

Shedrovitsky, Petr et al (2001), *Seminar 'Upravlenie Regionalnym Razvitiem'*. Available at http://www.csr-nw.ru/doings.php?code=39.

Smirnyagin, Leonid (2001), *Federalizm po Putinu, ili Putin po Federalizmu: Zheleznoj Pyatoj?* Briefings Vol. 3(3), Moscow, Moscow Carnegie Centre.

Tompson, William (2002), 'Putin's Challenge: The Politics of Structural Reform in Russia', *Europe-Asia Studies*, Vol. 54(6), pp. 933-57.

Ulykaev, Aleksei (1999), *Pravyi Povorot*, Polit.Ru:. Available at http://www.polit.ru/documents/147910.html.

Volkov, Vadim (1999), 'Violent Entrepreneurship in Post-Communist Russia', *Europe-Asia Studies*, Vol. 51(5), pp. 741-54.

Zudin, Alexei (2003), *Putin: Itogi Pervogo Sroka*. Available at http://www.politcom.ru.

PART IV

FUTURE MOTORS OF REGIONAL COOPERATION

Chapter 9

Accounting for the Role of Cities in Regional Cooperation: The Case of Europe's North

Pertti Joenniemi

Cities as an Inroad

Is there any advantage – theoretically as well as in practice – in viewing the Baltic Sea region and Europe's North more generally from the perspective of cities? Are there any reasons to explore cities as a rather interesting set of actors, despite their limited size and resources and, more particularly, do they have any potential left that could be of value at the current juncture after the dual enlargements of NATO and the EU?

The argument advanced here is that this is very much the case. In recent years cities, as civil society-oriented actors, have offered important inroads and some potential is arguably still there that may be distilled through a critical probing of some of the departures that bolstered and underpinned what might be called the first wave of regionalisation during the immediate post-Cold War years.

The reasons for embarking upon such an endeavour are twofold. First, there appears to be a need for fresh departures as region-building has recently showed some signs of stalling. It seems that the rather rapid and perhaps somewhat unexpected transformation process of the last decade has come to a halt. It was unexpected to start with, as during the Cold War years Northern Europe stood out as a rather strictly delineated and bordered political landscape. It was almost exclusively premised on statist departures and the only features of de-bordering and region-building consisted of the tight and inward-oriented Nordic cooperation.

However, this changed quickly in the aftermath of the Cold War with Northern Europe rapidly turning into one of the most regionalised parts of Europe. A rich patchwork of various border-crossing and border-transcending endeavours – with cities as one of the elements breaking actively out of their previous confinement – emerged. In fact, Europe's North developed into a laboratory of innovative ways of dealing with the divisive nature of borders and exclusionary politics (Hedegaard and Lindström, 2002). Two scholars, Helmut Hubel and Stefan Gänzle (2001, p.5), have emphasised the 'open-ended' character of region-building in the Baltic Sea area. They have noted that the policies pursued in the region increasingly rely on informal contacts, flexible networks, and private rather than public actors. Overall, they conclude that a 'third space' – one of continuous motion (i.e., based on flow rather than location) – is no longer just a theoretical notion or a mere vision. This is to say that there has not merely been a discourse present providing perspectives for change and a different way of organising political space; instead, quite concrete steps have also been taken to implement at least some of the visions.

It has to be added, however, that the constitutive debates have remained predominantly anchored in the past. For many of the actors in the region – including the Baltic States, Poland and Finland – the end of the Cold War did not signify the end of the East-West divide. It was rather comprehended as presenting a new context within which one's position might be shifted further to the West. Thus, despite rhetorical efforts of overcoming the Cold War divide, the deeper discursive structures retained the East-West schism as a foundational basis. Security remained, it appears, a core argument. In this context, region-building was largely comprehended as a way of achieving security, rather than security being something to be left behind. Whilst dominant conceptions changed, to some extent, from an emphasis on 'hard' to 'soft' security, security nonetheless stood out as a crucial anchoring point bolstering the endeavours of region-building.

The more recently proclaimed 'endism', a feature seen as being entailed in the dual enlargement of the EU and NATO, might thus stand out as a profound challenge for the departures that have largely underpinned region-building in Europe's North. Whilst there is not much left of the East, security also appears to be on its way towards losing salience as a constitutive argument. Instead, debates appear to be increasingly focused on issues such as how to gain centrality and prominence in the process of Europe-making and how to avoid being pushed into the periphery in terms of power and influence.

The question posed here is thus whether the demise of security will play into the hands of actors such as cities. Can they capitalise on it or will they instead suffer from the stagnation of an argument that has previously been quite conducive to region-building? Would there be any advantage in increasingly using the lens provided by the region's cities, one that pays relatively little attention to the East-West distinction and leaves aside any heavy focus on security – at least when compared to the emphasis customarily placed on security by states – in outlining the current dynamics of political space in Europe's North? It might be argued, in this latter regard, that the singling out of cities carries with it a certain emancipatory impact, one applicable also at the current juncture, a period which presents somewhat different challenges than the immediate post-Cold War period. Precisely because of their non-state character, and in being devoid of much of the baggage usually associated with state-centred approaches, cities arguably offer an horizon of expectations and possibilities now called for in Northern Europe. Whilst such a perspective entails theoretical and conceptual challenges, it can also be comprehended as pointing to some concrete challenges of a rather practical nature.

It should be noted that there is, as such, no categorical lack of studies using cities as an inroad into networking and region-building. As a matter of fact, the theme has been covered reasonably well and some of the analysis that has been done is even based on efforts of drawing upon a conceptual and theoretical frame. However, in essence, it seems that the issues at stake have remained in some sense under-theorised in that they have left potential openings still to be explored, or – to put it differently – the theoretical departures used have remained too attached to ordinary statist and sovereignty-related theories. In some cases this is done rather openly, whereas in other analyses the reproduction and reinforcing of statism takes place more unwittingly. Arguably, such approaches are not sufficiently 'post-sovereign' and detached from various state-related concerns in order to offer the insight required.

Hence, the second task to be pursued here consists of an effort of reviewing some of the theoretical and conceptual literature that has been produced in recent years in discourses pertaining to the role of cities in Europe's North. This is done so that alternative avenues can be explored, thereby leaving space for the conclusion to address some of the more profound theory-related issues unavoidably stirred up by such an endeavour.

Reaching Across Borders

The increasing networking of cities has stood out as one important indication of the crumbling of previous walls. Actually, already since the 1970s individual cities, along with other subnational as well as transnational regional players, have made their mark also in the international sphere. Their specific strength lies in being *avant garde*, i.e., in what is dynamic, flexible, participation-oriented, and not in structures, institutional machineries, enforcement mechanisms, regulation and control. By reaching across state borders and transcending traditional hierarchies, these actors have established themselves as players in international relations. They no longer seem to reside, as before, merely in their local and marginal roles, leaving 'high politics' for state authorities to handle. On the contrary, 'low' politics increasingly seems to penetrate the sphere of 'high' politics, and consequently a number of situations now seem to empower authorities of various urban centres to deal with international relations as well. This is to say that the political space relevant for international relations is no longer confined to state territory. To put it differently, a certain de-territorialisation of political space seems to have occurred (cf., Sassen, 1991; Hobbs, 1994; Dunford and Kaflakas, 1992) as an 'urban logic' has made itself increasingly felt, both discursively as well as in practice.

The trend towards the increased involvement of cities in external affairs shows every indication of continuing and, indeed, accelerating. Cities, for example, have organised themselves into various networks of Leagues of Cities, Capital Cities, Harbour Cities, Sister Cities and trading groups. In general the globalisation of economic relations, revolutions in communications and transportation, as well as the demise of the Cold War, has greatly eroded the monopoly of national governments over foreign policy. John Friedman uses the phrase 'world cities' in reflecting upon the new linkages that have emerged. He argues that some cities have escaped the constraints imposed by the nation-states as they articulate regional, national and international economics into a global economy. Not least, he points out that such cities serve as organising nodes of a global economic system (Friedman, 1993). If organised into a hierarchy, the top cities consist of New York, London and Tokyo, which function as command centres of the global economy. Others, like Singapore and Miami, have a commanding multinational role.

The erosion of a number of established borderlines also implies that the domestic sphere is no longer as clearly separated from the foreign as it used to be. In a similar vein, special interests appear to be competing rather successfully with more general ones. The recent talk about 'bi-national' or cross-border cities testifies to this trend, even if among the opponents to such claims Ehlers (2001), for example, argues that these concepts remain visions rather than something firmly established and grounded. However, in Northern Europe some cases would seem to substantiate the usage of such concepts: Tornio and Haparanda being a case in point due to their far-reaching integration across the Finnish-Swedish border (see, Ronkainen and Westman, 1999).

Overall, there is a persistent view that crucial changes are underway. For example, Young and Morris (1990) claim that there are features evident of a revival and re-emergence of cities as actors and loci of political decision-making. In other words, they do not aspire to set up cities as an innocent and non-political set of actors dealing basically with functional matters. In their view, there has been a disruption of static spatial categories between centre and periphery, as well as between high and low politics, which in turn is opening up space for critical engagement. Cities are seen as endowed with competence to utilise such a situation and impact on the unfolding of political space for functional, but also for moral or identity-related reasons.

If traced back, it appears that the rise of cities started some time towards the end of the 1940s in the form of 'twinning'. This is to say that the departure was explicitly ideological in being furnished with the explicit aim of establishing positive relations to achieve reconciliation across previously troubled borders (cf., Széll, 1998). Initially 'twinning' stood out as a largely state-driven enterprise, but more recently this appears to have changed with cities acting increasingly on their own initiative. Moreover, town-to-town relations are not only restricted to the spheres of the symbolic – for example, exchanging flags or naming streets on the basis of friendship – or cultural relations, as has been the case with what Detlef Weigel (1998, p.47) has called the 'first generation partnerships'. Instead, they increasingly pertain to various functional motivations, above all those related to competitive vitality and economic growth. Today, and particularly in the European context, partners are predominantly searched for to link up to transnational networks in order to remain on the cutting edge, and not behind, in global competition. The relations established serve as conduits for the transfer of knowledge, thereby stimulating innovation in the sphere of technology, whilst they also serve as a catalyst for further cooperation, or may be useful in the context of enhancing one's voice in the context of lobbying for European resources. As argued by Sari Söderlund (1998, p.74), national integration has been increasingly replaced by supranational forces and mechanisms. Söderlund locates the origins of change basically with the states and claims that this is also strongly felt in the case of cities: 'Thus the individual locality depends increasingly on its international relations rather than on its place in the national urban system. Urban governments can no longer count on locational advantages in the national system or national politics to protect them from market forces'. They are thus compelled, for reasons of subjectivity, to rethink and expand their political horizons beyond the traditional national setting.

If reflected upon from this perspective, it appears that twinning, in many cases, initially developed as a kind of door-opener. This is to say that it has been easier and appeared more 'innocent' to establish reconciliatory relations between local actors than to come together on the politically loaded state level, even if state interests have nonetheless been of decisive influence. However, in the longer run town-to-town relations seem to have assumed a more independent and pragmatic character. Hence, cities no longer need some general 'excuse' for going international as the agendas now pertain to trade, industrial projects, travel, cultural contacts, student exchanges, immigration, border-related issues and other such items of an instrumental, moral or identity-related character. Indeed, nowadays simple self-interest is taken to be important enough for cities to gain subjectivity in the sphere of international relations. Moreover, what initially consisted of bilateral relations and was conditioned by geographic as well as cultural proximity has over time turned into a rather diverse and dense network of multilateral relations (cf., Batten, 1995).

With the urban conglomerations no longer sticking to their traditional roles and with the city halls looking abroad, there is a growing linkage between local politics and the broader international sphere. This, no doubt, contrasts with the customary way of conceptualising foreign policy and international relations. Statist formations are no longer privileged to quite the extent they have been traditionally. The primacy of statist policies, statist spatialisations and the understanding of state boundaries as the ultimate demarcations of societies, community and political life have been increasingly challenged. The appearance of new actors and forces on the scene – cities being one of these – tends to de-centre many of the traditional state-centred discourses on territorially fixed sovereignty as the key constitutive principle underlying international relations. Such a trend involves aspects of de-regulation and in some cases perhaps even mutiny against established hierarchies that amount to an emphasis on translocalism rather than international cooperation in the traditional, state-centred meaning of the word.

Notably, cities today take themselves more seriously in this sphere than they did only some years back. In particular, the periods of stagnation in national economies during the 1990s seem to have driven home the lesson that states are on occasions unable to offer remedies to their economic and social problems. In being compelled to take responsibility for their strategic development, cities have thus begun to search for links that might be conducive to their future development and in doing so turn increasingly, it seems, into actors in their own right.

This is to say that in addition to various 'pull factors' related to a number of access points that now allow for and invite cities to go international, there are also 'push factors' related to the declining tendency of states to engage in interventionist policies domestically. This has been discernible particularly on the European scene with states, on the one hand, increasingly going international and, on the other hand, leaving more domestic tasks to sub-state actors such as cities. In the relative vacuum created, major cities and urban centres tend to find themselves more or less on their own. Therefore, whilst there are undoubtedly features of the centralisation of power in the new Europe, the other side of the coin consists of the decentralisation of political space. These changes might be rather profound in the sense that they pertain to the underpinning constitutive principles. Whilst during the modern era sovereignty has been the primary and self-evident constitutive principle of European politics, room might have opened up for regionality to also impact on the unfolding of political space. If so, it also plays into the hands of actors such as cities. In any case, there is simultaneously a push and a pull present in the sense that there appears to be both the freedom as well as the need for cities to act.

Trends in Europe's North

These trends are also present in Northern Europe, and they appear to be particularly relevant in the case of the Baltic Rim. The twinning of cities has been a part of the Nordic scene already since the 1950s. Such policies also had a certain role to play in Northern Europe across the East-West divide during the Cold War, whereas the networking of cities on a larger scale is basically a post-Cold War phenomenon. If measured in empirical terms, it may be noted that the increased prominence of cities resembles a pattern that has been discernible in other parts of Europe as well (Groth, 2001; Johansson and Stålvant, 1998; Kanninen and Schulman, 2000; Söderlund, 1998; Vartiainen, 1998), although the north European experience seems to have gone particularly far in terms of city-networking. One example of this is that already in 1991 the cities of the Baltic Sea region established the Union of Baltic Cities (UBC) as a joint organisation covering the region as a whole.

In the immediate aftermath of the end of the Cold War Northern Europe's cities clearly stood out as a considerable discursive resource. For example, various forms of region-formation have often been justified and brought into view by referring to the legacy of the Hanseatic League of the mercantilist period. In this perspective, the growing importance of the region's cities could be seen in terms of the re-enactment of an old drama, in which the region's cities would be understood to be actors of key political importance (and not merely seen as non-political or semi-political in essence, as they are usually depicted). From such a perspective the cities could have been seen as core constituent actors within a system void of states and with regionality high on the agenda. In other words, the story could hence have been comprehended as not merely pertaining to the revival of cities, but as one premised more broadly on the re-emergence of regionality as a key constitutive principle. Within such a setting cities could consequently be thematised, not only as alternative actors to states in the regional context, but as such providing an insight into a different, far less state-based system as to the configuring of political space at large.

It appears, however, that this is not the way the stories pertaining to the Hanseatic League have actually been told. Instead, the stress has been confined to focusing on the increasing subjectivity of the cities. This is to say that the new constitutive stories have not been taken very far. Regionality might have re-appeared in the cracks of the pavements of sovereignty, but without ever directly challenging it. Thus, the Hanseatic stories have merely stood out as hints and a reminder of the fact that Northern Europe at some previous juncture was host to a rather peaceful period characterised by less border-drawing, more interaction, and a period in which there was much space for various non-statist actors to be engaged, all of which catapulted Northern Europe into prosperity and considerable prominence on the European scene. In all, the narrative has not been brought to the fore as an oppositional one, but has rather been utilised in the more recent discourses as a somewhat vague vision pointing to the fact that political space could, in principle, be constructed differently.

It may also be noted, in this perspective, that the problems with the usage of the story, as a rule, have not had their background in fears about being exposed to an overdose of regionality. Instead, the concern has resided in worries about the possible eventual return of German dominance in the region, and the somewhat related concern that in the end the Hanseatic League gained a formidable military dimension. After all, during its final stages it was far from an harmonious and peaceful solution. Taken together, the story has showed itself to be too biased in order for it really to have a chance of unifying the region as a whole. Obviously, as the principal challenges inherent in the Hanseatic narrative have shown themselves to be somewhat problematic, it has been more convenient to place one's trust in the potency of the cities as such, without resorting to the help possibly provided by an historical legacy.

The theme of cities as an important inroad has thus been strongly present in post-Cold War discourse, and this has been the case particularly in the spheres of spatial planning and urban and regional studies, i.e., studies which tend to have a rather strong empirical and functional orientation. It has hence been possible to address the actorness of the cities in a very factual manner, to comprehend it as a rather natural theme and to do this without raising any broader, system-related issues. One reason underpinning the somewhat narrow focus on cities might also have consisted of the wish to avoid stories like those told, for example, in the context of Catalonia where regionalism is linked to a local kind of nationalism. These connotations have been absent and deliberately avoided in Europe's North as nationalism has been rather categorically tied to the state.

The attitude towards cities coalescing has thus remained rather favourable. They have been expected to take stock of the openness evident in the post-Cold War political landscape, albeit to do so in tandem with various statist efforts of regionalisation and cross-border cooperation. However, if seen as breaking beyond the existing barriers and developing into something novel in terms of being unbounded, non-centred and supra-territorial in a too radical manner, voices of caution – if not outright critique – have tended to quickly emerge (cf. Vesa, 1998) and in ways that display clear statist predispositions. Such attitudes have, for example, hampered the development of the Öresund region (with Copenhagen, Malmö, Helsingborg and Helsingør as key participants) with the relevant states (Denmark and Sweden) being rather slow in harmonising their respective legislation in ways that would enable the region to push further. Similarly, Russia has discouraged the Kaliningrad region from too actively plugging into various euro-regions and other similar arrangements that have been set up with the participation of local actors in Lithuania and Poland.

One of the new joint pan-Baltic processes in the sphere of urban planning has been the 'Visions and Strategies around the Baltic Sea 2010' (VASAB 2010) project. The project has been undertaken by the region's planning ministries. Cities and urban networks have, in that context, been seen as one of the basic departures essential for the overall regional configuration. However, this favouring of cities and urban networks notwithstanding, the project itself has remained basically on the level of states. It has remained statist rather than developing into an inter-urban endeavour between actors such as the cities of the region, this testifying to the existence of a constant contest and the efforts of the states to preserve their unchallenged pre-eminence.

It may be observed, however, that cities have more recently tended to form the functional core of region-building in Northern Europe, although some obstacles to further progress remain to be tackled. One of these consists of a certain imbalance among the cities themselves in the sense that in the case of the Nordic and the Baltic countries relevant cities tend to lie at the national core, whereas in the case of the other countries of the region they have a rather more peripheral location in the national context. Vartiainen (2001, p.123) describes this latter aspect by talking about cities that constitute 'an antithesis to the national core areas and capitals'. In other words, they are kept at some distance from the core. In the German, Polish and Russian cases a genuine orientation towards the North should be based, he remarks, 'on local and regional empowerment'.

Stating it somewhat differently, there seems to be a significant difference between the south-eastern and the north-western parts of the Baltic Rim. Cooperation, until recent years, has mostly consisted of the latter assisting the former, for example in the fields of social and environmental policies. In essence, cooperation has basically boiled down to an unequal exchange and one-way street in terms of communication. There has, in other words, been a lack of a genuine partnership among the cities taking part with the less developed ones detracting from the possibilities of Northern Europe being able to compete forcefully on the all-European scene. In their own environment the cities that are part of the north-western sphere of the region have, above all, been reacting to a crisis of the welfare state and/or their respective states going increasingly international, while at the same time assisting cities in the south-eastern parts of the region in coping with the various socio-economic and administrative challenges posed by the post-communist era.

It may also be noted that as to the former, the most densely populated and economically more powerful areas are located in the deeper hinterland (in Germany, Poland and Lithuania), whereas the most populated areas of the Nordic countries, Estonia, Latvia and the Russian part of the region are located in the coastal areas. In consequence, major cities are in one part of the Baltic Sea area located in the hinterlands (e.g., Berlin, Warsaw, Krakow, and Katowice), while they are concentrated along the Baltic coastline in the Nordic/Northern part of the area (Stockholm, Helsinki, St. Petersburg and Tallinn). No doubt, the coastal cities are in a somewhat better position to take stock of the option of cooperation in the Baltic Sea region, although one may observe that there is also considerable competition among the coastal cities. One example here is whether the dynamic centre of the Baltic Rim should be seen as formed by the Copenhagen-Malmö-Gothenburg region, or if it is to be found closer to Helsinki, Tallinn, Vilnius, Stockholm and St. Petersburg. The latter grouping is cooperating through a joint endeavour called the Baltic Palette, whereas the former is pulling its forces together in the context of the Öresund project. The cities in the more Northern parts of the region have, for their part, activated themselves mainly through the Bothnian Arc, a formation consisting chiefly of the Finnish town of Oulu and the Swedish town of Luleå. The Swedish town of Haparanda and the Finnish town of Tornio have, as mentioned above, also become known for their far-reaching cooperation across the national borders, including the establishment of some common institutions providing joint communal services (*BBC Online*, 2002). Their true cross-border character – one that also pertains to their self-understanding – has been evidenced by a proposal to organise joint municipal elections, though this suggestion has proved to be too much for the respective statist authorities in Finland and Sweden to digest.

Another variation in the overall constellation relates to the latitude provided by the respective states to their cities in terms of freedom of action. Germany, being a federation, appears to be the most liberal in this regard (with the cities of Hamburg and Bremen in a category of their own in having the status of *Länder*), whereas the political institutions of the Nordic countries are far more centralised, and with Poland and the Baltic countries somewhere in between. However, in the case of the Baltic countries the stress has tended to be on the development of a national identity, with this process often being contrasted with the unfolding of a local and regional identity and thereby curtailing the options available to the cities. Russia has, for its part, displayed a trend of its own in the sense that during the years of President Yeltsin there was – at least occasionally – considerable leeway for regional and local actors to pursue policies of their own. With President Putin at the helm a more centralised approach to governance has emerged. However, alongside an emphasis on the consolidation of Russia at the federal level, under Putin there has also been a certain preparedness to consider various border-breaking policies at the regional and local levels. The 300th anniversary of St. Petersburg in 2003, which was organised and set up very much with the federal and the local authorities working in tandem, is a case in point. More recent signs, however, point to renewed efforts of tightening the centralising tendencies with less room for local initiatives being provided.

A general theme that describes well much of the recent discourse and which is valid for Europe's North more generally, appears to be that over the years much progress has been made, although more could have been wished for particularly if viewed against the hopes expressed towards the end of the 1980s and early-1990s. Although there has been much that divides, there is also a civil society tradition in Northern Europe (albeit one that followed somewhat different paths in the Northern and Eastern parts of the region) that may now be re-activated (cf., Götz and Hackmann, 2003, p.5). Overall, over the years developing relations have reached far beyond a 'getting-acquainted-with-each-other' phase and in terms of regionalisation cities and major urban areas form, in many cases, its true core. Gradually some inter-institutional interaction and synergy has emerged allowing one to speak of a localised and networked institutional thickness (Vartiainen, 2001, p.127). The Öresund region between Copenhagen and Malmö exemplifies this general story quite well in the sense that initially there were high hopes, these were then followed by a process of implementation that gradually generated pessimism and perhaps even disappointment, for the process finally to take off albeit with a slower speed than originally expected (cf., Matthiessen, 2004). The motors of the project have largely consisted of the cities of the region. They have been the driving forces while the two states of the area, Denmark and Sweden, have mainly been allotted with the task of keeping up the pace in the sphere of harmonising legislation in order that the project will not stall. In this sense, the two Nordic states have been under pressure to deliver in order not to be blamed for undermining the prospects of progress within the project.

Issues Pertaining to Theory

In order to make normative sense of the city-oriented approach, a closer look into the theoretical frames and the conceptual departures applied in the various studies focusing on the role of cities in Northern Europe might be called for. The question is then whether frames and departures have emerged that enable the cities to make use of their full potential and what the use of such frames means more generally.

In most cases these studies appear to lack such properties. They tend to be void of theory in the sense that no particular theoretical frame is used. Intensified contacts between cities are just categorised as one indication of internationalisation, Europeanisation and the growth of transnational contacts. However, twinning seems to stand out as a deviation as the assumptions used in that context are clearly more normative in character and contain elements of theory. Cities are then treated and approached as civil society actors that hence offer an escape from a variety of aspects and approaches usually associated with statist policies. Cities are, in this context, purported to be 'bottom-up' types of actors; they are seen as pragmatic and are assumed to harbour a more accommodating attitude to conflicts than do states. Moreover, it is asserted that they 'do usually not claim to be superior to each other' (cf., Galtung, 1998, p.23). Along similar lines, it is also argued that they tend to tolerate plurality and do not ascribe to ordering relations between each other according to some strict and hierarchic principles. In other words, they are less rule-bound in their international conduct. Above all, cities are seen as being prone to enhancing peace. They do so – as argued by Christian Wellmann (1998, p.10) – in bringing about contacts, facilitating integration, working for depolarisation, advancing mutual understanding between people, aspiring for conflict prevention, being engaged in development aid and also due to assistance they provide in overcoming prejudices. Cities thus arguably contribute to peace, both in adding to contacts on a personal as well as city-level, and due to their functioning in various ways as structural impediments against war and violence.

Beate Wagner (1998) stands out, among the various analysts probing the policies of cities, as an author equipped with an explicit theory. She leans, more particularly, on the idea of pluralistic security communities originally developed by Karl W. Deutsch. The central explanation as to the allegedly peaceful effects brought about by town-to-town relations resides, in her view, in that these relations amount to a considerable number of independent transnational contacts. These influence, by bringing about increased plurality and a broader variety of voices, the overall relations between states. In her view, cities can be seen as being engaged in a kind of 'paradiplomacy' that takes issues beyond statist relations. In exploring the policies of twinning pursued by a number of German cities, Wagner basically argues that the relations established bring about added value. She claims that longstanding enmities may be overcome on a local level by sufficiently independent initiatives, which may then spread to have an impact on a wider sphere.

To be more precise, Wagner is not altogether alone in her stress on an interactionist approach and efforts of theorising, but her approach does seem to be the most elaborate and explicit in this regard. However, such thinking can arguably be pushed further. Whereas Wagner, in her application of the security community concept, primarily pays attention to the impact and the effects of the town-to-town contacts established, one could also explore the extent to which developing inter-city relations represent an inroad into an alternative discourse of international relations that escapes the usual confines of security-speak. Such an approach would work on the level of the discourse itself and would do so by making it possible to bypass and exclude from the agenda many of the concerns specific to states, and in particular issues pertaining to security. Cities would hence not try to assist or complement, or even circumvent, states in this sphere, but would instead focus on other things. They would operate on a different 'wave-length' and speak in a different 'code' compared to the statist discourse, thereby contributing to opening up spaces and channels of communication that are not linked to security in the first place. In doing so they would rather bolster the terrain of asecurity (on this term see, Wæver, 1997).

However, it may be noted that such a move should not be perceived as one of capitulation – as could be claimed on the basis of views premised on the idea that security is an omnipresent condition – nor should it be interpreted as ducking important issues. This is so as one mode of operation does not translate into the other. The move of avoiding the theme of security rather works in terms of a division of labour with states privileged in the security sphere and engaged in their mandatory security-speak, whereas cities focus on more mundane matters that are void of security-related concerns in the first place. In the context of this thinking, one should perhaps not talk about town-to-town relations as a form of 'paradiplomacy' (thereby too much buying into ordinary statist discourses to start with), or try to prove, by the usage of rather strongly security-geared departures such as the Deutschian one on security communities, that cities may – for one reason or another – contribute to bringing about peace and security. They may rather be seen as being important precisely because they focus on other things. Cities are doing politics in different keys, thereby leaving security-related talk aside. By pointing to an agenda of their own they provide discourses pertaining to the construction of political space with a different point of anchorage and further contribute by strengthening the various non-security-related discourses. In other words, their main contribution may reside in contributing to a framing of politics in a manner that by-passes security as a constitutive argument.

In the end, by using a different lens and inroad into regional matters, either the traditional statist security logic will prevail or it will be gradually undermined with security as an argument losing in credibility. The experience of the Nordic countries seems to testify that in fact the latter option may be the outcome. At some juncture, and as a result of bottom-up types of forces gaining considerable influence, the use of the security argument in relations between the Nordic countries lost its relevance. Consequently, intra-Nordic relations took a positive turn with an intra-Nordic war becoming seen as inconceivable.[1] In tapping into such a logic it could be argued that the networking of cities and their intense cooperation will have a similar impact. Whilst they are not contributing to security in any direct manner, and should perhaps not even endeavour to do so, the impact

---

[1]   For an account along these lines, see Joenniemi (2003).

of their coalescing is of considerable importance precisely in opening up perspectives that go beyond security.

Another, although related avenue is offered by the use of the concept of networking. The concept – as well as the more general theoretical notions underpinning it – goes some way in fulfilling the requirements of deconstruction and, in that context, downgrading statist concerns pertaining to security. In the first place, in the form developed by Manuel Castells (1993), a networking approach tends to be premised on the claim that there is a new spatial logic at work, one being determined by the pre-eminence of the 'space of flows' over the 'space of places'. The former concept refers to a system of exchange – of information, capital and power – that structures the basic processes of societies, economies and states among different localities. It is argued, in this context, that city networks are based on these flows. Depending on the quality of the flows, city networking complies either with a 'competitive logic' or a 'network logic' that tends to undermine much of the previous bordering and implies, among other things, that statist security-talk is downgraded if not entirely substituted with a focusing on 'risks' and various socio-economic issues.

In general the network-related theory appears to argue that the very framework that moulds spatial and temporal articulations might be undergoing radical change, and that the break might favour urban agglomerations. Some accounts refer to an urban logic determined by the pre-eminence of the 'space of flows', a concept that – in addition to a system of exchange – refers to the advanced, information-based technologies, over the space of places, i.e., terrestrial barriers. The argument is, more particularly, that various factors that do not have a spatial materiality have drastically grown in importance (with small entities being favoured if they are smart and well informed). Systems of speed and acceleration are collapsing time and space into new, simultaneous, non-geopolitical politics where barriers cannot be geographical in the old sense. It is argued that within such a system power becomes informational (although it might be better to speak of potency rather than power), and politics become 'cronopolitics', relating to the pace of exchange and depending upon the flexibility to be able to accommodate various challenges.

Obviously, this general move from place to flow highlights the importance of some sites and downplays others. Those who lack access to networked space, and control over its nodes, are disempowered while those who manage the new environment are privileged. It has been argued, among others by Castells (1993), that cities belong to the latter category.

Unsurprisingly, the network approach has spread in the sphere of research with considerable speed, and has done so particularly in the sphere of regional studies and spatial planning. However, it may be observed that the concept of networks is often employed in a somewhat flat manner by just singling out and mapping contacts, such as cross-border relations, without using the full force of the theory. This also appears to apply to those studies dealing with Northern Europe and the Baltic Sea area. On the one hand, the concept of networking has been employed in the region and contributes to a circumvention of much of the baggage originating with traditional state-centred approaches. It has thus had a liberating impact by making it possible to address relevant issues by reverting to a different 'code'. On the other hand, however, ideas pertaining to the declining importance of territorially devised national borders, and the emergence of a kind of immaterial territory in the form of networks, in which cities gain increased prominence, have to a large extent remained untested. Moreover, the broader implications of the theory relating to the unfolding of political space and the impact that may be entailed for the core categories of such space have remained at the sidelines. This appears to be the case also in Europe's North, despite the fact that over recent years the position of cities in the region has changed in a significant manner.

Concluding Remarks

Clearly, cities have stood out as an horizon of expectations in Northern Europe after the demise of the Cold War. They occupy a much more prominent place in contemporary political discourses than they had enjoyed previously. Moreover, they are seen as harbouring considerable potential through processes of networking. As such, the initial debate immediately after the Cold War carried with it relatively high hopes that cities would be a major spur in the context of region-building, as well as cross-border and trans-border activities. As noted, though, such hopes were soon scaled down, as the concrete realities that emerged were too slow in catching up with expectations. However, recently the mood has again turned more optimistic, among other reasons because a number of steps forward have been realised in cooperation between cities.

In the case of cities in Northern Europe divisive issues do not appear to pertain to questions of democracy (as in the context of debating civil societies in the purview of globalisation), but to security. Mostly security has stood out as a stumbling block as the very concept has been so strongly associated with states and statist activities. The debate has been rife with voices claiming that in the end only states can provide security, and if cities turn into too much of a novelty, they tend to endanger security, i.e., they interfere with what is to be viewed as an exclusive jurisdiction of states. The ordinary statist discourses appear, in this manner, to remain so strong that they pre-empt any thorough exploration of the potential that cities – as one category of civil society-related actors – might have in terms of emancipation and as an inroad into differently premised and constructed political spaces. If the boundaries between cities and states show signs of being in danger of getting blurred, then cities are quickly categorised as 'city-states', with the discourse turning into a re-enactment of historical themes ending in cities being pushed back into local and marginal roles. Cities are conceptualised as pre-political entities along the lines of the Hanseatic story and are consequently regarded as relics of the past rather than seen as representing some relevant future trends. As relics they are equated with entities that used to be on the scene prior to states conquering their current status as sovereign and prime political actors, an outcome to which cities were related either through subjugation or consent. The providing of cities with increased subjectivity of their own appears, in this perspective, to be a highly questionable direction.

All this seems to point to that there exists, in general, a conceptual interdependence making it, by and large, impossible to thematise cities in the context of international relations without always falling back on states and statist ideas. The conceptual boundaries and the specific ontological departures available pertaining to cities do not seem to be strong enough not to cave in once security-speak is brought into the picture. States belong to the category of master distinctions, which in conjunction with other concepts such as the nation condition the intelligibility of modern political life in the first place. As such, efforts of furnishing cities with a stronger and more autonomous position in that context are thus doomed to fail already for ontological reasons. Within such a context security can always be invoked as an argument to be turned against non-state actors, and the option of moving into a sphere of a-security by riding on cities remains a foreclosed alternative.

It therefore seems that leaning on cities alone will not suffice if they are to appear as a horizon of expectations in a more determined manner. However, help could be offered by the concept of globalisation, if this is comprehended as an autonomous process of transformation taking place both above and beneath (i.e., in the form of regionalisation) the level of states. As a transformation occurring at a system level, it affects the quality of the system, as well as impacting on states at the unit level. As outlined by Jens Bartelson (2003, p.117), globalisation is thus, by definition, a multidimensional process taking place *outside-in*. 'To the extent that this process involves states, it does so by turning them into reproductive circuits for those systemic processes and forces which ultimately alter their identity, as well as, eventually, the constitutive rules or organizing principles of the system in which they are situated.' By treating globalisation as a distinct field of knowledge and 'the global' as a distinct object of investigation, many of the ontological barriers also arresting cities and subordinating them to the logic of states are removed. As argued by Philip Cerny (1995, p.625), notions of sovereignty get relativised and the modern warfare/welfare state is being gradually replaced with a competitive and market-oriented state which ultimately will 'lose its structural primacy and autonomy as a unitary actor in the international system'. Notably, Zygmunt Bauman (1998, p.25) belongs to the same category of theorists exploring alternative avenues and he argues, for his part, that 'the dynamics of globalization have turned states into executors and plenipotentiaries of forces which they have no hope of controlling politically'. And finally, Saskia Sassen (1996, p.28) claims – spinning also along similar lines – that while sovereignty and territory remain key features of the international system, 'they have been reconstituted and partly displaced onto other arenas outside the state and outside the frame of nationalized territory'.

If these claims hold true, such transformative processes would provide the energy and the insight needed for a set of actors, among them cities, to break out of the modern and state-centred confines. They would be increasingly at liberty to pursue policies of their own and to do this without the security-argument almost automatically being turned against them. Pursuing such arguments would enable the opening of important questions in the context of exploring the role of cities and would displace, in that context, a number of rigidities that have so far seriously hampered the discourse waged.

References

Bartelson, Jens (2003), 'On the Redundancy of Civil Society', in Jan Hallenberg, Bertil Nygren and Alexandra Robertson (eds.), *Transitions. In Honour of Kjell Goldmann*, Stockholm University, Stockholm, pp. 111-22.

Batten, D. F. (1998), 'Network cities: Creative urban agglomerations for the 21st century', *Urban Studies*, Vol. 32(2), pp. 202-18.

Bauman, Zygmunt (1996), *Globalization. The Human Consequences*, Cambridge, Cambridge Polity Press.

BBC Online (2002), 'Finland and Sweden plan Eurocity', 8 July. Available at http://news.bbc.co.uk/1/hi/world/europe/2115938.stm.

Castells, Manuel (1993), 'European Cities, the Informational Society and the Global Economy', *Tijdschrift voor economische en sociale geografie*, Vol. 84(4), pp. 247-57.

Cerny, Philip (1995), 'Globalization and the Changing Logic of Collective Action', *International Organization*. Vol. 49(4), pp. 595-625.

Dunford, M. and Kaflakas, G. (eds.), (1992), *Cities and Regions in the New Europe. The Global-Local Interplay and Spatial Development Strategies*, London, Belhaven Press.

Ehlers, N. (2001), 'The Utopia of the Bi-national City', *GeoJournal*, Vol. 54(1), pp. 21-32.

Galtung, Johan (1998), 'Local Authorities and Peace Factors, Actors and Workers', in Christian Wellmann (ed.), *From Town to Town. Local Authorities as Transnational Actors*, Hamburg, Band 8. Lit Verlag, pp. 15-27.

Groth, Niels Boje (2001) (eds.), *Cities and Networking. Urban Systems and Urban Networking in the Baltic Sea Region*, Reports no. 8. Danish Centre for Forest, Landscape and Planning.

Götz, Norbert and Hackmann, Jörg (2003), 'Civil Socety in the Baltic Sea Region: Towards a Hybrid Theory', in Norbert Götz and Jörg Hackmann (eds.), *Civil Society in the Baltic Sea Region*, Aldershot, Ashgate, pp. 3-16.

Hedegaard, Lars and Lindström, Bjarne (2002), 'EU Enlargement and Integration in the NRBI Area', in Lars Hedegaard and Bjarne Lindström (eds.), *The NEBI Yearbook 2001/2002. The North European and Baltic Sea Integration*, Berlin, Springer Verlag, pp. 3-20.

Hobbs, Heidi, H. (1994), *The City Hall Goes Abroad. The Foreign Policy of Local Politics*, London, Sage Publications.

Hubel, Helmut and Gänzle, Stefan (2001), 'The Council of the Baltic States (CBSS) as the sub-regional organization for "soft security risk management" in the North-East of

Europe', *Report to the Presidency of the CBSS*, 18 May 21. Documents.27 Jan.2003. Available at http://www.cbss.st/documents/cbsspresidencies/9german7thecouncil/.

Joenniemi, Pertti (2004), 'A Deutschian Security Community? Nordic Peace Reframed', in Stefano Guzzini and Dietrich Jung (eds.), *Contemporary Security Analysis and Copenhagen Peace Research*, London and New York, Routledge, pp. 143-53.

Johansson, Torbjörn and Stålvant, Carl-Einar (1998), 'Twin City Relationships: A Code for Neighbourhood Co-operation in the Baltic Sea Area?', in Christian Wellmann (ed.), *From Town to Town. Local Authorities as Transnational Actors*, Hamburg, Band 8. Lit Verlag, pp. 141-71.

Kanninen, Vesa and Schulman, Harry (2000), *Cities as Hubs for Co-operation in the Baltic Sea Region. Urban Systems and Urban Networking in the Baltic Sea Region*, Reports no. 17, Danish Forest and Landscape Research Institute.

Matthiessen, Christian W. (2004), 'The Öresund Area: Pre- and post-bridge cross-border functional integration: the bi-national regional question', *GeoJournal*, forthcoming.

Ronkainen, R., and Westman, B. (1999), 'Tornio-Haparanda – A Unique Result of City Twinning', in *Vital North! Security, Democracy, Civil Society*, Calotte Academy and Finnish Academy for European Security, pp. 10-13.

Sassen, Saskia (1991), *The Global City: New York, London, Tokyo*, Princeton, Princeton University Press.

Sassen, Saskia (1996), *Losing Control? Sovereignty in the Age of Globalization*, New York, Columbia University Press.

Széll, György (1998), 'Development and Co-operation in Global Twinning', in Christian Wellmann (ed.), *From Town to Town. Local Authorities as Transnational Actors*, Hamburg, Band 8. Lit Verlag, pp. 61-68.

Söderlund, Sari (1998), 'Developing Networks in the Baltic Sea Economic Region: The Role of Cities in the Economic Development of the Baltic Sea Region', in Christian Wellmann (ed.), *From Town to Town. Local Authorities as Transnational Actors*, Hamburg, Band 8. Lit Verlag, pp. 69-83.

Young, I. and Morris, M. (1990), *Justice and Political Difference*, Princeton, Princeton University Press.

Vartiainen, Perttu (1998), 'Experience from Research on Urban Networking and Urban Systems in the Baltic Sea Region', in Jesper Manniche (ed.), *Searching and Researching the Baltic Sea Region*, Report 17, Research Centre of Bornholm, pp. 133-38.

Vartiainen, Perttu (2001), 'Urban Networking in the Balticd Sea Region. A Nordic View', in Heikki Eskelinen, Ilkka Liikanen and Jukka Oksa (eds.), *Curtains of Iron and Gold. Reconstructing Borders and Scales of Interaction*, Aldershot, Ashgate, pp. 117-30.

Vesa, Unto (1998), 'What is Old, What is New in the Transnational Contacts of Local Authorities? Some Notes on Recent Developments in the Baltic Sea Region', in Christian Wellmann (ed.), *From Town to Town. Local Authorities as Transnational Actors*, Hamburg, Band 8. Lit Verlag, pp. 51-68.

Wæver, Ole (1997), 'The Baltic Sea: A Region of Post-Modernity?', in Pertti Joenniemi (ed.), *Neo-nationalism or Regionality? The Restructuring of Political Space around the Baltic Rim*, Stockholm, Nordregio, pp. 293-342.

Wagner, Beate (1998), 'Twinnings – a Transnational Contribution to More International Security?', in Christian Wellmann (ed.), *From Town to Town. Local Authorities as Transnational Actors*, Hamburg, Band 8. Lit Verlag, pp. 37-44.

Weigel, Detlef (1998), 'Transnational Co-operation between Towns and Regions. A Foreign Policy Perspective', in Christian Wellmann (ed.), *From Town to Town. Local Authorities as Transnational Actors*, Hamburg, Band 8. Lit Verlag, pp. 45-49.

Wellmann, Christian (1990), 'Introduction', in Christian Wellmann (ed.), *From Town to Town. Local Authorities as Transnational Actors*, Hamburg, Band 8. Lit Verlag, pp. 9-12.

Chapter 10

The Paradiplomacy of St. Petersburg

Stanislav Tkachenko

Introduction

For the last twenty years, especially since the end of the Cold War, scholars from a variety of different disciplines and countries have been increasingly inclined to consider cities and regions as important actors in international relations, which partly form the phenomenon of globalisation. Large and successful cities can create positive images for their countries. By their character and reputation, therefore, cities are able to improve or to reduce the prestige of states and nations, and to attract or frighten off foreign investors and tourists. Impressive international projects in the service sector, ecology, education and science are being implemented at the city level in many countries. St. Petersburg, being the Northern capital of the Russian Federation, is one of the national leaders in the development of international links in Russia. The primary aim of this article is to describe and analyse the 'paradiplomacy' of St. Petersburg, which should be understood as the activities of public bodies and institutions of civil society oriented towards the development of international links and the integration of St. Petersburg into a system of cooperation of Northern European cities and regions.

According to one point of view prevalent in the academic literature, the rise of paradiplomacy, being a process closely interrelated with globalisation, is seen as undermining sovereign states and transforming them into an institution with still unclear characteristics (Kuzmin, 1999). A study of the history and present of St. Petersburg, however, makes it possible to draw another conclusion, where paradiplomacy on the part of Russian regions is actually a part of modernisation processes in these regions. On the one hand, the growth in paradiplomacy is opening regional economies to the world market and in doing so improves democratic institutions in Russia. At the same time, however, paradiplomacy can be seen to exist easily alongside more traditional means of developing the Russian economy and of conducting international relations based on traditional concepts of 'power politics'. The Russian Federation, especially since the second Chechen war and NATO's campaign in Kosovo, is far from championing post-modern interstate relations that exist in other regions of the world, especially in Northern Europe. The main argument of this chapter is that Russia, since 1991, has instead been preoccupied with trying to secure its status in world politics, as inherited from the

Soviet Union. The pragmatism of modern Russia's internal and foreign policy is therefore based on the idea that the highest priority for the country's leaders should be that of reconstituting Russia as a great power. In this context, Russia's regions are free to utilise their international relations for developing regional economies and infrastructure just so long, however, as the interests of the state are not jeopardised. That is why it is federal government and the presidential administration that are playing the central role in defining the frameworks for cooperation of Russia's regions in regional and global affairs.

St. Petersburg and the Russian National Project

During recent decades many cities and regions around the world have been using images such as being a 'meeting point' or 'gate' etc., as a way to define their intermediate function as a place of combining business and political and cultural activities. Such images have been applied to St. Petersburg throughout its 300 years of history, but especially since 1833 when the famous Russian poet, Alexander Pushkin, wrote the poem: 'The Bronze Horseman: A Tale of St. Petersburg'. In this poem Pushkin spoke of St. Petersburg as 'a window to Europe', an image that has remained the most famous definition of the city's historical mission ever since.

After Peter the Great established the city his successors generally shifted away from policies of radical reforms, although Catherine the Great and Alexander I were not totally devoid of liberal leanings, whilst Alexander II came into history as a great reformer, despite all the unpleasant distortions that followed the abolition of serfdom. However, whatever the general direction that has dominated in Russia's politics at different points in time, whether liberal or reactionary, St. Petersburg has always been the most sensitive of Russia's regions to Western influence and has been a centre of liberalism and free thought, from where it has spread across the whole country.

Only during the 70 years of the Soviet regime was the city unable to fulfil what might be seen as its historical mission. However, even at that time millions of tourists from the USSR and all around the world visited Leningrad, attracted by its architecture and unique urban culture. For example, many museums were functioning and UNESCO recognised Leningrad as an historical zone of global importance. During this period, though, the city was excluded from world political and cultural processes and any new construction in the historical centre of the city was forbidden. Indeed, Leningrad was close to repeating the history of another great European city of medieval times – Bruges. At the end of the nineteenth century the Belgian writer, Georges Rodenbach (1855-1898), published the novel *Bruges la morte* (Bruges the Dead), as an attempt to describe the tragedy of a great European city which had apparently lost its historical mission and died. After the Second World War the situation in Leningrad was similar: the huge historical centre was slowly being destroyed, the city's industry was very ineffective and environmentally damaging, whilst the most talented and energetic of the city's people were either emigrating or leaving the city for Moscow. Of course, this process was one that would take decades to unfold; however, the trend was obvious to everybody. It was time to start writing a Russian version of the Flemish book – 'St. Petersburg the Dead'.

Openness to foreign countries has been a special feature of St. Petersburg during all three centuries of its history. It has been demonstrated by the continual development of the city as a leading national transportation centre, through sea and river ports, railway links to different parts of Russia, as well through the construction of highways and airports. Similarly, the city has always attracted talented people and capital from different corners of Europe and Asia – though this was less the case during the Soviet period (1917-1991). Notably, St. Petersburg was also the first Russian city since the mid-nineteenth century to attract massive foreign investments into its industry, financial sector, transportation and communications. After the re-opening of the Russian economy for close cooperation with foreign partners in the late 1980s, the city regained its status as being an attractive Russian region for transnational investments. The whole post-Soviet period has been one in which the city has witnessed a continuous expansion in the volume of goods exported and imported through the city. This trend was further encouraged in 1999 when the Russian Federal Government announced as an economic and strategic priority plans to develop the transport infrastructure of the regions of north-western Russia in order to reduce Russia's dependence on Finland and the three Baltic States in this regard. Nowadays, St. Petersburg is connected by all existing types of transportation with neighbouring European countries, and due to the further development of Pulkovo International Airport, also with countries on four continents.

During the post-Soviet period it can be argued that St. Petersburg has gone through three distinct stages. *The first stage* (1991-1996) was characterised by the ascendancy to power in the city of democratic forces led by Anatoly Sobchak. During this stage significant efforts were made to integrate the city into the European economic and cultural area and to create an attractive image of the city for foreign investors, tourists, artists and scientists.

The second stage (1996-2002) was characterised by a declining interest on the part of the administration of Vladimir Yakovlev in the development of international cooperation and preservation for the city of a special place in Russian foreign policy as a sort of 'ice-breaker', formulating and testing on itself new forms of cooperation with foreign partners of the Russian Federation. Consequently, St. Petersburg rather quickly lost attractiveness for foreign investors who instead began looking to other Russian regions, including the neighbouring Leningrad region, for opportunities.

The current third stage started in early 2003. At that time President Vladimir Putin sent Valentina Matvienko, Deputy Prime Minister of Russia, to St. Petersburg as his official Representative to the North-Western Federal District. She appeared as the focus of media and public attention during St. Petersburg's 300th anniversary celebrations in May-June 2003 and was rather easily elected as the Governor of St. Petersburg in October 2003. Since then St. Petersburg, as in the beginning of the 1990s, has again reconfirmed its image as a city where reforms take place, and even more important, as a place where the federal and city authorities are trying to present the city to the outside world as 'the cultural and diplomatic capital' of Russia.

It is impossible to imagine nowadays, that any other Russian city, including the nation's capital, could attract so many world leaders to celebrate the day or even year of its foundation. In fact, there are few cities of this type in the world. Of course, few cities in the world have exact dates of their foundation. However, this is only a minor part of the explanation of the 'St. Petersburg 300th anniversary phenomenon' that saw leaders from around the world descend on the city in 2003. Another element is that the great majority of cities were established in, so to say, a 'natural way' – due to the growth of population, economic interests, the need to protect the country's territory, and so on. St. Petersburg is totally different. The main reason for Peter the Great's decision in May 1703 to found a new capital was completely geopolitical: with St. Petersburg's location being the closest point of the economically and militarily great Asian power to its European neighbours. The decision was also symbolic of a desire to be part of another community and to choose a new historical destiny for the nation. As mentioned elsewhere, there has been discussion going on in Russia for centuries as to whether Russia is a European nation or not (see Neumann, 1995). There is no possibility here to mention all the arguments of both sides of the dispute, but one thing is absolutely clear, without the establishment of St. Petersburg in 1703 and its two centuries of being the capital of Russia, the arguments for those in Russia who consider the country to be an integral part of Asian politics and culture would be much stronger.

St. Petersburg in the post-Cold War Period

The idea of the 'city-state' can be usefully utilised in evaluating St. Petersburg today. This is not just because of the city's glorious imperial past. Recent activities of the city's authorities, private institutions, civil society institutions and the whole population of the city give us an opportunity to find important elements of 'statehood' in St. Petersburg. This includes elements of local identity, the active and rather competitive political life of the city, and the existence of 44 foreign consulates and dozens of representative offices of international governmental and non-governmental organisations in the city.

The lack of its own status as a capital city is considered within St. Petersburg itself and by many observers in other regions as a fatal misunderstanding. The city has created around itself a sort of metropolitan area, a network of special relationships of different regions, as well as a special relationship with the federal centre in Moscow. Active participants in these relations are bodies of legislative, executive and judicial power, business circles, media, the scientific community and artists. It is important to note that St. Petersburg is often named by Russian and foreign observers as the most Western, cosmopolitan, and advanced of all Russian cities (Hedenskog, 2000, p.62). The results of all post-Soviet federal and regional elections have demonstrated that the city is a democratic stronghold chiefly voting for reformist parties and politicians. Being the leading national economic, scientific and cultural centre, the city has always been open to cooperation with foreign countries. Following the dissolution of the USSR this mission has become even more obvious. For the city's economy the import of capital, goods and services has great importance in creating new forms and channels of cooperation with foreign countries. Meanwhile, St. Petersburg's credit rating is currently Aa2 (rus).[1] As such it has one of the highest ratings of Russia's regions due to the strong diversification of the regional economy and the income of the city budget, the low rate of debt and the city government's effective strategy of debt management, and finally, the relatively stable development of the city's economy in recent years and the independence of St. Petersburg's budget from donations to the federal budget.

Within St. Petersburg there are many representative offices of foreign cities, regions and countries, as well as of various transnational corporations and financial institutions. More then 30 countries are connected with St. Petersburg by regular flights from the city's two airports. Passenger ferries and cruise liners go from St. Petersburg to the biggest ports of the Baltic Sea and the Atlantic Ocean. Although still behind Moscow in the development of international business contacts, St. Petersburg has maintained its leadership as the largest national tourist centre, with more then 3 million foreign tourists visiting the city every year. At the same time, the city's tourist infrastructure is out-of-date, and to some extent non-existent. Indeed, the city needs at least 20-30,000 more hotel rooms at moderate prices in order to accommodate the several millions of middle-class foreign tourists who every year would like to visit the city, but many of whom now have to cancel their plans. In short, the city is losing its attractiveness for foreign tourists and businessmen due to the fact that St. Petersburg is now one of the top ten most expensive cities in the world. Consequently, a special programme directed towards creating a favourable investment climate for national and foreign investors, is now under consideration in the city's Government and Legislative Assembly (Matvienko, 2004).

St. Petersburg is the national leader in the development of telecommunication technologies. It is here that the first Russian company providing a mobile telephone service was established in 1992. Now several leading Nordic companies of mobile telecommunications are operating in the local market via their Russian subsidiaries. St. Petersburg is close to the average European level in mobile telephone use (73.9 per cent of the city's citizens have a mobile phone). The

---

[1]   The share of foreign debt in the combined debt of St. Petersburg in July 2004 was 16 per cent (RUR 1.6 billion, i.e., €450 million) and St. Petersburg is faithfully paying all internal and foreign debts (*Kommersant*, 16 August 2004, p.16). The whole debt of the city at the end of 2003 was equal to only 20 per cent of the city's annual budget.

national Internet network was also connected to the European segment of the world-wide-web via St. Petersburg and Finland. A number of foreign newspapers, news agencies and TV channels (mostly from Baltic rim countries) have correspondents in St. Petersburg, whilst hundreds of big and small international conferences and seminars are held annually in the city. Music festivals hosted by the city, like 'The White Nights' Stars' and the 'Christmas Musical Festival' are internationally renowned and embed St. Petersburg in the international cultural sphere. Moreover, when it comes to international contacts it should be noted that Leningrad/St. Petersburg has been developing 'twin-city' partnerships for over fifty years. Currently 71 cities from all five continents are twinned with St. Petersburg. Notably, the number of partner-cities has doubled since Vladimir Yakovlev was elected as the Governor of St. Petersburg (from 35 cities in May 1996 to 71 cities in August 2004). Among these partners many are located in the area of the Commonwealth of Independent States (11 of the 36 new partners). However, twin-city relations have also been strong with the major economic and cultural centres of the Baltic region: with Turku (since 1953, St. Petersburg's very first foreign partner), Hamburg (1957), Gdansk (1961), Goteborg (1962), Århus (1989), Stockholm (1992), Helsinki (1993), Tampere (1993), Mikkeli (1996), Imatra (1997), Kotka (1997), Lappeenranta (1997), Riga (1997), Tallinn (1999), Daugavpils (2002).

Similarly, in June 2004 St. Petersburg's chamber of trade and commerce had cooperation agreements with 60 chambers of commerce in 36 countries on five continents. Among its partners are the unions of traders and industrialists of Western Sweden, Turku, Stockholm, Helsinki and Central Finland.

Both the St. Petersburg Administration (regional government) and the Legislative Assembly (regional parliament) have experience of international activities and well-trained staff for this sphere of activity. After fundamental changes in regional government in autumn 2003, when Valentina Matvienko was elected as the new Governor, dozens of young businessmen joined the new regional government. Many of them have experience of successful international cooperation in many sectors of business. Today, St. Petersburg is probably the national leader in attracting leaders of the business community into public office in order to assist in the transformation of the regional economy in line with international standards.

It is important to emphasise that St. Petersburg (like Moscow) is not typical of the whole of Russia. Living standards in the city are much higher compared to average levels in the country. In fact, if we use such indicators as living standards of the majority of the population, the transport and telecommunications infrastructure, the number and quality of trade centres, the financing of museums and theatres, and the construction of sea ports and new metro lines, etc., it is possible to predict that in 20 years the level of development of the city's infrastructure will be close to average European standards. After the end of the anniversary celebrations in the city in autumn 2003 the Russian President and Government made an important promise to maintain the same high levels of financing from the Federal budget in order to support the continued reconstruction of the city's infrastructure. This will give the city the chance to be not just a better place to live, but also to make it a more attractive place for foreign tourists, investors, students, etc.

All these elements noted above are important in that they illustrate that St. Petersburg is not a 'normal' Russian city, and is instead playing a rather fundamental role in Russia's post-Cold War transformation process, but also in locating Russia in the context of international relations. Thus, St. Petersburg currently has significant and growing importance for the internal and foreign policy of the Russian Federation. There are several reasons that can explain why it is that St. Petersburg has become an important actor in the international context.

First, St. Petersburg is playing an important role as a 'contact centre' and 'meeting point' between Russia and its most important partners in the international arena, i.e., European and North American countries. The city has been among the most active Russian regions in establishing external relations (Kuzmin, 1999, p.109). This is important since one of the priorities of Russian foreign policy has been to utilise existing avenues of cooperation in different spheres and to develop new forms of partnership.

Second, the city is one of the biggest regions of the Russian Federation in terms of economic potential, being the locomotive of economic development of neighbouring regions and north-west Russia in general. Securing favourable economic growth in St. Petersburg and the consequent positive influence this will have on the economic situation of north-west Russian regions are understood as very important conditions in transforming the Russian economy away from crisis and towards the principles of market economy.

Third, the city is located in the Baltic Sea region where during the Cold War, as well as in the 1990s, unique mechanisms maintaining peace and stability were established, and where Russia undertook radical measures to reduce the likelihood of a military confrontation. The preservation of stability in the Baltic rim, especially in the current context of the international war on terrorism and the recent enlargements of the EU and NATO to include the Baltic States, is a major priority for Russia, and one where St. Petersburg and nearby regions will play a special role. Not least this is because St. Petersburg is developing as a major urban area, second in size in Russia and one of the largest in Northern Europe.

Moreover, and also a part of this third factor, is that it is important to emphasise that there has been a radical change in the perception of threats to national security in Russia since 2000. Issues of economic security and the correlation between economic growth and rising living standards in Russia are now closely interrelated in the formulation of Russia's foreign policy strategy and tactics. The Ministry of Foreign Affairs is playing a leading role in the attempt of governmental agencies to double Russia's GDP by 2010. On the one hand, the 'campaign' to double Russia's GDP has strong parallels with 'the age of socialism', with mass-media propaganda and the mobilisation of national resources for the implementation of the strategic policy of the Russian President and Federal Government. On the other hand, an important symbol of change is that this prioritisation of economics is not purely political. The 'economisation' of Russian foreign policy gives Russia a chance to look like other European countries, which are the major political and economic partners of the Russian Federation. Notably, the economisation of international contacts is also becoming typical for St. Petersburg as well. Many visits of St. Petersburg's official delegations since 1996 have been to CIS and Baltic countries. Included in these delegations are usually a number of representatives of large regional industrial and transportation companies, research centres and universities, museums and theatres. The main aim of these visits has been to develop better contacts with different types of foreign partners. The personal participation of the Governor, Vladimir Yakovlev (nowadays Valentina Matvienko), has been a clear message that regional authorities are supporting local business, and the cultural and academic community, whilst at the same time such participation is also seen as enhancing Russia's broadly defined foreign policy agenda. For example, in the first half of 2004 official delegations from St. Petersburg, headed by Governor Matvienko, visited Azerbaijan, Finland, Kazakhstan, Kyrgyzstan, Turkmenistan and Ukraine. Moreover, it should also be noted that the status of local companies in their contacts with partners in the CIS is changing significantly. Today, they are not just trade partners, but increasingly also investors, acting on behalf of their own companies or together with foreign companies from Europe or North America.

Regional Actors

To get a better idea of the role that St. Petersburg is playing in post-Cold War Russian politics it is useful to take a look at the activities of some of the major regional actors.

The Government of St. Petersburg

The Administration of St. Petersburg comprises the regional government. It consists of a number of committees, whose chairpersons are appointed by the Governor. The Governor is elected by a direct vote of all the citizens of St. Petersburg for a four-year term and can be re-elected once. There are also seven Vice Governors, who are appointed by the Governor after consultation and approval from the Legislative Assembly of St. Petersburg.

Since Professor Anatoly Sobchak was elected as the first post-Soviet Governor (then called Mayor) of the city, the local government has actively developed the city's international cooperation with foreign partners. St. Petersburg is a member of such European and regional organisations as Eurocities and the Union of Baltic Cities (UBC). Recently, St. Petersburg supported a proposal to hold an international conference of 'Baltic Metropolises', a group comprising 10 of the largest Baltic cities from 9 countries.[2]

For many years the St. Petersburg Administration has been cooperating successfully with international financial institutions. For example, in June 2004 the Russian Government approved an agreement between St. Petersburg's Government and the World Bank for a loan of $161.1 million for the 'economic development of St. Petersburg', with the main objective being the transformation of St. Petersburg's economy through the privatisation of a number of companies currently owned by the city. The deal is rather unusual in the context of current relations between the Russian Federation and international financial institutions. Since 2000 the official position of the Russian President and Government has been that the financial situation of the country is good enough to avoid applying for more credits from international financial institutions and private banks, especially at a time when the Russian foreign debt is more then $150 billion. The policy is still effective, however, the June 2004 deal between the World Bank and St. Petersburg Administration has broken the ice in the relationship between Russia and one of the leading international financial institutions (Klepikov, 2004, p.7).

Both the Government and Parliament of St. Petersburg have significant influence on the development of the international business links of local companies. They may give permission to rent land plots for the construction of new industries, as well as discuss terms for foreign investments including different types of tax exemptions and tax relief. For example, recently they agreed to a project to construct a new 'China Town' on 300 hectares of land with total Chinese investments of about $1 billion.

Probably a unique example of institutionalised international cooperation in Russia is 'The Group of Finnish Advisors to the Governor of St. Petersburg'. The group was established about 10 years ago when Vladimir Putin was the Chairman of the Committee on Foreign Relations of St. Petersburg Administration. The group consists of CEOs of leading Finnish companies: Neste, Fazer, Sonera, Finnair, Skanska, Fortum and others. The group conducts one or two sessions annually where they discuss the implementation of concrete projects of these and other Finnish companies in St. Petersburg. The Governor, Vice Governors, Chairmen of governmental committees, their Deputies and Heads of Departments take part in these sessions. Due to these meetings, representatives of the business communities of St. Petersburg and Finland, as well as regional authorities responsible for establishing a positive investment climate, have the opportunity to discuss common problems and report results directly to the Governor of St. Petersburg.

A couple of examples of the regional diplomacy of St. Petersburg can well highlight the important role that international contacts play for St. Petersburg, but also the role that through such paradiplomacy St. Petersburg can also play for

---

[2]   The first 'Baltic Metropolises' conference took place on 12-13 October 2002 in Copenhagen.

Russia. During the first half of 2004 Governor Matvienko took part in three official visits of delegations from St. Petersburg abroad. The first of these visits was in February to Finland. During the visit meetings were held with the Finnish President, the Speaker of the Finnish Parliament, the Mayor of Helsinki, the Minister of Foreign Trade and Development, the management of the Finnish railway system and with the staff of the Mayor's Office of Turku. Besides the usefulness of direct contacts with leaders of a neighbouring country, among the positive results of the visit was progress in implementing a project to construct in St. Petersburg a 'Finnish Village' – a techno-park for the organisation of high-tech industrial production and the implementation of a number of innovative technological projects. Other results of the visit were an agreement to open in 2004 a new St. Petersburg-Tallinn-Helsinki ferry link to be operated by the Finnish company Silja Line; another ferry link between Tallinn-St. Petersburg-Rostok (Silja Line together with Tallinn Group AS (Ageev, 2004, pp.8-12)); and a decision to open in 2004 several new customs offices on the Russian-Finnish border.

The second visit was also in February, when Matvienko and other members of the delegation visited Kazakhstan, Turkmenistan and Kyrgyzstan and met the Heads of State and Governments of all three countries. This visit can be seen as somewhat unique because of the 'foreign policy' part of its agenda. For example, Matvienko met President Putin just before the visit and at his request had a meeting with the President of Turkmenistan, Saparmurat Niyazov. It was exactly during those days when Turkmenistan's President took additional measures further worsening the status of the country's Russian-speaking population, as well as against those citizens of Turkmenistan who had graduated from universities of the Russian Federation. Even before these measures were taken the status of the Russian-speaking population, including whose with dual Russian-Turkmen citizenship, was very problematic. Notably, many Russian and international NGOs consider the situation in Turkmenistan as part of a growing humanitarian crisis. The visit of the St. Petersburg delegation to the country was timed to coincide with Turkmenistan's National Flag Day, with St. Petersburg's Governor acting as the plenipotentiary representative of the Russian President at the celebrations. From one point of view, it was a Russian message to Niyazov that the level of contacts between the two nations will be lower for so long as Niyazov's repressive policies continued. At the same time, the personal participation of the Governor of Russia's second principal region in the celebrations was symbolic of Russia's desire to maintain positive relations with Turkmenistan and its President. Confirming this observation, Matvienko signed with President Niyazov an agreement on economic, research and technological and cultural cooperation between Turkmenistan and St. Petersburg. It was the first agreement that Turkmenistan has signed with a separate Russian region.

The visit of Matvienko to Kyrgyzstan was equally surprising. During this visit Matvienko had a meeting at the newly opened Russian military airbase in Kant, near Kyrgyzstan's capital of Bishkek. The airbase was opened by President Putin following a Russia-Kyrgyzstan intergovernmental agreement of 22 September 2003, which was notably much criticised by foreign policy and military experts from NATO countries. The official explanation for the visit of the St. Petersburg delegation to Kant was rather unusual and somewhat unprecedented in the conduct of Russian foreign policy: St. Petersburg decided to establish its official patronage of the military airbase! The nature of this 'patronage' is still very mysterious, but it is important to emphasise that in implementing its foreign policy the Russian leadership, including the President and Ministries of Defence and Foreign Affairs, are increasingly recruiting non-federal institutions, including Russia's regions.

Matvienko's third visit was to Sweden in May 2004. It included meetings with the governors of Stockholm and Uppsala provinces, lunch with prominent Swedish businessmen, a reception with the Crown Princess, and meetings with the Mayor of Stockholm and the Minister of Finance. A number of agreements between St. Petersburg companies and Swedish corporations were signed during the visit. There was also intensive discussion regarding further Swedish investments into the industry and infrastructure of St. Petersburg.

Political Parties

The 1960-70s were years of crucial importance for the city's destiny. At that time the city's military industrial complex faced its biggest period of development and turned into a centre of high-tech military production. The consequences of that process were ambiguous. On the one hand, the social and economic appearance of St. Petersburg hardly changed. On the other hand, however, a new social group emerged (Soviet middle class) with relatively high education and income and which despite its close ties to the ruling regime was also well aware of the regime's inadequacies.

The 1989 elections to the Congress of the People's Deputies resulted in the defeat of the Communist Party. Representatives from Leningrad, especially Anatoly Sobchak, played an important role in the interregional faction in the Congress of the People's Deputies. At the 1990 elections to the Russian Supreme Soviet and the Leningrad City Council representatives of the democratic forces gained the opportunity to establish control over the local parliament as well as to become an integral part of the reformist group in the Russian Supreme Soviet, headed by Boris Yeltsin.

In summer 1991 radical economic, social and political reforms started in Russia. St. Petersburg became the testing area for the new democratic and market-oriented legislation. As part of the reforms a multiparty system was established at the regional level, with St. Petersburg again playing the leading role in the process. The 1989 and 1990 city elections were free and in September 1991 the city voted to change its name back to St. Petersburg, in one of the most symbolic actions indicating Russia's intention to cut its links with the Soviet past and as such in a sense place St. Petersburg at the symbolic heart of the transformation process. Notably, therefore, the City Council played a key role in maintaining peace and stability in St. Petersburg during the *coup d'etat* in August 1991, remaining loyal to President Boris Yeltsin and his democratic reforms.

The percentage of votes for democratic and liberal parties in St. Petersburg in the Russian Parliamentary elections of 1993, 1995 and 1999 was also much higher than in general for all Russian regions. More generally the city has been considered to be a stronghold of the Yabloko party of Gregory Yavlinski, as well as of more liberal parties, like Democratic Choice of Russia (DVR – especially in 1993 and 1995) and the Union of Right-wing Forces (SPS – especially in 1999). The results of the Parliamentary elections of December 2003 were a shock for all Russian political parties, except for the amorphous coalition of political forces whose political programme consisted of total and unconditional support of Vladimir Putin. Due to the fact that Putin was born and lived for many years in Leningrad/St. Petersburg, but also because of the tremendous celebrations of St. Petersburg's 300th anniversary, the results of the Parliamentary elections in St. Petersburg mirrored those in Russia more generally, with more than 70 per cent supporting United Russia (ER). Local members of the party are currently trying to establish contacts with similar political parties in European countries. However, due to the fact that United Russia is a 'centrist party' with a very unclear location along the left-right political spectrum, it has been difficult to find real partners among the leading European parties of Germany, France or the United Kingdom. Anyway, political life in St. Petersburg is still rather intensive, with hundreds of political activists coming to the city from different countries. It is easy find all of Europe's major political forces represented in St. Petersburg or having close relations with political groups and/or NGOs in the city, all indicating that outsiders see St. Petersburg as an important place for access into Russian political debate more generally.

The role of St. Petersburg as a democratic testing ground is still very important for the political life of Russia in general. Strong democratic traditions in the city have had a rather significant impact on regional and federal political life, preventing the concentration of political and economic power only at the federal centre of the country. Since the late 1980s there have been, and still are, many political parties and groups in the city, which are truly democratic according to high international standards, and which also have close links to similar European groups and parties, thereby locating regional politics in a broader international context.

The Business Community

During Soviet times Leningrad was one of the major centres of the military industry. One reason for this was the existence in the city of research institutions in all major spheres of weaponry from missiles and space technologies, to naval ships and submarines, to artillery systems, etc. It was this sector which suffered first after the disintegration of the USSR due to the sharp reduction of the military budget and spending on new military technologies in post-Soviet Russia. A minor growth of the military budget began following the outbreak of the first Chechen war in autumn 1994. Further increases were made following Putin's initiation of a new round of military reform in 2000. This precipitated a revival of St. Petersburg's military industry. It should also be mentioned that those producers able to export their military technologies (e.g., shipyards producing naval ships for China and India) were able not just to survive, but even to invest in their infrastructure, production and research. Even today these shipyards play an important role in securing high research and production capabilities within St. Petersburg.

Since the beginning of economic reforms in post-Soviet Russia the general evaluation of St. Petersburg's economic situation has been rather stable. According to official statistics and the estimation of experts, the level of employment in the city is very high, unemployment very low, whilst strong demand exists for specialists in many sectors of industry and services (especially high-tech sectors of industry in private companies or joint ventures). However, despite the positive labour market situation there is growing tension in the sector of low-paid employment and pensioners. Being one of the most developed regional markets in Russia, St. Petersburg combines a limited number of very wealthy people with a growing middle class and a still significant number of people who are just able to survive in a city with high prices for food and services. The general socio-economic situation in St. Petersburg is difficult and changes for the better have been very slow.

With the break-up of the USSR, the newly independent Baltic countries acquired a number of oversized ports, at least compared to the needs of their internal economies. Being formerly integral parts of the Soviet economy these ports have retained special geopolitical importance, not least because 70-95 per cent of the cargoes handled are '*en route*' to or from Russia. From the point of view of the Russian government, this dependence on these small countries, which have heavily drawn on anti-Russian rhetoric in strengthening their newly established national states, is unacceptable. Notably, many official representatives of the administrations of St. Petersburg and the Leningrad region have supported this image of the Balts as unpredictable and unfriendly neighbours. Importantly, these two regions have benefited from Putin's decision in 1999 to construct several new large port terminals in order to reduce Russia's dependence on the ports of the Baltic States. As a result, more than $1 billion has been invested into the transport infrastructure, industry and services of St. Petersburg and the regions around the city. Being the biggest single investment project in the economic history of the city for many decades, this significantly 'anti-Western' project faced no opposition, either from inside the Russian government, or in the community of institutions of paradiplomacy.

Many foreign companies have been working in the local market for more than 10 years and in general have evaluated their experience in a very positive way. Over the past decade the city administration and the business community have developed a rather friendly business environment. Therefore, it seems natural that since 2000 St. Petersburg has attracted over $2.2 billion of foreign direct and portfolio investments, more than ever before in the post-Soviet history of the city. St. Petersburg is also returning to its pre-Soviet image of being the Russian capital of culture (meaning Europe-oriented culture) and the centre of education and the arts.

Tourism is potentially the biggest (together with transport services and industry) and the most underdeveloped sector of St. Petersburg's economy. According to UNESCO estimates St. Petersburg is the eighth most attractive place for tourists in the world. Annually some 30 million people wish to visit the city. In practice, though, the number of foreign tourists is a fraction of this total, indicating that the city's tourist industry is unable to provide the required level of services.

As an important confirmation of the changes for the better in St. Petersburg we can note recent results of an analysis of the investment climate of all 89 Russian regions, which every year is conducted by the Russian business weekly, *Expert*. In 2003 St. Petersburg was the only Russian region to receive the highest rating of 1A. This rating means the city has the highest potential opportunities for all types of investors and at the same time the lowest level of investment risks (*Expert*, November 17-23, 2003, p.134).

The growing private sector of St. Petersburg's economy is becoming a significant factor in regional paradiplomacy. The sector is formulating its interests in a very transparent way and in clear distinction from the public sector of the Russian economy. The growing number of private companies are becoming a major force that support the deeper economic integration of the regional economy with neighbouring regions in Europe and in accordance with ordinary, 'civilised' standards, existing in neighbouring countries of the European Union.

Institutions of Federal Power in St. Petersburg

Arguably there were three important reasons that provided the rationale behind the large scale of St. Petersburg's 300th anniversary celebrations. These reasons derived from the Russian Government and through their participation in the celebrations were essentially endorsed by leaders of the EU, the Commonwealth of Independent States, the G-8 and some other countries.[3] First, there was the *aspiration* of the Russian leadership to convince their own citizens that Russia is still a great power and that the period of crisis that started in the late-1980s had come to an end. Second, there was a *wish* to demonstrate to the world that Russia is intent on securing a role as a leading power in world politics. The global scale of the celebrations was a clear message to other countries that Russia is going to play a prominent role, not just in its nearby regions, but also in other parts of the world as well. Third, the celebrations were also an *attempt* to rapidly change the country's image, which it was felt had been negatively affected by 70 years of Soviet rule and 12 years of painful and inconsistent economic and political

---

[3]   Leaders of 43 countries took part in the celebrations in May-June 2003, together with leaders of international organisations (for example, the EU), regions, cities, and NGOs.

reforms. It is important to emphasise in this context that the unique combination of St. Petersburg's European nature and its imperial history made the implementation of each of these tasks easier.

President Putin, ministers and leaders of Parliament frequently use the city for organising important summits, international conferences, festivals and unofficial meetings. Although it is too early to speak about a new 'St. Petersburg stage' in Russian political and diplomatic history, it is notable that important events for Russian diplomacy, such as the first unofficial meeting of Putin with British Prime-Minister Tony Blair, as well as the Russian-German joint initiative to start the 'St. Petersburg Dialogue' between the political, economic and cultural elites of the two countries, took place in the city. When in 2003 the new Presidential Residence was opened in St. Petersburg for organising summits and other high-level diplomatic events, the special status of the city in Russian diplomacy became even more obvious. It is also important to emphasise that during the 2003 celebrations the leaders of Russia and St. Petersburg did not mention any event from the Soviet history of the city. Even the most tragic and heroic period of the city's history – the 900 day 'Siege of Leningrad' (1941-1944) was forgotten. The reason was that the Kremlin urgently needed a positive, friendly, non-problematic image of Russia and that image should be an integral part of national foreign policy strategy.

Possible Future Developments

300 years ago Peter the Great began the construction of the Russian Empire with a war to gain access to the Baltic Sea for the development of economic relations with Russia's Western neighbours and to promote modernisation via adapting the heritage of Western civilisation to Russian realities. Today, in an attempt to re-assert itself as an international great power Russia is using a variety of social and economic strategies. During the 2003 celebrations in St. Petersburg, President Putin told journalists that in this context the 'Role of St. Petersburg, from my point of view, is very important, because the city is really fulfilling the role of a bridge, which gives citizens of Europe better understanding of Russia. By their mentality citizens of St. Petersburg are much closer to Europe [than other Russians]' (http://www.kremlin.ru, 28 May 2003). The ideas expressed by the President are very significant indicating a broader strategy of bringing Russia closer to Europe in terms of mentality and identity, a policy that is likely to remain important in the future.

Discussion of the role of St. Petersburg in Russian history, in particular its past and future as a European country, was always in the background of the celebrations. This discussion began at the very foundation of the city, or at the latest since 1712, when St. Petersburg was officially proclaimed the capital of the Russian Empire. For Tsar Peter the Great, moving the capital from Moscow to the Baltic Sea was important for accelerating reforms and integrating Russia into a new system of international relations, which appeared in 1648 after the Peace of

Westphalia at the end of the Thirty Years War. So, from the early eighteenth century Russia began integrating into a new international system with its distinctive features of sovereignty, diplomacy, the balance of power and international law. Peter the Great's reforms and his transfer of the capital closer to Europe did not stop conflicts between Russia and its Western neighbours, but these conflicts and even wars became an integral part of trans-European politics, and it established Russia as a significant player in the society of European countries.

The city's cosmopolitanism inherited from the times of Peter the Great prevents 'St. Petersburg patriotism' from attaining a clear-cut profile and becoming a significant phenomenon in the city's life. This could become problematic in the context of the future federalisation of Russian political life. The city has its imperial, glorious past and a desire to reinvent this. However, in the context of a new international situation, where interstate borders are losing their significance, St. Petersburg would be better to play on a new 'invented' history of cooperation with European neighbours rather than a history of territorial disputes, wars and 'Iron Curtains'. Key partners for St. Petersburg are located in Europe, which is why it has to be a long-term strategy for both politicians and non-governmental organisations in St. Petersburg to develop new forms of cooperation and to re-establish St. Petersburg as one of the political and cultural centres of Northern Europe.

The development of European politics since 1999 demonstrates a clear and stable tendency of the growing importance of national borders as a watershed between countries in the eastern corner of the continent. 1999 has become crucial in recent European and world history in the development from the Cold War era to a new architecture and philosophy of international relations. So what makes 1999 a watershed? In March 1999, despite the active opposition of the Russian Federation, the first post-Cold War eastward enlargement of NATO took place. A few days later, without UN approval, NATO began a war against Slobodan Milosevic's Yugoslavia. One consequence of this was that Russia adopted a more pro-active policy in the CIS area, it started the second Chechen war and began taking measures to protect the civil rights of the Russian-speaking population of the Baltic States. Combined with the March 2003 war in Iraq, the whole structure of international relations has been severely damaged. At the same time, very impressive growth of the Russian economy has begun. As a result Russia is no longer the 'ill man' of Europe and has returned to a foreign policy focused on a post-Soviet interpretation of 'national interests'. For all intents and purposes it seems that the experiment of establishing in the Baltic region a special, non-conflict based system of relations between Moscow and NATO/EU member-states has ended without desired results.

Since autumn 1999, when Putin was appointed Prime Minister, Russian diplomacy has been defined by the notion of 'pragmatism'. The combination of the international terrorist threat and the reduction of active US involvement in the affairs of the post-Soviet territory gave Russia an opportunity to adopt an active foreign policy based on the balance of power and economic nationalism. These days Russian policy in the Baltic region is still the same as it was formulated in 1999, with a strong belief in military and economic power as 'real arguments' for the protection and promotion of national interests.

Since 2000, when Putin was elected President, the idea of the 'diplomacy of Russia's regions' has begun to be filled with new content. As has been common practice for all the post-Soviet period, in the sphere of 'high foreign policy' Russia's regions have coordinated every step in their foreign policy contacts with such institutions as the Ministry of Foreign Affairs, the Ministry of Defence, the Federal Security Service, but most importantly, with the Presidential Administration. The recent novelty is related to the scale of involvement of Russia's regions in elaborating and implementing Russian foreign policy. Federal institutions in Moscow are increasingly inclined to believe that the regions are playing according to the existing 'rules of the game' in foreign policy, with St. Petersburg being one of the most active players. At the same time, there is no doubt that it is the Federal institutions that set the 'rules of the game' in the international arena, and it is too optimistic to expect that something will change radically in the near future.

The role of the 'St. Petersburg factor' in this *anti-postmodern* genesis of Russian foreign policy is small. Whilst it is true that nationalist politicians and academics have sometimes portrayed the West, and more particularly NATO enlargement, as a military threat to Russia, such arguments are no longer convincing, especially given that throughout the post-Soviet period Russian leaders have continuously emphasised that the country's main political and economic partners lie in Europe. Since 11 September 2001 and 11 March 2004 (attacks of terrorists in Madrid), this thesis has received new and more precise meaning. From our point of view, it is possible to verify that due to the proximity of St. Petersburg to European countries, Russia's political elite has become convinced of the positive historic role of Europe in Russian history. European countries provided Russia with assistance in the most difficult years of transition (1990-1992). They have also been a zone of stability during numerous ethnic conflicts and civil wars in former Soviet republics in the 1990s. However, another important explanation of the positive image of Europe is based on the successful years of St. Petersburg's paradiplomacy, the main object of which has always been making connections with European countries, their regions, civil society and ordinary people.

There is a significant paradox between two distinctive features of St. Petersburg's standing in the Russian Federation. From one point of view the city is one of Russia's symbols most closely related to the country's military history and the 'power politics' of the Russian Empire from the eighteenth-twentieth centuries. From another perspective, however, St. Petersburg is one of only a few Russian regions that are neighbours of the EU and where globalisation/localisation processes influence regional policy. Due to the peculiarities of its history St. Petersburg is interesting in being able, to some extent, to integrate into the wider European space, where it might find its proper place among the leading cities of the continent. For Russia, St. Petersburg has not been a 'trouble-maker', as might be expected would be the case by many theories of regionalisation/globalisation. For the EU and close neighbours of Russia (Finland, Sweden, Denmark, Germany, the Baltic States) St. Petersburg is becoming an increasingly attractive region for all types of possible cooperation. In the near future, for many Russian regions, the EU will begin in St. Petersburg, not politically, but economically and culturally, and as such there is growing need for active paradiplomacy of local institutions.

References

Ageev, Sergey (2004), 'Solo na parome' [Ferry's Solo], *Expert – Severo-Zapad*, Vol. 22(179), June 14-20, pp. 8-12.

Browning, Christopher S. (2001), *The Region-Building Approach Revisited: The Continued Othering of Russia in Discourses of Region-Building in the European North*, Copenhagen, Copenhagen Peace Research Institute, Working Papers 6.

Brzezinski, Zbignew (2000), 'Living with Russia', *The National Interest*, No. 61, Fall.

Chernitzyn, V. (2000), Tranzitnaya Zona. *Expert-Severo-Zapad*, No. 12, July 24.

Dynamics of the economic and social development of St.Petersburg in 2002. Administration of St.-Petersburg, Official web-site: http://www.gov.spb.ru/day/statistika/stat/2.

Ershov, A. (2000), 'Primorsk stal razmennoy monetoi', *Delovoi Peterburg*, 24 April.

The European Union Northern Dimension: view from St.Petersburg (2002), News Agency 'Baltic Research Center'.

Haukkala, H. (2001), *Two Reluctant Regionalizers? The European Union and Russia in Europe's North*, Working Papers 32, Helsinki, Ulkopoliittinen instituutti.

Hedenskog, Jacob (2000), 'The Foreign Relations of Russia's Western Regions', in Ingmar Oldberg and Jacob Hedenskog (eds.), *In Dire Straits: Russia's Western Regions between Moscow and the West*, Stockholm, Defence Research Establishment.

Joenniemi, Pertti (1994), 'Region-Building as Europe-Building', in Olav Schram Stokke and Ola Tunander (eds.), *The Barents Region: Cooperation in Arctic Europe*, London, Sage Publications, pp. 213-26.

Joenniemi, Pertti and Sergounin, Alexander (2003), *Russia and the European Union's Northern Dimension. Encounter or Clash of Civilisations?*, Nizhny Novgorod, Nizhny Novgorod Linguistic University Press.

Khudoley, K. (2000), 'Rossija i severnoe izmerenie Evropejskogo soyuza' [Russia and EU's Northern Dimension], in S. Pogodin (ed.), *Formula Rossii: tsentr i periferia* [Formula of Russia: Center and Periphery], St. Petersburg, Nestor, pp. 223-26.

Khudoley, K. and Tkachenko, S. (2001) 'The Russian Debate on the Role of St. Petersburg', in Pertti Joenniemi (ed.), *St. Petersburg: Russian, European and Beyond*, St. Petersburg: University Press, pp. 53-66.

Klepikov, Alexey (2004), 'Kredit pod prismotrom' [Credit under surveillance], *Expert – Severo-Zapad*, Vol. 22(179), June 14-20.

Kommersant, 16 August 2004.

Kostrov, Vladimir (2001), 'Pravye golodayut. V Pitere im ne chvataet politichaskih kadrov', *Izvestiya*, January 31.

Kuzmin, Eduard (1999), 'Russia: The Center, the Regions, and the Outside World,' *International Affairs (Moscow)*, Vol. 45(1), pp. 26-36.

Matvienko, Valentina (2004), Annual Address of the Governor of St. Petersburg. Available at http://www.gov.spb.ru/gov/governor/zaks_09.06.04.

McAuley, Mary (1997), *Russia's Politics of Uncertainty*, Cambridge, Cambridge University Press.

Neumann, Iver B. (1995), *Russia and the Idea of Europe*, London, Routledge.

Orlov, V. (2000), 'Vneshnya politika i rossiyskie regiony', *Mezhdunarodnaya Zhizn,* No.10.

Rezultaty investitsionnogo reitinga [Results of investment rating] (2003), in *Expert* (Weekly), no. 43 (396), 17-23 November 2003.

The Strategic Plan for St. Petersburg (1998), The Ignatief Centre.

Yakovlev, V. (2002), 'St. Petersburg 300 years – The role of the city in the Baltic Sea region', in *Baltic Sea – Ways of Integration and Co-operation*, The 11th Baltic Sea Parliamentary Conference, St.-Petersburg, September 30 – October 1.

Zhiharevich, B. (2000), 'Replika iz-za shirmy. Chto skruvaet Strategiccheskiy Plan Sankt-Petersburga', *Expert-Severo-Zapad*, No. 17, October.

Zimine, D. (2002), 'Limits of Integration: The Vase of North-Western Russia', in Lars Hedegaard and Bjarne Lindström (eds.), *The NEBI Yearbook 2001/2002. North European and Baltic Sea Integration*, Berlin, Springer Verlag, pp. 63-78.

Chapter 11

Transnational Forces, States and International Institutions: Three Perspectives on Change in Baltic Sea Affairs

Carl-Einar Stålvant

Baltic Sea 2004: New Horizons

Over a period of some fifteen years the Baltic Sea formation has sprung from relative oblivion into a European success story. Achievements have been noticeable, particularly in terms of transcending the divisive East-West barrier in Northern Europe. Epochal changes in the late 1980s spurred on regional activism and social dynamism to redefine, and even to recast, long-standing political identities and commonalities. Within a very short period, an immense and dense number of direct contacts have been established between neighbouring peoples and communities who had previously shared barriers, but not many bridges. After a sharp downturn, intensified interactions have boosted economic growth and, for all countries, the aggregate regional weight of financial transactions, production networks and the exchange of goods, has increased in absolute terms. For most of the countries of the region one can also note a relative gain in inter-regional interactions,[1] and many figures can be provided to support the claim that the area of the Baltic basin is one of the most economically dynamic regions in Europe.

With regard to security governance, soft power assistance has propped up weak state institutions in the Baltic States, Poland and Russia, and has contributed to the reduction of tensions and the dissolution of traditional enemy images. In the 1990s strategies were devised that supported the efforts of neighbouring countries to change and transform themselves, whilst foreign policy reorientations have coalesced with domestic reforms in stabilising turbulent conditions. Although latent flash points are conceivable that could ignite future crises, existential threats are now located elsewhere, further beyond the region.

---

[1] For the transport sector, see Nilsson (2003). For economic and trade developments, see Laaser and Schröder (2003).

In this context, spring 2004 marked a watershed for the Baltic States and Poland in their incremental march towards international institutions. With their accession to NATO (the Baltic States) and the European Union (the Baltic States and Poland) these countries have accomplished their primary foreign policy objectives. The significance of this political reorganisation has been underscored by concomitant changes in the wider Euro-Atlantic framework. Strategic partnerships with Russia, on the part of both the US and the EU, and realignments caused by the global War on Terrorism have created a different and contradictory matrix of interests. The creation of the NATO-Russia Council has furthermore enhanced Russia's position and expanded its diplomatic options, also with regard to security relations with the Baltic States. The role of external pressures in shaping the region's future has been notable, and taken together all these developments have altered the basis for regional dialogue between governments and peoples in the region.

In this context, this chapter starts from the position that the 'master word' that has usually been used to describe such developments, and in particular the transformation process in the southern and eastern parts of the region and in the post-Soviet space in general – transition – has not always been able to capture the dynamics at play, whilst in today's context it appears somewhat outdated, despite persistent structural disparities in Northern Europe. Instead, this chapter argues that Baltic Sea politics and developments have been driven by several national and collectively shared motives, which analytically can be divided into three perspectives of *regionalisation, stabilisation* and *normalisation.*

Three Modes of Change: A Few Assertions and their Implications

Although cooperation is driven by a multitude of interests and covers substantive issues in all walks of life, the three perspectives alluded to give a sound basis for a theoretical interpretation of changes in Baltic Sea regional conditions. A certain sequential order is also expressed by the terms. This means that the chronology of events is, to a certain extent, subordinated to the logic of the perspectives. However, whilst no exact temporal fixing points exist certain actions and policy reversals do stand out.[2]

First, the underlying conceptualisation is one of *regionalisation* that has been promoted by new concepts of political organisation. In the 1990s a shared framework of action emerged, visualised by a spatial core of untapped potentials. Following this, dispersed contacts and uncoordinated interactions were soon given direction and purpose by *stabilisation* policies designed to provide security and to promote the institutionalisation of policy-making. The third phase of *normalisation*

---

[2]   Some of the arguments and the sequential identification of trends presented here are in line with a theoretical interpretation of security and cooperation developments in the Baltic Sea Region in the post-Cold War period as presented in Tassinari (2004).

is trickier to define as one could of course argue indefinitely about what a 'normal' state of affairs should look like. However, it is not necessary to explore the political meanings of normalisation beyond making a few simple observations. The term is associated with legal and diplomatic practices connoting the mutual recognition of states and the pursuit of 'correct' inter-state relations. It is consonant with the propensity of regional members to assess, exploit and acquiesce to unfolding new political realities and alignments. It is a relative term, not necessarily describing amicable relations, and might even be consistent with tension and divergent and even opposing political principles. Finally, it also denotes a process of arriving at a crossroads and turning from one pattern of conducting business in a concerned and tense way to an altogether less confrontational mode.

Similarly, each term also tends to emphasise the role of particular entities in sustaining Baltic Sea cooperation: with regionalisation connecting most clearly with civil society, stabilisation highlighting state actions, and normalisation pointing to a shifting focus towards the role of international institutions. Second, the terms also identify changing strategic nexuses on the regional agenda. And third, they also point to a variety of bottom-up and top-down approaches to political and social cooperation.

As an initial illustration of these points, it is useful to take a brief look at Swedish Baltic Sea programmes and to show how the framing of Sweden's neighbourhood policies has changed since the end of the Cold War, and in ways that have reflected shifts in the general mood and orientation of these three periods. The three perspectives are then explored at a regional level in more detail in later sections of the chapter.

First, then, whilst each of the entities (civil society, states, international institutions) has influenced the unfolding of developments in the region, many indicators suggest that their relative importance has varied over time and within the three dimensions. The conventional and rather established view is that civil society and local transnational structures have been the most forceful agents of regionalisation. In Sweden, for example, this pattern was evident when environmental action groups took initiatives to ameliorate worrying conditions in Poland. At a broader level, in 1989 a programme for *emergency aid* was launched, with the general public giving generously in order to alleviate the harsh living conditions and poverty in the post-Soviet Baltic space. Although much popular Swedish concern and solidarity actions were concentrated on the Baltic States, activities were also directed to nearby areas in Russia and Poland as well. In autumn 1991, a strategy designed to support *sovereignty* in weak and reborn states was then put forward and which was built around broader ideas of promoting regionalisation (*Från Visby to Riga*, 1998, p.10).

Following, and alongside this initial emphasis on regionalisation, in the early 1990s a concern with the idea of stabilisation also became evident. In contrast, however, the national governments and their collective instruments have primarily handled issues of stabilisation and security. The terminology of 'security enhancing support', adopted by a Swedish assistance programme in 1995, was illustrative of a shift towards more inter-governmental relations in the pursuit of *security and stability* (*Sveriges Samarbete med Central- och Östeuropa*, 1994, p.17). This tended to overshadow the role of social bonds and civil society organisational networks created during the initial phase of regionalisation. Reading the story from a Polish or Baltic perspective the periodisation between regionalisation and stabilisation might, of course, be different to the emphasis evident in Sweden. For example, a campaign for the maximum objective of achieving stability via their inclusion in the EU and NATO, even before these organisations had declared their doors open for eastern enlargement, was already among their earliest national priorities. Given the mixture of small and big states in the region, it is noteworthy that for quite some time 'a club of smaller states' emerged as the principal initiators of cooperation. The larger states were much more preoccupied with their own internal agendas and more pressing diplomatic issues. Thus, when harder security questions in the military and strategic field were at stake, much caution prevailed. When proposals were tabled also to include such issues on the regional agenda, smaller states – and Germany – preferred to anchor them in the wider international context.

Third, it should be noted that various regional bodies and a number of international institutions also contributed at an early stage to region building, not least by rendering services in renovating legal standards and in monitoring international law and minority questions. Support was given to assist democratic developments and the adaptation of national economies to the rules and standards of market economies. *Development cooperation* later entered regional parlance as a comprehensive description for capacity building during pre-accession EU preparations (and as a part of NATO's Membership Action Plans) in an increasingly multilateralised relationship (*Att utveckla ett grannlandssamarbete*, 1997). With the 2002 decisions to enlarge NATO and the EU, transition policies without clear objectives and time targets faded into the background. It is this developing institutionalisation that both proceeds and sustains a new post-enlargement agenda, and that has characterised the third phase of normalisation. The emergent period of 'normalisation' entails the prospect that many regional matters will now be dealt with at decision-making tables in dominant international structures. One of the main challenges facing the region is now to sustain the particular blend of popular engagement and purposeful collective action by the various actors in the Baltic Sea region now that political attention has begun to shift elsewhere, precisely as a consequence of the shift towards more normalised relations in the north.

Reflecting on this brief overview a number of questions raise themselves for consideration. First, it is important to ask what the central dynamics in the region have been since the end of the Cold War. Or put more pithily, what has made the region tick? Second, how has the emerging pattern been consolidated? Third, how will regional affairs be affected by the post-enlargement agenda and decision-making in the new constellations? Whilst such questions are easier to pose than to answer, utilising the theoretical framework noted above, and drawing on diverse empirical evidence, this chapter explores and provides one explanation of how structural factors and political tendencies have variously interacted under changing conditions within Northern Europe since the end of the Cold War.

Regionalisation

Early Drivers

Regionalisation is an accomplishment. Although Churchill only located the Iron Curtain between Trieste and Lübeck, leaving Northern Europe as a less central area in the East-West contest, modern Baltic Sea regionalism could be rationalised as a policy and strategy precisely for overcoming this barrier. Many forces and happenstance coalesced in creating this opportunity. During the late 1980s, scholars of the arts and humanities emphasised with some justification that their intuitive grasp of overstretched Soviet ambitions and socialism's shaky cultural foundations were more accurate guides to understand unfolding events in Eastern Europe than the categories used by social scientists trained in the realist school of power relations. The relevance of explanations based on economic exhaustion and strategic checkmate to the demise of the socialist system should not, of course, be dismissed. However, it is a fact that the banners of the velvet revolution – 'the contagious strength of new ideas in times of accelerating upheavals', to quote the renaissance historian Jacob Burckhardt (1982, pp.348-49) – were in the Baltic Sea region carried by musicians, artists, poets and an outstanding electricity repair worker. Old political hands, bureaucrats and scientists played more marginal roles.

So, within a short period of time, the Baltic Sea area turned from a militarised borderland into a sub-regional 'laboratory of all-European unification' (Hubel, 1994, p.59), or even a 'microcosm of wider Europe society' (Stålvant, 1999, p.55). The outer contours of the formation were and remain undetermined; an attribute that enhanced the attraction of the region as a *frame of reference* for action. This territorial flexibility was instrumental in construing relations between various types of actors at different levels of society. Once the Cold War overlay shattered, older maps resurfaced, and a different historical cartography of borders and connections in all walks of life was brought to the agenda.

A Plurality of Actors

The regional formation took further strength from the synergetic effects of many decentralised efforts, collaborating institutions and networks. Relatively uninhibited by formal rules, local actors and civic organisations grasped a window of opportunity to establish and cultivate relations with ancient but unknown neighbours. In the economic sphere, the networks of Chambers of Commerce guided and stimulated enterprises and companies in their search for new economic partners and projects. Such genuine bottom-up processes and contacts between members of different civil societies accelerated the shift in public discourses and the creation of institutions. The story of Baltic Sea cooperation is filled with entrepreneurial spirit and direct networking. Popular movements and associations, local communities and civic interests, both stimulated the growth of the region and gave shape to some of its institutional and substantive innovations.[3]

Within a very short period, an immense and dense number of such contacts were established. However, many initial initiatives and projects turned out to be short-lived efforts during the first years of transition. Ongoing cooperation is nevertheless broad and reaches into all walks of life. Much direct support has been given to democratic development and the strengthening of public law, economic development and banking, commerce and transportation, environmental problems and sustainable development, energy and nuclear safety, physical planning and small enterprise, cultural exchange, research and education. Moreover, a variety of international political frameworks and national assistance programmes structured cooperation and provided new incentives for societal actors to solidify their contacts. It also inspired many national authorities, public agencies and MNCs to open 'regional windows' and to establish a regional presence. Meanwhile, the ensuing pattern of bottom-up processes sustained more formal decision-making.

The effect of these developments, and the move towards more open borders, was perhaps even more dramatic in the peripheral High North on the 'Skull-cap' of the Baltic region. Regional dynamics spilled over into the contiguous parts of Russia as well: areas that carry a strategic role for nuclear strategy and the supply of scarce minerals, and that remained a cause of apprehension to Russia's neighbours despite the fact that the Russian successor state was much weaker than its Soviet predecessor. A sub-regional cooperation process between the Nordic countries and Russia was therefore consciously initiated for mitigating threats stemming from the legacy of nuclear infrastructures and cross-border ills. If Baltic Sea regionalism was inspired by and profited from the Hansa metaphor, so in the Barents Sea the impetus to convert barriers into bridges was found in old Pomor trading routes and sea-lanes. Obviously, the appeals for regionalism fell onto fertile ground at a time when changing cultural, social and political needs coincided and interacted with natural and physical environments.

Within the new European architecture, a Northern wing established itself. The emerging and enlarged North developed from fundamental reassessments in combination with the particular traditions and national experiences that characterise these parts of the continent. In the late 1980s, some efforts were made to extend the field of action of Nordic cooperation by inviting foreign participation in issue-specific conferences. Despite changes in the Nordic Council's structure and competences it was found that the institution could not accommodate the dynamics of political transformation underway. Elements of Nordic ideology and

---

[3]   For an early identification of actors and forces, see Joenniemi and Wæver (1992). An inventory of initiatives and actors can be found in Stålvant (1996).

modes of cooperation, therefore, were instead projected onto the emerging networks and proliferating translocal contacts (Wæver, 1992).

. Baltic Sea regionalisation rests on a solid material foundation. Different indicators for trading patterns, economic relations, investments, transport and social communication all bear witness to the extent to which the Baltic Sea basin countries and Norway and Iceland are interacting with each other, and have become interdependent in many walks of life. Not least, large region-based international companies and financial institutions have invested heavily and expanded their activities throughout the region through foreign direct investment (FDI), mergers and acquisitions of new plants.

Common Interest

Different answers have been given to the question as to what factors have been conducive to region building in Northern Europe. A very modest degree of regional cooperation emerged only early in the 1970s as a rational response to shared environmental problems (see, Johnson, 1973; 1986). Two conventions were signed, one on the management of fisheries and one on the environmental protection of the Baltic Sea. These two Baltic Sea Conventions were among the few instruments and relations that were not affected by negative spill-over from worsening political and military relations in the early 1980s. Evidently they embodied both a symbolic and substantial value, although within limited fields.

In the absence of direct legacies, however, it is noteworthy how national cultural institutions and educational grant schemes in the Nordic countries were turned into diplomatic assets in the early years of cooperation in the vicinity areas. A Finnish estimate of a decade of allocations to supporting political and economic change in Central and Eastern Europe claims that more than €600 million was spent on grants (*From Support to Partnership*, 2004). A former Director of the Danish Cultural Institute has confirmed that his organisation was turned into an asset and foreign policy tool in the late 1980s. The foreign minister proposed a considerable expansion of the means available to a scholarly and cultural exchange programme and called for the swift establishment of information centres in vicinity areas.[4]

Second to culture was concern for the environment. The securitisation of the environment mirrored the gravity of the situation, but also resonated well with public opinion and donor countries' willingness to assist. Sometimes the many projects also corresponded with the recipient's concerns. Not least, after the Chernobyl nuclear catastrophe and Gorbachev's Murmansk speech in 1987, the notion of 'comprehensive environmental security' came to legitimise direct cooperation within committed domestic partners and with actors in the field. Securitisation of life-sustaining processes and alarming conditions in ailing

---

[4]   Personal communication. The step-up of activities is described in the yearly reports, 'Årsberetning' of the Danish Cultural Institute between 1990-1993.

industries and chemical-intensive agricultural practices made 'comprehensive environmental security' a legitimate objective for foreign assistance. Not least, Poland became a favoured target.

In fact, a widely shared perception of environmental deterioration interacted with political developments and precipitated a number of decisive turning points. In the 1980s resistance against Moscow-directed projects with negative environmental consequences mobilised public opinion and encouraged people to rally behind the banners of national front movements in the struggle for Baltic independence. Oil spills and an infectious disease among seals effectively brought home the message of the Baltic Sea as being something of common concern over which there should be shared responsibility. Moreover, following the fall of the Berlin Wall such issues persuaded the Swedish and Polish Prime Ministers jointly to arrange the region's first post-Cold War conference that reflected the new realities and the different political geography in the region. The meeting, held in Ronneby in Sweden in September 1990, gathered together a variety of participants, with the aim of framing an action programme. Present were not only the riparian states, but also autonomous and semi-autonomous regions, international organisations, and international banks and NGOs. Also present were observer states with an interest in the region.[5] The inclusiveness of representation set a precedent for other issue areas of regional cooperation that would develop later.

Whilst, many small project schemes saw the light of day, environmental protection received the lion's share of financial and technical assistance. An overall calculation of total transfers of European assistance aid, however, shows that from 1988-96 a higher proportion of projects were justified using environmental arguments in the Baltic Sea region than in central or southern Europe (Bergh, 1996). At the same time, it also took some time before loans, grants and corporate FDI could be properly coordinated and geared to costly infrastructural projects and commercial investments.

Security Downplayed

Certainly security concerns were also prominent in promoting regional cooperation, but only as a mute motive. A common assertion in small state theory is that when great power alliances and the international environment are 'fixed', then small states have a great amount of security, but little freedom of action. When, on the other hand, the system collapses, breaks up and changes its character, small states are then presented with considerable freedom of movement, but many uncertainties. In retrospect, however, it seems that in the 1990s a combination of both freedom and security prevailed in Northern Europe, with the small Nordic group of states provided with considerable room for manoeuvre, which they used

---

[5]   When commenting on his life-long political career, former Swedish Prime Minister, Ingvar Carlsson, mentioned this meeting as being a primary achievement and more important than, for example, Sweden's EU membership.

to sustain regionalisation. Bo Huldt (2004) even claims that such a situation was not only a unique incidence in the history of the region, but might also have been a unique event in small state history *per se.*

The role played by the Nordic countries in inventing *institutional responses* at the sub-regional level in order to deal with the new conditions of the post-Cold War environment is particularly noteworthy. The Barents Euro-Arctic Council, the Arctic Council and the later EU Northern Dimension proposal have distinctly Nordic roots, whilst the proposal to establish the Council of Baltic Sea States (CBSS) was made jointly by the Danish and German foreign ministers. The Nordic and Baltic Councils, in combination with their associated networks, have also impacted on the shape of the political landscape. Despite separate priorities in the national foreign policies of various states of the region to become members of, or to develop special relations with, NATO and the EU, it took almost a decade before processes based on the two main collective organisations within Europe actually became prominent also in a regional perspective

The tendency to base cooperative proposals on a security-conscious strategy while excluding security elements from the explicit mandate of regional bodies managing cooperation reflects an old Nordic tradition. The Nordic Council itself only accepted security as a proper topic for cooperation with the demise of the Cold War. Only in 1991 did the five heads of government conclude that, 'on the interests and needs of their citizens, the Nordic countries must try to influence developments in Europe and among their neighbours' and that this would require a renewal of Nordic international consultations. However, they carefully circumscribed the mandates of the emerging new Councils (Nordic Council, 1992).

Thus, security was not considered to be a proper object for the CBSS to handle, even if members could introduce 'other matters or possible subjects for cooperation should they so decide' (*Declaration*, 1992). A similar duality was also expressed in the Finnish proposal for an EU Northern Dimension initiative, and where it was feared that the inclusion of overt security questions would impede, rather than facilitate, any progress. Moreover, including security questions, it was feared, might elevate the Northern Dimension to a purely intergovernmental mode of foreign policy decision-making, rather than keeping it within the confines of the Union's 'external relations', where there was also the possibility of it having recourse to the Commission's expenditures. The Barents Council also stayed away from matters of high political contention. The view has been that should the need arise such issues can be raised on the sidelines of meetings, without this entailing any pressure to reach agreement, and which in turn will have only negligible repercussions on other items on the agenda.

Regionalisation cum Laboratory

So, by happenstance and calculation, a number of different organising principles and institutions have both created and integrated a system of cooperative multilevel relations among public and private actors. From a theoretical point of view a number of interpretative designations have been proposed for describing and characterising the ensuing Baltic Sea formation. A significant number of studies concur in their view of the significance of bottom-up processes in fostering a regional perspective (Hubel and Gänzle, 2001; Schymik, 2003). However, the exact nature of the Baltic Sea constellation defies simple classification. It clearly differs from the Nordic community of small states based on homogenous civic values and similar institutions. In contrast, in the Baltic Sea area regional cooperation flourished thanks to, rather than despite, heterogeneous background factors, divided histories and a diversity of actors.

At the same time, the nature of the constellation is an argument for caution. The Baltic Sea area is a peripheral sub-region, linking peoples and authorities in Europe's key regions, the EU, Nordic non-EU states, and Russia. To no surprise, relations encompass many contradictions between and across the countries. For example, regionalisation and decentralised cooperation unfolds as part of government strategy among the Nordic states, or as a consequence of a basic political trait in German political culture. In contrast, in Russian politics, this trait is seen by many as a policy of default, or as a token of weakness and incapacity on the part of state authority. Furthermore, the policies pursued by Putin's Russia have also differed from the turbulent years of the early 1990s, which was a period of considerable struggle between the centre and the regions. The Federation's good economic record over several consecutive years has facilitated national consolidation, whilst administrative reforms impacting on internal centre-periphery relations have partly halted the further decentralisation of foreign relations, but have also given certain established cross-border contacts a more solid basis.[6]

A neoliberal argument concerning conditions for stability and order can be used to summarise the essentials of 'the Baltic Sea laboratory'. Ideas about the virtues of pluralism have been transferred to the international realm. Overlapping authorities and competing organisational solutions to different concerns now underpin stability. Fuzzy borders of competence have become depicted as frontiers and meeting grounds to explore 'win-win' situations at the expense of clear demarcations and exclusions that might only reach sub-optimal gains. Not least, cities and local municipal cooperation have functioned as inroads into transnational networking and region building. With the risk of oversimplification, it seems a vibrant civil society has begun to emerge at the transnational level, a view which epitomises much of the social science discourses about Baltic Sea regional cooperation. Finally, this neomedieval or postmodern vision is distinctly different from a modern order of sovereign states characterised by clear delineations between self-controlled national spaces.

This portrait obviously entails a positive appreciation of restrained top-handed governmental guidance, national funding opportunities, and self-sustained transnational contacts and cooperation between functional authorities, private corporations and NGOs, all of which have been apparent in the Baltic Sea region

---

[6]   See Prozorov's chapter in this volume.

since the end of the Cold War. However, to what an extent are such developments still tenable?

Stabilisation - Bringing States In

The dynamic elements of regionalisation nurtured by Baltic Sea regionalism and its underlying logic have been described above. Closer scrutiny, however, reveals that in setting national objectives, and while adjusting to accelerating changes, the distinction between high and low politics has impacted on the appreciation of the nature of the European strategic environment. Politics have rather been framed on the logic of *a dual agenda* (Joenniemi and Stålvant, 1995, p.30).[7] Civilian security concerns of a non-military nature have been a strong driver behind regionalism. A different type of game and national utility calculations guided national governments when strategic possibilities were opened by reforms in European and Atlantic institutions, not least with the gradual opening of doors towards enlargement. The core question – the conditions for inclusion in European and Transatlantic structures – brought the diplomatic heterogeneity of the Baltic constellation into the open. Not least the Nordic states were (and remain) notably divided. However, differing formal affiliations did not impede these countries – and a number of interested outsiders as well – from engaging in 'competitive cooperation' in cultivating links with the new democracies and neighbours. As multilateral negotiations and national preparations for membership either in the EU or NATO dragged on, more pressing threats from areas in the vicinity made inroads on the regional agenda. The new challenges were mainly of two kinds: civic security risks yielded by intensified exchanges and trans-boundary effects, and common problems stemming from the socialist legacy (Hubel and Gänzle, 2002).

So, with the demise of the Cold War confrontation and the advent of conflicts rooted in internal conditions, the security spectrum of contingencies widened. The new range of potential threats suggested a need to rethink national security strategies to include other violent disruptions and societal vulnerabilities to non-military challenges. To mitigate and tackle such threats, according to Anders Bjurner (1999, p.9), not only are inter-governmental actions called for, but increasingly also *'trans-state'* actions. Upon this conflation of security and stability, national governments in the Baltic Sea region embarked on a course whereby soft security measures were accepted as a major focus of action. Enhancing broad-based cooperation and providing targeted support to assist the transition process in individual countries was seen as central to international and national security and stability policies. Uncertainties in institutional capacity and the institutions of law and order in the transition countries also prompted the

---

[7]   For a critical review of academic and political uses of soft and hard security, see Knudsen (1998, pp.47-50).

provision of concrete assistance, not least through training agreements and cooperation in the improvement of norms and rules. All this occurred in order to try and prevent the weakening, or even break-up, of important state security and law enforcement structures ranging from the military sector to the tasks performed by border guards, customs services, legal services and police and rescue organisations. Amongst other things, liaison officers were exchanged between twin authorities, and some spectacular law enforcement operations were synchronised (*Från Visby to Riga*, pp.36-7).

Focusing on low politics and promoting soft security therefore implies engaging in costly and concerted action. Policies of this kind differ from the traditional national positioning strategies of diplomatic politics, and are instead increasingly framed and implemented through negotiated bilateral and multilateral programmes. Because such policies engage partners across different states and nations the interaction between ideas, decisions and institutions is particularly important for making such policies succeed.

However, improvements in security, protection measures, and actions to build up the capacity to cope with different sorts of crises, are at the mercy of budget lines, programme conditions and application procedures. Shifting priorities between successive tenders can also inhibit the functioning of long-term and ongoing projects. The framing and operationalisation of the Northern Dimension, for example, has revealed the problems inherent in coordinating the many funds and instruments of the European Commission (Stålvant, 2001). Some of these instruments, action plans and stock of experience were transferred into EU programmes when Sweden and Finland became members in 1995, since in preparation for their membership and for the later adoption of the Schengen regime in the region, significant investments were made in Poland and the Baltic States as regards border protection, border crossing posts and border surveillance capabilities.

However, improvements in civil security and less threatening military contingency postures notwithstanding, more traditional security concerns regarding the Baltic States were also evident throughout the 1990s. For example, there was a widely shared appreciation of the vulnerable situation of the three small Baltic States that prompted many donor governments also to assist in helping them build-up their military security capabilities (Möttölä, 1998). However, the main political question in this respect revolved around the reconciliation of NATO expansion with regional stability. While Poland's prospective membership in 1999 was met with fierce resistance in Russia, but was grudgingly accepted, the inclusion of the former Soviet territory of the Baltic republics was felt to be absolutely unacceptable. There was also hesitation among many NATO allies, bar Denmark, before the Bush administration decided to go along with a big bang approach to enlargement. However, it should be noted that already in May 1996 the Swedish Prime Minister surprisingly announced that the decisions and preferences of the Baltic States should be respected (Huldt, 2004, p.404). The legitimising argument for such a statement was that over the long run, if the Baltic States would feel more secure as a result of membership, and would no longer feel caught in an unpalatable grey zone between NATO and Russia, then ultimately this might also be beneficial to Russia as well. In contrast, Finnish politicians continued to air concerns about the Baltic States' possible inclusion in NATO right up until 2002, by which time their future membership had become an open secret.

By that time, American policy in the aftermath of 9/11 had upset the global agenda. Putin's Russia had lowered its fierce resistance to the Baltic States' NATO membership by admitting that the step would not be a tragedy for Russia, although it would not do the Balts any good. NATO-Russian relations had been placed on a firmer footing by the creation of the NATO-Russia Council (NRC), already before the Prague summit, in May 2002. Therefore, although alliance membership signifies a triumph for the three small ex-Soviet republics, it has occurred under radically altered transatlantic and global conditions. Russia has also noted that the NRC could be a diplomatic asset in monitoring the evolution of NATO, including the policies pursued by its Baltic neighbours. Also important, in this regard, is that the non-Article 5 'new threats' identified by NATO include the global War on Terrorism – in which Russia is a privileged partner – and which is increasingly shaping the security preparations and threat perceptions of NATO members. To some extent this is also doing the same within the Baltic region as well.

Normalisation: Steps Towards Different Games?

As stated earlier, the year 2004 marks a watershed. Not least this is because political discourses and national strategies will likely change with EU and NATO enlargement. Initially, of course, Russia's strong campaign against new NATO members in 1996-99 did succeed in postponing the Baltic States' inclusion in NATO. However, whilst Russia proposed a variety of alternative security arrangements and guarantees, backed up by clear measures and conditions, they were all dismissed. At the same time, NATO's desire to develop good relations with Russia probably acted as a restraint on the Baltic States' relations with their eastern neighbour. For example, aspirant members have been expected to conform to specific Membership Action Plans in which a number of political and military conditions have been laid down, the most notable in the case of the Baltics being that future members should settle ethnic and territorial disputes by peaceful means. Meanwhile, domestic reforms during the pre-membership period have also profoundly reshaped the social and economic fabric of new members.

Therefore, with membership in the EU and NATO the Baltic States, like Poland, have accomplished their primary foreign policy objectives. Their security concerns have been salved and their economic, legal and administrative progress has been endorsed by EU accession. Supported by the Nordics and Germany, and with Russia acquiescing to the new European realities of the post-Cold War period, *normalisation* has become the catchword for the new rules of the game. Indicative of this is a statement made by President Putin whilst on a visit to Finland in

September 2001 that, in his opinion, the enlargement process should not be understood in terms of gaining security guarantees, since nobody was being threatened by anybody in Europe. Nevertheless, he declared that Russia would not start 'a hysterical campaign' against the Baltic States, indicating that some tensions were perhaps still evident.[8]

Much restraint and caution characterises the military and deployment aspects of alliance extension. Already in 1997, with the signing of the Founding Act on Mutual Relations, Cooperation and Security with Russia, NATO gave reassurances that it had 'no intention, no plan and no reason to deploy nuclear weapons on the territory of new members'. Baltic politicians have also, in various statements, signalled their reluctance for establishing both new, and/or foreign, bases on their soil. Actual deployments have also been modest in volume. The one exceptional issue, however, has been the symbolic air patrols undertaken by Belgian pilots in NATO aircraft on the eve of formal membership in April 2004.

The master notion of the previous decade – transition – is therefore outdated, whilst the language of donor and recipient is also no longer adequate or so appropriate. Consequently, it is therefore important to ponder some conceivable consequences of these developments for security, welfare and regional cooperation in Northern Europe.

Security

In the context of thinking about security, the first thing to note is that the emergence of new global threats and the War on Terrorism has diverted attention to other more distant unruly areas and hot spots. However, as the repercussions on Europe of America's new assertive policy, and the splits this has also occasioned between the countries of the Baltic Sea region have been noted in previous sections, when discussing security it is suffice to make some small observations on relations in the region.

Importantly, as a result of their membership of NATO and the EU, and as a result of the logic of collective diplomacy, the former East European countries of the region will now meet Russia as a strategic partner, be it in matters of security or economy. In consequence, however, the Baltic States' accession will leave Finland and Sweden in a shrinking camp of partners engaged in Partnership for Peace (PfP) exercises and activities. At the same time, the Nordic states' previous significant security-enhancing support for the Baltic States has left a Nordic legacy that emphasises preparations for total territorial defence in defence thinking. Today, however, such strategies are less in demand, as the new members will be assigned quite different roles and missions within the alliance. Reorienting the strategic nexus from homeland guarantees and being a 'security receiver', more towards participation in out-of-area operations, is in tune with the international agenda, but it is a costly exercise for a would-be 'security provider'. However, as

---

[8]   For an overview of NATO enlargement and the Baltic States, see Huang (2003).

an Estonian official maintains, 'In joint operations small states have the possibility of providing small but effective niche-capacities, both independently as well as in cooperation with other nations of similar size' (Tiido, 2002, p.12).

However, hard choices might be on the cards for small countries that have been a part of the dual enlargement of the EU and NATO. In general they have seen NATO as the main security provider. Problematically, though, the hope for a positive NATO-EU partnership in the aftermath of the 'Berlin-plus' agreement, which allows the EU to use NATO resources for military/peacekeeping operations that it may undertake as a part of its developing common security and defence policy, and the concurrent view on the division of labour between the two organisations, is not as straightforward as it initially seems. Indeed, there are significant chances that this balance might well be upset, especially in situations where there may well be more than one operation underway, each of which may require a contribution from relevant member states. The fact of the matter is that most of the new members simply are not in a position to contribute to more than one operation, raising the question of which operation (organisation) they should prioritise, or whether they should increase defence expenditure to enhance individual state capabilities.[9] This problem is less acute for the militarily non-aligned countries, Finland and Sweden; however, as they also aim to remain active in this field it is not an issue they can avoid. In current plans for cutting back defence costs and for restructuring military forces one preferred external option has emerged that envisages the build-up of European crisis management capabilities through the creation of integrated European battle groups. Beyond this, however, emerging new threats also challenge old security thinking. For example, the solidarity clause and the commitment for EU members to assist each other in cases of natural disasters or terrorism has also opened up new prospects for cooperation in the civilian field and with regard to functional security. In the latter field, Baltic Sea cooperation already has a good record, and appears as a possible stepping-stone when building up multinational support teams.

The expanded Union will face many different foreign commitments. The centre of gravity in the stabilisation policies pursued by NATO and the EU, respectively, will move towards the new eastern members. In this sense, non-alignment entails a dilemma of political marginalisation rather than a security problem for Finland and Sweden. Denmark has a certain advantage in being a dual member, and has forged links with the Eastern countries who have all opted to support the US-led coalition of the willing. In this situation, the new Baltic Sea EU members have also revealed an eagerness to take the lead in cultivating stability in the new neighbourhood regions of the EU and NATO. Poland's ascendancy as a regional and major European power and its plea for an Eastern Dimension to complement the EU's Northern Dimension has been the most poignant voice for this orientation. Polish activism and its pivotal position within the EU were put to a test early on in

---

[9]   On such problems concerning the dual use of NATO military capabilities, see Croft et al., (2000, pp.513-4).

connection with the disputed presidential election in Ukraine in November 2004. Baltic state activism in the Caucasus and in East Balkan states also reveals similar concerns and a willingness to export their experience to prospective listeners (e.g., see Miniotaite, 2004; Ilves, 2003, p.197).

Welfare

When it comes to questions of welfare European governance is set for a profound transformation with the *fifth enlargement*. A Union of 25 is different from one of 15 members. Membership will impact on a wide array of policies, and not only in the domestic field. Just to pinpoint the obvious, enlargement has left Russia as the only CEE partner in the Northern Dimension. Although economic cooperation and trade questions are important in Baltic Sea cooperation, it is not a system for legal integration and regulation. However, Baltic Sea countries will, in certain matters, become a regional intergovernmental lobby within a much more complicated system for shaping decisions.

Three aspects of Baltic Sea cooperation in the perspective of EU-Europeanisation should be highlighted.

First, the Swedish Prime Minister has made concerted efforts to orchestrate a unity of views among the new members before meetings in the Council of Ministers. The new Baltic-Nordic group has been recognised as the 3+3 group, in contrast to the 5+3 conceptualisation of Nordic-Baltic cooperation prevalent in the 1990s. The need to secure support from Poland and Germany has also been mentioned, but in this context institutionalised forms are absent (*Finland's Security and Defence Policy*, 2004). However, decision-making rules within the Council complicate matters. In majority voting this eight-member state caucus will neither be strong enough to block a proposal, nor to ensure that one gets accepted. This assessment is true, both for decisions taken according to Nice rules, and for those that may be taken as a result of the simplified EU Constitutional Treaty regulations.

Second, the Finnish researcher Esko Antola (2003) has commented that, 'the economic policy paradigm of New Europe might well emerge as an important element in the Baltic Sea Region. ...The Baltic countries are following the neo-liberal paradigm to an extent that is not unknown in "Old Europe", Ireland and Great Britain included'. This observation entails a number of consequences, some of which are already becoming politicised and embedded in national politics. For example, having secured enlargement, Swedish (and some Finnish) politicians have added their voices to criticisms of such 'libertarian' models and their applications. Notably, a government bill proposed that Sweden should introduce transition rules in order to invite 'social tourists' benefiting from generous welfare payments. Likewise, the prime minister reproached some of the new EU members, arguing that economic dynamism and fast achievements should not be attained in an irresponsible manner. Indeed, he publicly criticised Estonia for its low taxation rules and for maintaining an unfair competitive edge (*Dagens Nyheter*, 11 October

2003). Flexible regulatory frameworks might not only encourage low-cost seeking enterprises to relocate their production to other countries, but will probably also put pressures on social standards and welfare provisions.

Third, Sweden and Germany have also been joined by other net payers in a proposal to lower the proportion of national GDP that serves as the key for calculating state payments into the EU budget. Likewise, a difference of opinion between new and old members concerning the level of payments within the Common Agricultural Policy (CAP) also persists. In the CAP, however, EU funds are not an agent for redistribution, but rather reinforce already existing income disparities between member states.

In sum, it rather seems that family quarrels between Baltic Sea EU members will, in all likelihood, become more frequent in future.

Regionalisation Reappraised? The Prospects of Normalisation

A few indications from 2004 suggest that Baltic Sea regionalisation has lost much popular appeal and political zeal. For example, government ministers of the region now meet less often than they used to, whilst the frequently heard argument that this is a place where the inclusion of Russia can be realised makes less sense if a centralised Russia pursues strategic dialogues with Brussels over the heads of regional stakeholders. Also notable is that only a few of the ideas and proposals first probed by regional bodies have been emulated or deliberately transferred to the EU level. Indeed, despite commitments to the contrary made by EU civil servants in connection with the Northern Dimension, the Commission actually seems to downplay the utility of sub-regional institutions as initiators or executers of policy (Catellani, 2001, pp.58, 65-6). Further indicators of the loss of regionalisation's appeal include the fact that the services of the special office of the CBSS Commissioner are no longer in demand, whilst the workings of the CBSS secretariat in Stockholm are currently being reviewed by the incumbent president, Poland, with new proposals due to be put forward in 2005 as to the future of the organisation. Finally, support for some of the national, local and specialised Baltic Sea secretariats for regional cooperation has also disappeared, or their functions have been merged with other public tasks.

In Sweden the high tide of a decade of Baltic Sea activism was marked by three consecutive 'Baltic billions' spent on regional assistance projects using extraordinary procedures between 1996-2000.[10] However, these expenditures and other national programmes for vicinity areas have now been phased out. For

---

[10] It is a token of high political salience that these means were introduced outside of normal budgetary procedures and assigned to a special decision procedure on expenditures attached to the Prime Ministers's Office and later to the Ministry of Industry. As there was no emergency, the observation qualifies central assumptions in securitisation theory. On securitisation see Buzan, Wæver and de Wilde (1998, ch.2).

example, funding for an Estonian language-training programme for that country's Russian-speaking minority will now cease. Likewise, EU expenditures that spurred regional affairs and cross-border activities through the TACIS, PHARE and Interreg programmes, or in the context of the pre-accession process, will also be renegotiated and slimmed down in the future structural funds of the EU and in the next multi-annual budget.

At the same time, it has been argued that a dense network of civil society contacts and city and county twinning sustains the regional pattern. This is well supported and published figures reveal the many interconnections and city-chains created. However, people-to-people contacts seem to have reached saturation point. Although there are renewals and changes, the list of Baltic Sea secretariats, NGOs and action groups has remained quite stable since their founding a decade ago. The creation of new region-specific NGO networks and twinned sister institutions is due much more to organisational fusions and administrative reorganisations rather than any new innovations.

When promoting cooperation, solidarity and friendship motives have been overtaken by questions about utility and return. It is likely that some sister city-relations will contract as new generations of decision makers come into power and the initial zeal is lost. Likely winners are those that occupy hub positions within regional and European networks. Cities and municipalities that diversified contacts and engaged a broader section of municipal services and private interests in sustained economic exchanges with regional partners are also likely to stay in place.

So, to conclude, Baltic Sea developments are still likely to be influenced by different categories of actors. However, the passage of time reflects the fact that different discourses and a reassessment of motives and interests have become evident. As noted, the master signifier of the previous decade – transition – is now out. Whilst initially a dialogue between *donors and receivers* supported the rise of participatory transboundary regionalism, today such language does not hold any longer. Not least, the frequent misuse of funds by donor-country consultants in the provision of foreign assistance has discredited the tiered presumptions of such roles. Meanwhile, the creation of and increased emphasis on the language of *partnerships* suggests a more utilitarian and rational pursuit of interests between corporate business, bureaucracies and political authorities is emerging. In normalised but institutionalised settings for taking decisions governmental *parties* are becoming the pre-eminent players. They are resuming their formal roles, but at a risk of getting bogged down in diplomatic battles about trivial matters and in formal wrangling about subtle rules.

More significant is the changed nature of what is at stake. To a certain extent, the stakes have moved beyond internal regional preoccupations to a concern with external threats and international relations more broadly. The much less pronounced image of Russia as a tacit enemy has lessened the motives for Nordic security assistance. Normalisation, therefore, might well render the Baltic Sea region a less distinct profile in a wider Europe.

Institutional factors in Europe are also likely to redefine interests in tactical games. As the rift over the Iraq war in major international institutions has demonstrated, discord within cooperative organisations and political and military alliances seems to be part and parcel of normalisation. Such conditions, together with centralised and long-term bureaucratic planning, might, despite good intentions, slow down and impede issue-based networking and financially dependent, but routinised and local, cross-regional cooperation. If it turns out that the different corners of Europe are reconstituted as rather fixed alliances in distributive negotiations, stalemate might result. In such a situation new flexible frameworks have to be designed, allowing for more 'autonomy' at the sub-regional level. In this contingency Baltic Sea cooperation has a good record of reasserting itself and of working together at all levels of governance.

Beyond the Region: What Dynamics Will Unfold?

There is little doubt that the next set of states lying in a band further to the East will be a new testing ground for European security and stability. In this context, Russia is very reserved and is vehemently resisting the EU's emerging policies in the post-Soviet space. More generally, the Union has been criticised for its unilateral framing of policies and for its 'conceptual deficiency' in making the new neighbours and Russia simply 'objects' of its policies, rather than engaging with outsiders as subjects with a legitimate voice in the policy-framing debate (Emerson, 2004, pp.27-8).

For their part, Poland and the Baltic States have declared their willingness to seize 'a chance to contribute with their particular historical experience and know-how' to the effort of developing relations with these new neighbours (Ojuland, 2004, p.152). But what will the other Baltic Sea countries do? Will they take up the challenge and work side by side with the Baltic States and Poland, or will they redefine their roles to provide support to the new Eastern EU members behind the front lines? This might be a commendable course, but so far the prospects for this have been given rather scant attention. The course suffers from a lack of domestic popular engagement. Neither is there evidence of a self-generated dynamic bottom-up process, as there was in the initial phases of Baltic Sea regionalisation. The Baltic experience suggests that links between civil society associations make a difference by impacting on the development of political cultures and on development as such. Thus, a proliferation of such contacts between new member states and their near neighbours would be desirable. However, conditions apparently differ between these proto-democracies of today and the freedom of action that the demise of totalitarianism and socialism entailed fifteen years ago. There is apparently less certainty about the stakes and forces at play, and as a result popular mobilisation is more likely to follow the lead of public policy, rather than the other way around, and as was the case in the Baltic experience.

The pattern of change identified in this article outlined three different perspectives that it was argued tend to follow a separate logic of their own. Each is an essential element in international affairs and European sub-regional relations, however, much of the evidence pointed to a sequential order leading to the unfolding of contemporary politics. Whether the pattern and the particular interactions of structural factors and political tendencies that worked well in the Baltic Sea setting is tenable also for other political complexes is a matter for reflection. While the core terms are apt to identify and describe crucial processes, it would be a challenge to explore in a more systematic manner the conditions under which they yield benign results.

References

Antola, Esko (2003), 'Falling Apart? Diverging Trends in the Baltic Sea Region', *Mimeo*, seminar paper 26-27 September, Jean Monnet Centre, University of Turku.

Att utveckla ett grannlandssamarbete [Developing Neighbourhood Co-operation] Swedish Government Bill 1997/98:172.

Bergh, R. (1996), 'Environmental Cooperation with the Baltic States', Inventory Report, Swedish Environment Protection Agency, *Mimeo*.

Bjurner, Anders (1999), 'European Security at the End of the Twentieth Century: The Subregional Contribution', in A. Cottey (ed.), *Subregional Cooperation in the New Europe: Building Security, Prosperity and Solidarity from the Barents to the Black Sea*, London and New York, Macmillan, pp. 8-22.

Burckhardt, J (1982/1905), *Die Geschichtlichen Crisen. Über das Studium Der Geschichte*, München, Verlag C. H. Beck, new edition edited by Peter Ganz.

Buzan, Barry, Wæver, Ole and de Wilde, Jaap (1998), *Security. A New Framework for Analysis*, London, Lynne Rienner.

Catellani, Nicola (2001), 'The Multilevel Implementation of the Northern Dimension', in Hanna Ojanen (ed.), *The Northern Dimension: Fuel for the EU?* Helsinki and Berlin, Ulkopoliittinen instituutti and Institut für Europäische Politik, pp. 54-77.

Croft, Stuart., Howorth, Jolyon., Terriff, Terry and Webber, Mark (2000), 'NATO's Triple Challenge', *International Affairs*, Vol. 76(3), pp. 495-518.

Dagens Nyheter, 11 October 2003.

Declaration, Foreign Ministers of the Baltic Sea States, Copenhagen March 5-6, 1992.

Emerson, Michael (2004), *The Wider Europe Matrix*, Brussels, Brussels, CEPS.

Finland's Security and Defence Policy (2004), Helsinki: Prime Minister's Office.

Från Visby to Riga [From Visby to Riga] (1998), Stockholm, The Prime Minister's Office.

From Support to Partnership – Finland's Strategy for Cooperation in its Neighbouring Areas (2004), Helsinki, Ministry of Foreign Affairs.

Huang, Mel (2003), 'Climbing Down from the Summit: Estonia's Road Towards NATO', in Andreas Kasekamp (ed.), *The Estonian Foreign Policy Yearbook 2003*, Tallinn, The Estonian Foreign Policy Institute, pp. 76-90.

Hubel, Helmut (1994), 'The Baltic Dimension of European Unification', in Kaisa Lahteenmäki (ed.), *Dimensions of Conflict and Cooperation in the Baltic Sea Rim*, Tampere: TAPRI Research reports no. 58.

Hubel, Helmut and Gänzle, Stefan (2001), *CBSS as a sub-regional organisation for 'soft security' management in the North East of Europe*, Report to the Presidency of the Council of Baltic Sea States. Available at http://www.cbss.st.

Hubel, Helmut and Gänzle, Stefan (2002), 'The Soft Security Agenda at the Sub-regional Level: Policy Responses of the Council of Baltic Sea States', in Holger Moroff (ed.), *European Soft Security Policies: The Northern Dimension*, Helsinki and Berlin, Ulkopoliittinen instituutti and Institut für Europäische Politik, pp. 251-280.

Huldt, Bo (2004), 'The post-Cold War Transition in the Baltic Sea Region: A decade of Small State Activism', in *International Security in a Time of Change: Threats, Concepts, Institutions*. Festschrift für Daniel Adam Rotfeld, Serie Demokratie, Sicherheit, Frieden no. 164, Baden-Baden, NOMOS, pp. 392-406.

Ilves, Toomas Hendrik (2003), 'The Grand Enlargement and the Great Wall of Europe', in Andres Kasekamp (ed.), *The Estonian Foreign Policy Yearbook 2003*, Tallinn, Estonian Foreign Policy Institute, pp. 181-200.

Joenniemi, Pertti and Stålvant, Carl-Einar (1995) 'Baltic Sea Politics: Achievements and Challenges', in *NORD*, no.35, Stockholm, The Nordic Council of Ministers, pp. 9-54.

Joenniemi, Pertti and Wæver, Ole (1992), 'Regionalisation around the Baltic Rim', Background Report to the 2nd Parliamentary Conference on Co-operation in the Baltic Sea Area, Stockholm, Nordic seminars and working groups reports.

Johnson, B. (1973), 'The Baltic', in Robin Churchill (ed.), *New Directions in the Law of the Sea*, New York, Dobbs Ferry.

Johnson, B. (1986), *Folkrätt och Säkerhetspolitik* [International Law and Security Politics], Stockholm, Norstedts.

Knudsen, Olav F. (1998), 'Cooperative Security in the Baltic Sea Region', *Chaillot Papers 33*, Paris, Institute for Security Policy.

Laaser, Claus-Friedrich and Schröder, Klaus (2003), 'Knocking on the Door: the Baltic Rim Transition Countries Ready for Europe?', in Lars Hedegaard and Bjarne Lindström (eds.), *The NEBI Yearbook 2003: North European and Baltic Sea Integration*, Berlin, Springer Verlag, pp. 21-45.

Miniotaite, Grazina (2004), 'Lithuania's New Neighbours Policy in the Framework of the EU's "Wider Europe-Neighbourhood" Initiative', Vilnius, March, (Unpublished research report).

Möttölä, Kari (1998), 'The Nordic Countries and an Updated Security Agenda for the Baltic Sea Region', in *Hard and Soft Security in the Baltic Sea Region*, Seminar report, Stockholm, The Olof Palme International Center, pp. 108-125.

Nilsson, Jan H. (2003), *Östersjöområdet. Studiet av Interaction och Barriärer* [The Baltic Sea Area. Studies of Interactions and Barriers], Lund, Sifysos Förlag.

Nordic Council (1992), Report from the 42nd Session, Stockholm.

Ojuland, Kristiina (2004), 'EU 25 is more than 15+10', in *Baltic Defence Review*, Vol. 1(11), pp. 147-153.

Schymik, C. (2003), 'Networking Civil Society in the Baltic Sea Region', in Norbert Götz and Jörg Hackmann (eds.), *Civil Society in the Baltic Sea Region*, Aldershot, Ashgate, pp. 217-234.

Stalvant, Carl-Einar (1996), *Actors around the Baltic Sea*, Stockholm: Swedish Ministry for Foreign Affairs.

Stålvant, Carl-Einar (1999), 'The Council of Baltic Sea States', in A. Cottey (ed.), *Subregional Cooperation in the New Europe: Building Security, Prosperity and Stability from the Barents to the Black Sea*, London and New York, Macmillan.

Stålvant, Carl-Einar (2001), *The Northern Dimension - A Policy in Need of An Institution?*, Working Paper 1, Berlin, BaltSeaNet, Nord-Europa Institut, Humboldt University.

Sveriges Samarbete med Central- och Östeuropa [Sweden's Co-operation with East and Central Europe] Swedish Government Bill 1994/95:160.

Tassinari, Fabrizio (2004), *Mare Europaeum: Baltic Sea Region Security and Cooperation from Post-Wall to Post-Enlargement Europe*, Copenhagen, Department of Political Science, Ph.D. Dissertation.

Tiido, H. (2002), 'Estonia Anchoring Itself in the Euro-Atlantic Security Structures', in *Estonian Ministry of Foreign Affairs Yearbook*, Tallinn, pp. 11-12.

Wæver, Ole (1992) 'From Nordism to Baltism', in Mare Kukk, Sverre Jervell and Pertti Joenniemi (eds.), *The Baltic Sea Area: A region in the Making*, Karlskrona, Baltic Sea Institute.

PART V

CONCLUSION

Chapter 12

Conclusion:
Europe-Making and the North after Enlargement

Christopher S. Browning and Pertti Joenniemi

Introduction

The rationale underlying this book has been to reflect on a number of issues that have arisen with the emergence of the War on Terrorism from 2001 onwards, and the dual enlargement of the EU (to the Baltic States and Poland) and NATO (to the Baltic States) in 2004, in the context of Northern Europe. More particularly, the chapters in the book have speculated to varying degrees about two questions. On the one hand, there has been a concern with analysing what these developments have meant for Northern Europe in general, and what they have meant for the future of regional cooperation and the construction of Northern regional subjectivity more specifically. Second, however, the chapters have also sought to analyse how developments in Northern Europe since the end of the Cold War have impacted on how European political space has been constructed and what impact Northern Europe may have on this dynamic in the future.

In this concluding chapter we will therefore reflect on arguments made in the previous chapters, draw together a number of common arguments, as well as highlight some of the tensions identified by the different interventions. Beyond this, however, this chapter also looks ahead to where Europe's north is heading. Above all, we probe into whether the prospects for Europe's North contributing, for its part, to the emergence of a rather regionalised Europe are still valid (as seemed to be the case during the 1990s), or if it is rather the other way around, with Northern Europe being increasingly integrated into a concentric and EU-driven order. Is it to be concluded that Europe's North is now 'completed' with the EU-led enlargement now proceeding smoothly on a rather practical level, and with the unfolding of the EU-Russia relationship in the North being one of the few remaining items of larger importance still to be sorted out? And in this perspective, is the EU-Russia relationship the only one that increasingly impacts on the nature of the region, or are there also some other factors that have to be taken into account in passing judgement on where Europe's North is heading? Moreover, in the context of this latter category, we raise the question of whether it is conceivable that also the United States is to be viewed as a core constitutive actor, thus implying that Northern Europe may emerge as a kind of battle-ground between the American New/Old Europe, Russia's True/False Europe and the EU-related conceptualisations of Europe-making. In other words, our aim is to tap into a variety of key issues that seem to be on their way, or that might become, of fundamental importance for the unfolding of the region in the future, whilst also reflecting towards the end of the chapter on the preconditions that are there for conceptual analysis to grasp the dynamics at play in the unfolding of Northern Europe and European space more generally.

The Dual Enlargement and the North

Regionalisation, Idealism and Stabilisation in the 1990s

To start, it is worth reflecting on Northern Europe during the 1990s. As has been indicated in a number of the chapters, the 1990s was a period of innovation and rather rapid regionalisation in Northern Europe. Characteristic of this were efforts of 'indigenous' region building that gave grounds for thinking about the Baltic Sea region, and Europe's North more generally, as an emerging regionalised order. With the end of the Cold War and the disintegration of the Soviet Union the confines and divides of the Cold War period that had largely constrained interactions within the region (especially between the Baltic Sea's north-western and south-eastern shores) were replaced by a sense of openness and adventure. As Möller and Browning indicate in this volume, amongst the political community, and not least amongst academics, there was a certain amount of idealism present that the old divides and suspicions could be replaced by building a new sense of regional community in Northern Europe. In particular, foreign policy intellectuals inspired by the Constructivist/Reflectivist turn in the social sciences, played a notable role in providing the knowledge that was used to support various region building projects, with such intellectuals drawing on historical examples (Hansa region, Pomor trade) in order to naturalise common regional identities in the present (also see, Browning, 2003c, pp.46-7, 52-5; Neumann, 1994, 67).

However, as Stålvant and Joenniemi also indicate in this volume, such idealism was not confined to the intellectual and political elite. Civil society in the form of NGOs, local municipalities and cities also became engaged in a multitude of transnational linkages, particularly between the Nordic and Baltic States, and with a particular focus on cultural exchanges, but also on charity and self-sacrifice on the part of the Nordic partners. Thus, twinning arrangements also became a channel for humanitarian aid and technical development assistance, and not just for (re)-establishing cultural linkages (also see Bergman, 2004). It has been noted that in the Baltic Sea region altogether some 600 organisations were founded in order to, or have the capacity to, operate in a cross-border manner (Scott, 2002, p.142).

Alongside such idealism, and to draw again on the arguments of Stålvant and Archer, underlying much of this idealism there was also a more security-oriented concern with creating stability within Northern Europe. This became of enhanced concern in the early-1990s following the break-up of Yugoslavia and concerns that the Baltic Sea region should not turn into a Northern Balkans. In this respect, questions of security became rather conducive to promoting cooperation and regionalisation in the North. This is interesting in that, for the most part, during the Cold War questions of 'security' were a reason to avoid too much interaction. During the Cold War security was generally understood in the statist and zero-sum terms of Realism that places primary emphasis on self-sufficiency as the best security strategy (Waltz, 1979, p.118). Whilst cooperation was obviously limited across the East-West divide, this also tended to hinder cooperation more generally. Thus, intra-Nordic cooperation never extended to the realms of security and defence, primarily in deference to Soviet warnings that moves in such a direction would be viewed as aggressive and threatening.

In the post-Cold War period, however, security has become a reason precisely to cooperate. In the Northern context there have been two elements to this.[1] First, for the Baltic States and Poland traditional Realist concerns of alliance building against a possible resurgent Russian threat have been evident. In this respect, linking in with regional cooperation projects promoted by the Nordic countries and Germany was seen as one way of escaping the Russian sphere of influence, whilst at the same time making them eligible for future EU and NATO membership. Thus, the 1990's discourse of 'returning to Europe' was always understood as leaving something threatening and 'non/less-European' (Russia) behind (see Jæger, 1997).

Second, however, and as demonstrated by Archer, throughout the 1990s there has also been a strong emphasis on more Liberal Institutionalist approaches to security. Instead of an emphasis on zero-sum gains, security has been reconfigured and represented in terms of ideas of cooperative, collective and comprehensive security. This has reflected a dual realisation: first, that state security is best achieved through building trust with each other and; second, that with the end of the Cold War a range of new and pressing 'soft security' issues that now appeared on the regional agenda (e.g., economic, environmental, social and public health issues) simply could only be effectively tackled through cooperative action. Indeed, throughout the 1990s the Nordic States and Germany (and later the EU) promoted a certain strategic blurring between these Realist and Liberalist dimensions of security, with the (liberalist) belief being that by promoting cooperation over common 'soft security' issues, qualitative gains might also be made in the 'hard security' realm by fostering trust and cooperative relationships between Russia and the Baltic States, and between Russia and its Western neighbours more generally. The institutionalist element to this approach became

---

[1] For a more developed version of the following argument see, Browning and Joenniemi (2004b).

clearest in the creation of the Council of the Baltic Sea States (1992), the Barents Euro-Arctic Council (1993) and the Arctic Council (1996), as forums for dialogue between the states and various other entities within the region, but also as (potential) symbols of shared interests and identities.

A final thing to note in this context of the focus on regionalisation, idealism and stabilisation during the 1990s is that for much of the period the EU's approach to the region remained rather limited. That is to say that whilst the EU's presence in Northern Europe did increase markedly with Finland's and Sweden's membership in 1995, the EU was slow in developing a distinct approach and set of policies towards the region. The furthest the EU went in this regard was the 1996 Baltic Sea Region Initiative (Commission of the European Communities, 1996), which was rather limited in essence. As such, the EU's Northern members (and Northern actors more generally) were provided with considerable space and opportunity to shape the EU's Northern agenda, a task most notably taken on by Finland with its 1997 proposals for the Northern Dimension (ND) initiative. Similarly, it should also be noted that the United States was also supportive of Nordic-inspired regional cooperation initiatives in Northern Europe. Indeed, the United States was perhaps surprisingly supportive of some of the 'myth-making' dimensions of regional cooperation that were designed to build a sense of common purpose and identity in the region.[2] The American strategy, which was originally laid out in 1996 by Ronald Asmus and Robert Nurick (1996), and which was officially launched under the title of the Northern European Initiative (NEI) in 1997, was designed to maintain a low American profile in Northern Europe whilst promoting the security of the Baltic States in view of the first round of NATO enlargement to the Czech Republic, Hungary and Poland. Whereas highly visible American actions in the region, and in particular towards parts of the former Soviet space (i.e., the Baltic States), were seen as only likely to provoke Russia, promoting regional cooperation at the soft security level and encouraging the Nordic countries to take the lead in this regard was seen as much more profitable. Indeed, at its most ambitious American policy-makers even talked of Northern Europe as a laboratory for experimenting with developing a new West-Russia relationship more generally.[3] The overall point being, however, that in quite different ways the EU and the United States created space for Northern actors to take the lead and set the agenda of regional cooperation in the North. The catchword upon which both the EU and America could agree was of creating a 'Europe whole and free', this playing to a considerable degree into the hands of the regional and local actors in the case of Europe's North.

---

[2] For an excellent example see the following speech by Derek Shearer (1997), the then American Ambassador to Finland.

[3] For more detailed analyses of American policy towards Northern Europe in the 1990s see, Browning (2001, 2003a) and Rhodes (2000).

The Impact of Enlargement

Bearing these points in mind, what impact are the dual enlargement and the War on Terrorism likely to have on regional cooperation in Northern Europe in the future? On this point the book's chapters adopt several perspectives, though there is general agreement that, especially in view of the dual enlargement, certain elements might begin to change within the region. In Stålvant's view, for example, the period of 'stabilisation' that was dominated by various (statist) security concerns, is likely to give way to a period of 'normalisation' and pragmatic politics. The reason, he indicates, is that with the dual enlargement the major security concerns of the Baltic States and Poland have been salved. Indeed, with the War on Terrorism it rather seems that regional security threats are being replaced by a more global agenda, and as NATO members the Baltic States will now be dealing with Russia as a strategic partner in the fight against terrorism and transnational crime, instead of seeing it simply as a potential territorial threat. Bearing in mind that throughout the 1990s 'security' has been something of a driver of regional cooperation, this raises the question of what will happen to regional dynamics as traditional statist security matters become of less concern in the region.

At this level there are reasons to think that future regionalisation may well be in trouble, since with the security-rationale less important the states of the region may become less interested in it. Above all, it appears that the EU has increasingly 'hijacked' the efforts of region building, this being evidenced for example by the fact that the Union is well on its way to devising for itself a rather uniform framework in the form of the European Neighbourhood Policy (ENP). With such a programme in place there is, in all probability, less space for initiatives coming from the regional and local actors themselves. In the last couple of years signs of such an attitude have become evident, not least with a certain running down of the CBSS (which has announced it will reduce the frequency of its summit meetings) (Dauchert, 2004), with Sweden's phasing out of its Baltic Sea Billions funds, and also with the United States revamping its NEI policy into the much less ambitious (and seemingly less well financed)[4] enhanced Partnership in Northern Europe (e-PINE). A number of voices that are part of the current debate claim that bodies such as the CBSS have declined in importance since they were established in the context of somewhat different conditions than those prevailing today in the post-enlargement situation. As such, they need to be revised in order for a more coherent setting to emerge, one providing ground for a more uniform Northern European voice in the debate on Europe-making.[5]

In this regard, it is also worth noting Möller's argument that the homogenising myths of region building in the 1990s – that aimed to build a common sense of

---

[4] For example, see Conley (2003), in which no mention of new financing is made.

[5] See, for example, interventions such as those of Pär Nuder (2004), a Minister in the Swedish Government, and Paavo Lipponen (2004), Speaker of the Finnish Parliament.

Northern subjectivity around rather one-dimensional historical narratives that undermined the acceptability of differences in regional interpretations of history – have not been as successful at constructing a sense of common identity as initially anticipated.

Similarly, in his chapter Archer also posed the important question of whether the adoption in the 1990s of a Liberal Institutionalist agenda by the Baltic States represented a genuine acceptance of such ideas, or whether it was done for purely geo-strategic reasons in order to meet the EU's and NATO's membership criteria. The answer to this question will become apparent in due course, but there are two elements worth considering in this respect. First, there is a question of the extent to which the Baltic States saw participation in regionalisation projects in the North as a way to gain access to the EU and NATO and whether, now that they have membership, and therefore direct access, they will any longer devote the same attention to regional cooperation as previously. Second, it is also worth taking note of Russian criticisms since the Baltic States' membership of NATO, and their membership (with Poland) of the EU, that these states are trying to influence these organisations into adopting a tougher stance towards Russia, thereby indicating that the Baltic States' acceptance of a Liberal Institutionalist approach in the 1990s was simply a strategic guise hiding a more Realist agenda.[6] Whilst there may be some truth in this, it should also be remembered that throughout the 1990s Russia also played up criticisms of the Baltic States and emphasised what they saw as their anti-Russian tendencies in order to push other agendas, not least in order to try and stall the NATO enlargement process, and to try and gain various concessions from the West.

Finally, it is also worth reflecting a little more on what effect the War on Terrorism has had on Northern Europe, and how this may potentially undermine regional cooperation in the future. In this respect, the disagreements that emerged in transatlantic relations over the war in Iraq, and more particularly related to the distinction drawn between New and Old Europe by Donald Rumsfeld (*BBC Online*, 23 January 2003; Rumsfeld, 2003) have been particularly notable, with Northern Europe becoming divided along somewhat different axes to what we have become accustomed. On the one hand, there have been the Baltic States, Denmark, Poland, and not least Russia that fell in behind the United States. On the other hand, there have been Germany, Finland, Norway and Sweden who, to varying degrees, adopted much more critical approaches. In a sense, the issue here is a question of the extent to which this New/Old Europe distinction will become important in framing European politics in the future. To the extent that it does – although so far the United States has refrained from pressing the issue in a region-specific context – this may well undermine regional dynamics as states begin to align ever more with those in other parts of Europe sharing their views. This would

---

[6]   Notably, Sergei Yastrzhembski, a special representative of President Vladimir Putin, has also included Denmark and Finland as part of an emerging 'Russophobic' bloc within the EU (see, *Helsingin Sanomat International Edition*, 8 December 2004).

be the case in the sense that the United States' delineation places particularly the Baltic countries in the category of 'exemplary' new Europeans, whereas if seen against the background of the Russian conceptualisation of a 'True' and a 'False' Europe, they rather represent unwarranted cases unfit for true Europeanness (Morozov, 2004b, pp.319-21). In other words, the American and the Russian conceptualisations of a Europe into which they can project themselves, differ considerably from each other. On a rather practical level the theme of terrorism might in fact be conducive to security-related cooperation, but if aired as a principally important and ideological issue pertaining to conceptualisations of political space more broadly it is bound to have opposite effects.

At the same time, in Northern Europe the New/Old Europe split transcends the War on Terrorism to also include economic elements that may actually be a cause of considerable competition in the region. This is most notable in that whilst the Nordic countries may have been rather successful in exporting Liberal Institutionalist ideas of security to the Baltic States, they have been far less successful in exporting their 'third way' egalitarian social democratic economic model. In contrast, the Baltic States have rather become champions of a more neo-liberal, Anglo-American conception of capitalism that some in the Nordic countries find distinctly threatening (Lehti, 2004).

These pessimistic views regarding the future of regional cooperation in Northern Europe following the dual enlargements, however, can also be contrasted with more optimistic arguments evident in this book. For example, if a shift from a period of 'stabilisation' to one of 'normalisation' is taking place then this indicates that a certain level of desecuritisation (Wæver, 1995) has been achieved. Indeed, in this context it seems that Northern Europe has rather successfully managed to transform itself into a security community (Deutsch et al., 1957), and might even be on the trajectory to become part of a future expanded Nordic '(a)security community', a description used by Joenniemi (2003) to refer to the fact that in relations between the Nordic states traditional security questions are simply not on the agenda. In other words, with the major security issues seemingly resolved it might be argued that there is an enhanced possibility that region building might shift further away from the state towards municipalities, cities and other transnational actors. Or put another way, with much of Northern Europe now members of the EU (and with Norway integrated into the EU through its EEA agreement), the region has become ensconced within the EU's common social and economic spaces, with the result being that regionalisation shifts away from state directed activities to more local levels. Meanwhile, even though Russia remains a problem in this regard, not least being excluded by the Schengen visa regime, Moscow is also pushing its own 'common spaces' agenda with the EU.

The North and the Construction of European Political Space

So, having reflected on changing developments within Northern Europe in the context of the War on Terrorism and the dual enlargement of the EU and NATO, we now need to analyse how developments in Northern Europe since the end of the Cold War have impacted on Europe more generally. At the same time, we also need to reflect on changing EU approaches towards the region and how these are in turn impacting on what is possible there.

To start with the first issue, one of the principal arguments of this book has been that even marginal and peripheral regions like Northern Europe are able to 'bite back' and to have an impact on the ways in which European (and Russian) political space has, can and will develop. The theoretical arguments for this position were laid out in the book's Introduction, and as such it is simply enough to here note Parker's (2000) argument that being on the margins and edges of an entity can provide the margin with significant resources to define the nature of the boundary between the inside and outside of a particular territorial entity, thereby impacting on the nature of the entity in question. In the case of the North, the fact that the region includes a border between the EU and Russia has been particularly notable in this regard. Throughout the 1990s, in the North this border (and the more general problems of the region) was understood as a challenge to be overcome. Since the EU's approach to Northern Europe throughout much of the 1990s was largely passive it was the Northern actors themselves who began to take the lead in developing regional and cross-border cooperation. This was especially the case along the Finnish-Russian border, where cross-border cooperation was facilitated via the Nearby Region Agreement signed between Finland and Russia in 1992. This permitted municipalities on either side of the border to engage in cooperative dialogue outside of the states' direct control (Eskelinen, Haapanen and Druzhinin, 1999, p.333; Tikkanen and Käkönen, 1997, pp.169-70). As such, when the EU enlarged to Finland and Sweden in 1995 it incorporated a new external border with Russia along which cross-border interaction was becoming increasingly common.

Beyond this, however, it should also be noted that there was considerable recognition on the part of Northern actors that activism in Northern Europe could also have a much broader impact on the EU. As noted in Browning's chapter, the North has sometimes been presented as a 'blank space' upon which new stories of European identity that transcend East-West divides might be written. Likewise, Ojanen (1999) has argued that Finland's ND initiative should be seen as a rather successful attempt by Finland to 'customise' the EU, to make the EU more Finnish/Northern by orienting it towards Northern concerns, but also by framing just what those concerns should be understood to be and providing a framework laying out just what types of solutions might be considered. At a time when the EU was rather reluctant to engage with its new neighbour, through the ND it was all of a sudden presented with the question of just how to think of its new common border with Russia. Whilst many EU members were in favour of relatively closed borders, Finland was instead promoting active regional and cross-border cooperation in order to avoid Russia's isolation, and a policy that actually called for providing Russia with an equal voice in elements of EU policy formulation. However, as the chapters by Prozorov, Sergounin and Tkachenko demonstrate, Russia's Northern regions have also at times caused similar headaches for Moscow for how to think about Russia as a political entity and how to conceptualise the nature of its borders.

Whilst it is going too far to say that the North has become a postmodern playground for neomedievalist visions, it is certainly the case that the North has posed challenges for how we think about European politics, and for how the EU and Russia conceptualise political space and their relations with each other and other neighbours. In this respect, the North has, at times, been seen as a resource. The fact that the region did not implode like the Balkans, but rather managed to deal with a range of potentially conflictual issues in peaceful ways, and in the process became one of the most regionalised parts of Europe, has meant that it has stood out as something of an exception. Consequently, the idea that there might be lessons to be learned from the Northern experience has become quite widespread. As noted, for example, the United States has explicitly spoken about Northern Europe as a 'laboratory' for experimenting with new forms of governance, and has more recently suggested that the Baltic model might be thought about in the context of the problems of the Caucasus and Central Asia (Ries, 2002). Similarly, in his chapter, Vahl has noted how the EU has actually identified two Northern models: the EEA and the ND. Both of these have been seen as offering insights regarding how the EU should approach its near neighbours, with the ND being seen as a potential model for the EU's above mentioned new European Neighbourhood Policy (ENP), and Norway's EEA experience most recently being spoken about as a possible alternative to Turkish membership of the Union. In this context then, it might be concluded that since the end of the Cold War Northern Europe, a region usually considered as something of a marginal area in European politics, has been punching above its weight when it comes to shaping the development of European political space.

However, it would be wrong to suggest that these dynamics go in just one direction. Thus, whilst there have been clear issues raised by Northern developments that impact on the developing nature of Europe, it should also be noted that developments elsewhere in turn constrain just what that impact may be. Most notable in this context is the growing tendency of the EU, in the face of its recent enlargement, to turn its back on regionalised approaches to dealing with its near neighbours, in favour of a much more centralised agenda. Therefore, as Vahl has shown, despite reference to the ND in the ENP, the ENP does not seem to be in the same spirit as its Northern counterpart. This is not least evident in that it basically precludes outsiders from having an equal voice in policy formulation and agenda setting (also see Browning and Joenniemi, 2003). Moreover, if anything it rather seems that the ND will in future become somewhat subordinated to the more centralised ENP. One reason for this is that as a result of EU enlargement the ND is increasingly becoming focused around the EU-Russia axis, the consequence being that the policy is increasingly seen as just one instrument in EU-Russian relations, rather than as being a regional instrument. Moreover, the fact that since enlargement EU-Russian relations have not been working well, and have increasingly become focused around bilateral discussions between Brussels and Moscow, has also constrained what is possible through the ND. Put another way, at least for the moment it seems that the space available for heterogeneous approaches along the EU's borders is closing down. Meanwhile, and as demonstrated by Prozorov, much the same dynamic also appears evident in Putin's attempts to wrest power away from Russia's regions and to assert the 'power vertical'.

The EU and the Internal/External Security Paradox

In sum then, and as indicated in a number of the chapters in this book, a tension exists between processes of regionalisation in Northern Europe and attempts on the part of the EU and Russia to construct their territorial and political subjectivities in rather more unified terms. Broadly speaking, this tension might be characterised in terms of competing *modernist* and *postmodernist* approaches to political space and governance, where postmodernism stands for multiplicity and heterogeneity, and modernism for standardisation and universalism. More specifically, however, it can also be argued that both the EU and Russia find themselves trapped in what we might term the 'internal/external security paradox'. According to this paradox external security would seem to support taking a more relaxed approach to regionalisation and embracing external borders as opportunities for exploration and interaction. In contrast, though, the concerns of internal security on the part of both the EU and Moscow rather tend to promote a fear of regionalisation and the conceptualisation of external borders as problems and as lines of exclusion. In this and the following section, therefore, we will briefly illustrate how this paradox can be seen in both the attitudes of the EU and Russia, and as such also demonstrating why it is that Northern Europe provides considerable challenges to how political space is constructed in the EU and Russia, and in Europe more generally.

In the case of the EU the issue at hand is also one of identity, where the EU's *raison d'être* has often been understood as that of being a peace project with a mission to prevent a return to the fractious politics of the inter-war period (see, Wæver, 1996). In undertaking this mission the EU has generally adopted policies aimed at undermining the significance of borders between its member states, and has seen enlargement as a process of expanding Europe's area of freedom, security, prosperity and justice, by constructing a new European order no longer built around the concerns of power politics (Prodi cited in Grabbe, 2000, p.519). Indeed, within the Union the aim has been one of doing away with borders in favour of creating a space that can be easily traversed by flows of capital, goods and people. Moreover, there has also been a desire to avoid the emergence of sharp and divisive boundaries at the outer edges of the Union, and which largely explains the variety of arrangements the EU has negotiated with various partners in order to ameliorate the effects of exclusion from membership.

Increasingly, however, the effort of establishing internal freedoms has been accompanied by growing anxieties about the ability of the external borders to keep out various ills such as transnational crime, illegal immigration and terrorism (see, Andreas and Snyder, 2000; Geddes, 1999). It is in this context that the EU has begun moving towards the view that it needs to have an all-encompassing and continuous external border that operates on the basis of a uniform set of departures. This aim for more standardised policies has been evident in the context of the recent eastern enlargement, where the applicant countries/new members have been expected to apply the Schengen *acquis* in full, with very little flexibility in the application of Schengen being foreseen (see, den Boer, 2002). Similarly, the instigation of the ENP can also be read as an attempt to curtail the multiplicity currently evident in the EU's policies towards its near neighbours, and to instead provide some sense of future standardisation and to concentrate decision making back in Brussels. These are all efforts that are likely to undermine regionalisation processes and that instead promote a rather modernist understanding of the EU as a political entity with clearly defined borders between inside and outside.

In the case of Northern Europe these dynamics in EU practices have been most obviously apparent in its approaches towards Russia's Kaliningrad *oblast*, which with the recent enlargement has become (with the exception of its Baltic Sea coastline) surrounded by the EU. In the Kaliningrad case the EU is struggling with two apparently conflicting aims. On the one hand, it wants to prevent the infiltration of crime and illegal immigration from the Russian enclave in order that it might preserve its own internal freedoms. On the other hand, however, it also wants to enhance the Union's external security by developing its relationship with Russia. The tension arises in that preserving *internal security* is seen to require a strict border regime with Kaliningrad in order to prevent the infiltration of unwanted elements into the Union. However, the negative effects of EU enlargement on Kaliningrad, in terms of restricting Kaliningraders' freedom of movement and undermining the regional economy as a result of the imposition of EU standards and of the impact of the Schengen visa regime in restricting the activities of cross-border shuttle-traders, has threatened to destabilise the EU's relations with Russia.[7]

Thus, it is argued that in order to foster *external security* and preserve the EU-Russian relationship, the border with Kaliningrad should be relatively open and porous with the semi-integration of Kaliningrad into the EU space, perhaps in a manner similar to that of Norway. However, preserving external security through opening up the Union's external border is seen to undermine internal societal

---

[7]   On the problems that EU enlargement will cause for Kaliningrad see, Baxendale, Dewar and Gowan (2000) and Fairlie and Sergounin (2001). For a more detailed exposition of the current argument see, Browning (2003b).

security. In this context, the Kaliningrad question has become one of how best to manage these contradictory demands, of how to manage this boundary rather than of how to overcome it, whilst critics of the Schengen regime tend to argue that the balance has fallen too far in favour of internal security (Huisman, 2002, pp.6-7).

Thus, whilst the EU has conceptualised itself as a peace project and has rather successfully managed, through promoting cross-border networks and multiple overlapping local, regional and European identities, to overcome amongst its members the problems caused by the exclusive nationalisms of the past, when it comes to its external borders the Union remains stuck in rather modernist ways of thinking. As such, the outside remains seen as unstable and potentially threatening, with the security of insiders and outsiders seen as disconnected by claiming that the outsiders have to sort out their own problems. Thus, the Union's peace-policies, in their original form, are restricted to the internal sphere and not seen as applicable in a more general sense and therefore are not to be unquestioningly extended to the nearby regions.

In this context, in which clear distinctions are being drawn between insiders and outsiders, localised and regionalised solutions (as, for example, envisaged in the ND) are seen as potentially opening the EU to contamination, in this case from Kaliningrad. Instead, the alternative option is to press for uniform and unambiguous policies such as the ENP and to try and shift the locus of EU-Russian relations to bilateral discussions between Brussels and Moscow. In such a modernist frame of reference the external borders remain conceptualised as a first line of defence. However, the consequence of this perceptual frame may actually be to undermine peace and stability in Europe.

In order for the EU to be faithful to its peace mission, different (postmodern/postsovereign) conceptual lenses would be required that would embrace a much more regionalised approach to European governance in general. It would also require significantly rethinking the nature of the EU's subjectivity by accepting and encouraging action from the margins. The current perceptual frame of reference of the internal/external security paradox, however, instead reproduces rather modernist understandings of subjectivity, central to which is the notion that subjects require clearly demarcated territorial spaces and borders over which they exercise sovereign control. In turn, this conflation of identity, territory and sovereignty tends to lead to the reification of selfhood to the negative characterisation of those outside the borders of the EU as potential threats to the EU's security. Consequently, there is little space for outsiders to join in the construction of an integration-related Europe and gain subjectivity and a legitimate voice in the constitutive discourses pertaining to the configuration that unfolds.

It seems clear that, against this background, the idea of the EU as a peace project comes mentally to a halt, and remains restricted to the internal sphere. Consequently, the Union is not able to project its peace-related identity across the new borders. This shortcoming and restraint shows itself clearly in the case of Kaliningrad, but has implications for the discourse on borders with Russia more generally, with the Union basically treating Russia as a rather monolithic entity. It is no surprise, therefore, that the Union has thus far refrained from developing any clearly distinguishable regionalising policies in relation to the relevant Russian regions in the North, such as Karelia, Pskov, St. Petersburg, the Leningrad region, as well as Murmansk.

Russia and the Internal/External Security Paradox

More briefly, a similar internal/external security paradox can also be identified in the case of Russia. Again, and as with the EU, a certain duality can also be traced in Russian views on national identity, political space and how to think about borders. In the first instance, there is clearly a rather strong modernist legacy in Russian thinking that emphasises the need for strict territorial control and that draws a close link between national identity and the territorial state (see, Trenin, 2002). In this way of thinking national identity is elevated above other alternatives, thereby leaving little tolerance for any overlapping, loosely bordered spaces (Morozov, 2002, p.42). It is notable, therefore, that the Russian administration has tended to be suspicious of the concepts of globalisation and regionalisation. Preoccupied with consolidating Russian sovereignty following the end of the Cold War many Russian leaders have understood globalisation and regionalisation to be part of a subtle Western attempt designed to further marginalise Russia in world affairs, and perhaps even as aimed at promoting its further disintegration (Haukkala, 2001, pp.8-9; Makarychev, 2000, pp.26-7). In contrast to decentralisation, it has rather been felt that a strong centralised state is essential in order to keep Russia's diverse ethnic groups and territorial spaces together. Thus, throughout the 1990s, Moscow became increasingly concerned at the growing power of some of the regions *vis-à-vis* the centre, fearing that this was a prelude to separatist ambitions. Putin's federal reforms reasserting the 'power vertical' can be seen as a direct response to these concerns, and that are aimed at consolidating Moscow's control over the regions and borders of Russia.

Most recently, the prevalence of traditional geopolitical thinking has been evident in the spat between the EU/West and Russia over the Ukrainian presidential elections towards the end of 2004. Many Russian (but also European) leaders clearly saw the dispute over who the rightful winner actually was, as being a matter of whether or not Ukraine is moving outside the Russian sphere of influence. If, as argued in Browning's chapter, it makes sense to think of the EU as having imperial characteristics and tendencies, then it seems that Russia's fear is that it is being steadily pushed to the edges of European political space, and remains destined to be excluded. In this context, it is also worth noting the tendency that exists – as noted above – in Russian discourses on Europe to draw a distinction between *True* and *False* Europes. As Makarychev (2004) and Morozov (2004a) have both pointed out, according to this way of thinking Russia represents 'True' European values that are primarily built around ideas of the territorially sovereign nation-state. This contrasts with the debordering, postmodernising project of the 'False' Europe of EU projections. Whilst such a discourse enables Russia to locate itself at the normative heart of a particular reading of Europeanness, the Europe projected in the discourse is one that leaves little space for engaging in projects of regionalisation and cross-border cooperation. Indeed, it rather seems to support Prozorov's conclusion in his chapter that Russia is, to some extent, excluding itself – due to an inability to project itself into any of the prevailing forms of Europe-making – from the major developments in European governance.

However, alongside these rather modernist elements that result in regionalisation being viewed as an external threat to the territorial integrity of Russia, there are also contradictory tendencies present. Despite apparent efforts to keep European regionalisation at a distance, Russia has also at times taken a much more proactive stance, particularly in Northern Europe. The fact that some 50 per cent of Russia's foreign trade is now with the EU means that isolating Russia is not a realistic goal. In a sense, Russia simply has to engage with the regionalising, globalising EU. As noted, in this context it is precisely in Northern Europe that Russia has felt able to experiment to some extent with ideas of regionalisation and decentralisation that ultimately would entail rethinking dominant conceptions of Russia and the nature of Russian political space.

On the one hand, the ND has been seen as a positive development, even described by Deputy Prime Minister, Viktor Khristenko (2001), as a 'brave political experiment' calling for 'unconventional decisions' promoting sub-regional cooperation that ultimately might develop into 'a common European social and economic space'. The one complaint, however, has been that in practice Russia has not been given the equal voice in policy formulation originally planned for in the initiative. However, it is has been with regard to Kaliningrad that some of the most interesting interventions have been made, most notably the 1999 suggestion that Kaliningrad could become a 'pilot region' in the development of EU-Russian relations. Moreover, actors within the Kaliningrad regional administration have also called for Kaliningrad's greater internationalisation and for its partial inclusion within the EU's economic space, in ways similar to Norway's EEA arrangement. However, the tensions and the internal/external security paradox that Kaliningrad poses for the EU are also evident for Russia in this case.

Thus, alongside such openness and various innovative suggestions, there have also been periods of backlash and recurrent emphasis made to the fact that the territorial sovereignty of Russia in the case of Kaliningrad cannot be tampered with.[8] It has hence been in Northern Europe, perhaps more than anywhere else that different visions for the future configuration of European political space, and of the identities and subjectivities of the EU and Russia, have been most clearly evident.

---

[8] For an analysis of the different discourses surrounding the Kaliningrad issue see, Browning and Joenniemi, (2004a).

Conclusion: Future Visions/Models

In a broad perspective, the dynamism that originated mainly with the regional and local actors seems to have to some extent stalled in Europe's North, although the various institutions established are still there and continue to yield results. In some cases the structures have even expanded, as indicated by the fact that between 2003-2004 two more Euroregions were established, one in Kaliningrad (between Russia, Poland, Lithuania and Latvia) and another in Pskov (Russia and Estonia). It appears obvious, however, that Northern Europe is not on its way of spearheading the unfolding of a rather regionalised European configuration, an idea sometimes described in terms of a Europe of Olympic Rings. A demise in 'indigenous' region building is discernible – to the extent that it was there in the first place – and instead the initiative appears to rest increasingly with the EU in a rather centralised manner, this then speaking for a concentric rather than decentred European configuration. This is not to say that region building is coming to an end, but that to the extent that it moves forward, it will reflect a standardised EU-approach with relatively scant space for deviations and local peculiarities.

The political order emerging in Northern Europe is increasingly an EU-based one and it appears that Russia is also largely able to live with such a development. However, for Russia the important question appears to be whether within that order it gets positioned as an outsider, or if it can aspire for and acquire the position of being a 'close outsider', or in some spheres even a kind of 'semi-insider' with a voice that to some extent carries even in matters that are basically internal to the EU. The importance of the energy dialogue, Russia's position in view of various issues in the sphere of security that are also important for the EU, as well as Kaliningrad's posture as 'a little Russia in the sphere of the EU's policies', all provide inroads that allow Russia to bolster its weight and influence in European developments.

With regionalisation still a prominent feature of the political, economic and cultural landscape in Northern Europe, but increasingly reflecting dynamics of the Union's core as well as developments along the EU-Russia axis, what is the best way to visualise the unfolding pattern? In this respect, something is obviously needed between the models and visions of a concentric Europe and that of the Olympic Rings. One suggestion would be to think of a configuration with two cores, Brussels and Moscow, clearly in place, albeit with strong features of regionalisation labelling the overall pattern. Alternatively one could perhaps think of blades circling each core in a daisy-like fashion with some of the blades common to two different cores, those of Brussels and Moscow. Within this pattern, strong centredness would not constitute a hindrance to regionalisation, but would rather be a precondition for such a development. In contrast to much recent analysis which tends to perceive centredness as undermining any serious efforts of region building, the reading could be that it is rather to be seen as a precondition for regionalisation to unfold. The relationship is not one of either-or, but one of both-and.

If seen in this, less polarised light, Europe's North could still be seen as a kind of testing ground and experimental area. It exemplifies that two constitutive principles – that of a sovereign core and the one pertaining to regionality – can in fact co-exist and jointly shape the unfolding of post-Cold War Europe. Northern Europe stands out among the different parts of Europe as the sphere where the cores are able to lean on and buy into a departure that is usually seen as standing in outright opposition to the rule of the core. On a more theoretical level Europe's North invites for an analysis that is premised on a broader repertoire of options than just the ones of a concentric Europe and the one pertaining to the Europe of Olympic Rings. In other words, it calls for analytical approaches that do not categorically play constitutive departures such as sovereignty and regionality against each other from the very outset, but rather that aspire to go beyond such a bifurcated approach.

References

Andreas, P. and Snyder, T. (eds.), (2000), *The Wall around the West: State, Borders and Immigration Controls in the North America and Europe*, Rowman and Littlefield, Lanham.

Asmus, Ronald D., and Nurick, Robert C. (1996), 'NATO Enlargement and the Baltic States', *Survival*, Vol. 38(2), pp. 121-42.

Baxendale, James, Dewar, Stephen and Gowan, David (eds.) (2000), *The EU and Kaliningrad: Kaliningrad and the Impact of EU Enlargement*, London, The Federal Trust.

BBC Online, 'Outrage at "old Europe" remarks', 23 January 2003. Available at http://news.bbc.co.uk/2/hi/Europe/2687403.htm.

Bergman, Annika (2004), 'Nordic Integration Assistance: The Case of the Baltic States', paper presented at the conference, *The Baltic States: New or Old?*, University of Glasgow, 22-23 January 2004.

Browning, Christopher S. (2001), 'A Multi-Dimensional Approach to Regional Cooperation: The United States and the Northern European Initiative', *European Security*, Vol. 8(4), pp. 84-108.

Browning, Christopher S. (2003a), 'Complementarities and Differences in EU and US Policies in Northern Europe', *Journal of International Relations and Development*, Vol. 6(1), pp. 23-50.

Browning, Christopher S. (2003b), 'The Internal/External Security Paradox and the Reconstruction of Boundaries in the Baltic: The Case of Kaliningrad', *Alternatives: Global, Local, Political*, Vol. 28(5), pp. 545-81.

Browning, Christopher S. (2003c), 'The Region-Building Approach Revisited: The Continued Othering of Russia in Discourses of Region-Building in the European North', *Geopolitics*, Vol. 8(1), pp. 45-71.

Browning, Christopher S. and Joenniemi, Pertti (2003), 'The European Union's Two Dimensions: The Eastern and the Northern', *Security Dialogue*, Vol. 34(4), pp. 463-78.

Browning, Christopher S. and Joenniemi, Pertti (2004a), 'Contending Discourses of Marginality: The Case of Kaliningrad', *Geopolitics*, Vol. 9(3), pp. 699-730.

Browning, Christopher S. and Joenniemi, Pertti (2004b), 'Regionality Beyond Security? The Baltic Sea Region after Enlargement', *Cooperation and Conflict*, Vol. 39(3), pp. 233-53.

Commission of the European Communities (1996), *The Baltic Sea Region Initiative*, Brussels, 10.06.1996, SEC(96) 608 Final.

Conley, Heather (2003), 'Building on Success: The Enhanced Partnership in Northern Europe', remarks to the School for Advanced International Studies, Washington, D.C., 15 October 2003. Available at http://www.state.gov/p/eur/rls/rm/2003/25286pf.htm.

Dauchert, Helge (2004), 'No Future for the Council of Baltic Sea States? The Implications of Baltic States' EU and NATO Membership for the CBSS', paper presented at the BaltSeaNet conference in Tallinn, 5-8 February 2004.

den Boer, M. (2002), 'To what Extent Can There Be Flexibility on the Application of Schengen in the New Member States?', in M. Anderson and J. Apap (eds.), *The New European Borders and Security Cooperation: Promoting Trust in an Enlarged European Union*, Brussels, Centre for European Policy Studies and SITRA.

Deutsch, Karl W., Burrell, Sidney A., Kann, Robert A., Lee, Maurice, Lichterman, Martin, Lindgren, Raymond E., Loewenheim, Francis L. and Van Wagenen, Richard W. (1957), *Political Community and the North Atlantic Area: International Organization in the Light of Historical Experience*, New York, Greenwood Press.

Eskelinen, Heikki, Haapanen, Elisa, and Druzhinin, Pavel (1999), 'Where Russia Meets the EU. Across the Divide in the Karelian Borderlands', in Heikki Eskelinen, Ilkka Liikanen and Jukka Oksa (eds.), *Curtains of Iron and Gold: Reconstructing Borders and Scales of Interaction*, Aldershot, Ashgate, pp. 329-46.

Fairlie, Lyndelle D., and Sergounin, Alexander (2001), *Are Borders Barriers: EU Enlargement and the Russian Region of Kaliningrad*, Helsinki/Berlin, Ulkopoliittinen instituutti and Institut für Europäische Politik.

Geddes, A. (1999), *Immigration and European Integration: Towards Fortress Europe?*, Manchester, Manchester University Press.

Grabbe, Heather (2000), 'The Sharp Edges of Europe: Extending Schengen Eastwards', *International Affairs*, Vol. 76(2), pp. 519-36.

Haukkala, Hiski (2001), *Two Reluctant Regionalizers? The European Union and Russia in Europe's North*, Working Papers 32, Helsinki, Ulkopoliittinen instituutti.

Helsingin Sanomat International Edition, 'Putin spokesman says Finland part of "Russophobic block" in EU', 8 December 2004.

Huisman, Sander (2002), *A New European Union Policy for Kaliningrad*, Occasional Papers 33, Paris, European Union Institute for Security Studies.

Jæger, Øyvind (1997), *Securitising Russia: Discursive Practices of the Baltic States*, Copenhagen, COPRI Working Papers 10.

Joenniemi, Pertti (2003), 'Norden Beyond Security Community', in Clive Archer and Pertti Joenniemi (eds.), *The Nordic Peace*, Aldershot, Ashgate, pp. 198-212.

Khristenko, Viktor (2001), speech to the Northern Dimension Forum in Lappeenranta, Finland, 22 October, in *Results of the Northern Dimension Forum in Lappeenranta October 22-23 2001*, Helsinki, Prime Minister's Office.

Lehti, Marko (2004), 'Challenging the "Old" Europe: Estonia and Latvia in a "New" Europe', paper presented at the 5th Pan-European International Relations Conference of the Standing Group on International Relations, 'Constructing World Orders', The Hague, The Netherlands, 9-11 September 2004.

Lipponen, Paavo (2004), 'Vil sanere nordisk samarbeit', *Aftenposten*, 29 March. Available at http://www.aftenposten.no/nyheter/uriks/article757757.ece.

Makarychev, Andrey S. (2000), *Islands of Globalization: Regional Russia and the Outside World*, Working Paper 2, Zurich, Center for Security Studies and Conflict Research.

Makarychev, Andrey (2004), 'Russia's Discursive Construction of Europe and Herself: Towards New Spatial Imaginary', paper presented at the workshop: *EU and Russia: Conflict and Cooperation between two Subjects in Transformation*, Danish Institute for International Studies, 26-27 November.

Morozov, Viatcheslav (2002), *The Discourses of St. Petersburg and the Shaping of a Wider Europe: Territory, Space and Post-Sovereign Politics*, Copenhagen, COPRI Working Papers 13.

Morozov, Viatcheslav (2004a), 'Europe and the Boundaries of Russian Political Community', paper presented at the workshop: *EU and Russia: Conflict and Cooperation between two Subjects in Transformation*, Danish Institute for International Studies, 26-27 November.

Morozov, Viatcheslav (2004b), 'Russia in the Baltic Sea Region: Desecuritization or Deregionalization?', *Cooperation and Conflict*, Vol. 39(3), pp. 317-31.

Neumann, Iver B. (1994), 'A Region-building Approach to Northern Europe', *Review of International Studies*, Vol. 20 (1), pp. 53-74.

Nuder, Pär (2004), 'The Baltic Sea Countries are to Revise their Cooperation', *Helsingin Sanomat*, 25 May.

Ojanen, Hanna (1999), 'How to Customise Your Union: Finland and the Northern Dimension of the EU', *Northern Dimensions*, Helsinki, Finnish Institute of International Affairs, pp. 13-26.

Parker, Noel (2000), 'Integrated Europe and its "Margins": Action and Reaction', in Noel Parker and Bill Armstrong (eds.), *Margins in European Integration*, Houndmills, Macmillan Press, pp. 3-27.

Rhodes, Edward (2000), 'The American Vision of Baltic Security Architecture: Understanding the Northern European Initiative', *Baltic Defence Review*, (4), pp. 91-112.

Ries, Charles (2002), 'The Baltic Sea Region from a US Perspective', speech to the Baltic Development Forum Summit, Copenhagen, 15 October 2002. Available at http://www.state.gov/p/eur/rls/rm/2002/14539.htm.

Rumsfeld, Donald (2003), 'New Tools Needed Against Threats', speech at the George C. Marshall Center, Germany, 11 June 2003. Available at http://www.iwar.org.uk/news-archive/2003/06-13-4.htm.

Scott, James Wesley (2002), 'Baltic Sea Regionalism, EU Geopolitics and Symbolic Geographies of Cooperation', *Journal of Baltic Studies*, Vol. 33(2), pp. 137-55.

Shearer, Derek (1997), 'The New Hanseatic League: Creating a Zone of Stability in Northern Europe', speech delivered at the conference, *Towards a New Hanseatic League*, Helsinki, 8 October. Available at http://www.usemb.se/BalticSec/shearer.htm.

Tikkanen, Veikko and Käkönen, Jyrki (1997), 'The Evolution of Cooperation in the Kuhmo-Kostamuksha Region of the Finnish-Russian Border', in Paul Ganster Alan Sweedler, James Scott and Wolf Dieter-Eberwein (eds.), *Borders and Border Regions in Europe and North America*, San Diego, San Diego State University Press, pp. 163-75.

Trenin, Dmitri (2002), *The End of Eurasia: Russia at the Border between Geopolitics and Globalization*, Washington/Moscow, Carnegie Endowment for International Peace.

Waltz, Kenneth N. (1979), *Theory of International Politics* (New York: McGraw-Hill, Inc).

Wæver, Ole (1995), 'Securitization and Desecuritization', in Ronnie D. Lipschutz (ed.), *On Security*, New York, Columbia University Press, pp. 46-86.

Waever, Ole (1996), 'European Security Identities', *Journal of Common Market Studies*, Vol. 34(1), pp. 103-32.

Index